Go West, Young Woman!

From Military Wife to Country Life

NANCY QUINN

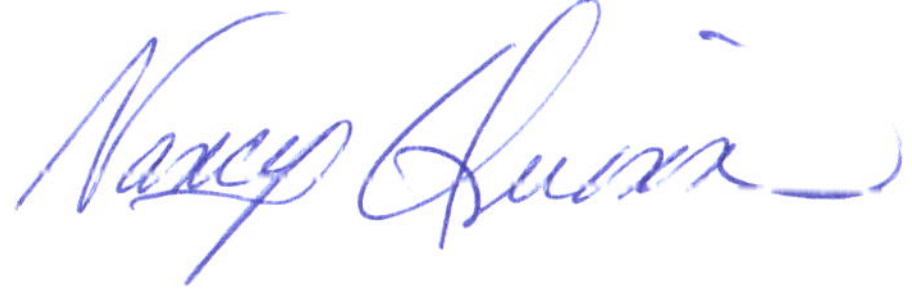

HELLGATE PRESS   ASHLAND, OREGON

GO WEST, YOUNG WOMAN!

©2016 Nancy Quinn

Published by Hellgate Press

(An imprint of L&R Publishing, LLC)

Hellgate Press
PO Box 3531
Ashland, OR 97520
email: sales@hellgatepress.com

Editor: Harley B. Patrick
Cover Design: L. Redding

Library of Congress Cataloging-in-Publication Data

Names: Quinn, Nancy (Nancy Z.), author.
Title: Go west, young woman! : from military wife to country life / Nancy
  Quinn.
Description: First edition. | Ashland, Oregon : Hellgate Press, [2016]
Identifiers: LCCN 2016022429 (print) | LCCN 2016026272 (ebook) | ISBN
  9781555718299 | ISBN 9781555718305 ()
Subjects: LCSH: Quinn, Nancy (Nancy Z.) | Quinn, Nancy (Nancy Z.)--Family. |
  Helena Region (Mont.)--Biography. | Helena Region (Mont.)--Social life and
  customs. | West (U.S.)--Social life and customs. | Country
  life--Montana--Helena Region. | Natural history--Montana--Helena Region. |
  Animals--Montana--Helena Region. | Wildlife artists--Montana--Helena
  Region--Biography.
Classification: LCC F739.H4 Q85 2016 (print) | LCC F739.H4 (ebook) | DDC
  978.6/615--dc23
LC record available at https://lccn.loc.gov/2016022429

Printed and bound in the United States of America
First edition 10 9 8 7 6 5 4 3 2 1

To you Bill, and our daughters.

Books have been an important influence in my life for as long as I can remember. I have always turned to them to entertain myself or just fill a lonely void. Through books I have enjoyed all kinds of new experiences, solved mysteries, explored foreign lands, and even learned how to cook. I hope reading my story gives you the kind of experience you are looking for. Thank you sincerely for spending your time with me.

If you have a comment or a question, I would be delighted to hear from you through my Facebook page: Nancy Quinn, Author, at https://www.facebook.com/nancyquinn0.

Contents

Introduction ....*ix*

Prologue ....*xi*

1 *Go West, Young Woman!* *1*

2 *Green Acres We Are Here* *11*

3 *A Creek Runs through It & A River Runs near It* *15*

4 *The Refrigerator Incident* *17*

5 *A Mouse in the House* *21*

6 *The Cows Come Home* *25*

7 *The Facts of Life* *29*

8 *Winter of Discontent* *33*

9 *A Dog's Life* *39*

10 *Houdini Dog* *51*

11 *Logjam* *55*

12 *Good Fences Make Good Neighbors or
Where the Buffalo Doesn't Roam* *57*

13 *A Horse is a Horse* *63*

14 *In Search of Mr. Good Horse* *67*

15 *A Cunning Plan* *73*

16 *Saddle Up* *85*

17 *A Stable Environment* *89*

18 *Belle and the Beast* *93*

19 *Sybil* *101*

20 *Misstep* *113*

21 *Winter World* *119*

22 *Trespassers* *125*

23 *Wait Until Dark* *127*

24 *I Am NOT The Grass* *133*

25 *Finding Linda* *139*

26 *Yard Wars* *151*

27 *Spoils of War* *157*

28 *Uptown Cowgirl* *161*

29 *She Thinks My Tractor's Sexy* *165*

30 *Hoarse Horse* *173*

31 *TKO* *177*

32 *Dressed to Kill* *183*

33 *Dead Heads and Dead Ends* *187*

34 *Rory* *201*

35 *Meet Mr. Wilson* 207

36 *Trouble's a Foot* 223

37 *Season of the Grizzly*...227

38 *A New World Odor*...245

39 *Swap Meat*...249

40 *Kickin' Cousins* 251

41 *Ride Like the Wind* 253

42 *A Horse of a Different Color* 257

43 *Ride On* 261

44 *Hello Dolly* 267

45 *Saddle Up* 271

46 *Goodbye Dolly* 283

47 *Bless This Mess?* 291

48 *Right-of-Way* 295

49 *Snow Days* 299

50 *How the West Was Fun* 303

51 *Everything's Normal* 311

52 *Missing Lynx* 313

53 *A "Swell" Time*...317

54 *"Porcupine in Parking Lot"* 321

55 *Batman and Robin* 325

56 *Home is the Hunter* 329

57 *Magnum* 335

58 *Whiskey for My Sandy* 339

59 *School Daze* 345

60 *Spring Has Sprung* 349

61 *The Good Earth*...351

62 *I Am No Lineman for the County* 355

63 *All Not Quiet on the Western Front* 357

64 *Night of the Predator* 359

65 *Let Them Eat Cake* 367

66 *The Price of Freedom* 369

Epilogue...373

Recipes 375

I have clinched and closed with the naked North,
I have learned to defy and defend;
Shoulder to shoulder we have fought it out—
yet the Wild must win in the end.

*—From The Heart of the Sourdough
by Robert Service (1874—1958)*

Introduction

I WAS VISITING A FRIEND WHO GREETED ME WARMLY, and said, "I've been waiting for your next horse story, tell me about your horses! I love your country life stories. Have you seen any more wild animals?" She was not the first person to tell me I should write a book about my experiences, both the good and the not so good.

After giving it some thought, I decided to share my experiences with you. I hope this book brings a smile to your face and, at times, makes you laugh out loud. If you are contemplating a change to a more pastoral life, I hope it helps prepare you better for success by avoiding some of the mistakes we made along the way! And for those interested in horses, I hope it brings you to a deeper understanding of them and how they can enrich our lives. And most importantly of all, no matter your background or experience, I hope it proves to you that with effort and patience, not only can you follow your dream, you can live it.

Go West, Young Woman!

Prologue

"IT LOOKS LIKE A MODERN-DAY COVERED WAGON," I quipped as I examined the heavy blue tarp that covered the back of our new pickup truck, a gunmetal grey Ford F250. Underneath, were stacked my husband's tools, along with other basic necessities we would need for our new life in Montana. They filled the eight-foot bed, and overflowed into the U-Haul trailer his mother had managed to secure for us. It was the last one available in the tri-state area, and thanks to her dogged efforts, we acquired it, instead of one of the thousands of graduating seniors who were disgorging this same week from nearby Florida State University.

As we hurried about, checking the lashings one last time before we departed, I scanned the scene. It was a bright and beautiful spring day, and the sun glinting off of the metal body contrasted sharply with the shimmering tarp. Colorful as it was, I tried to imagine it was not unlike the prairie schooners of the pioneer stories I loved reading in my childhood. The idea that I too was moving west was like a dream finally come true. But it had started as a nightmare...

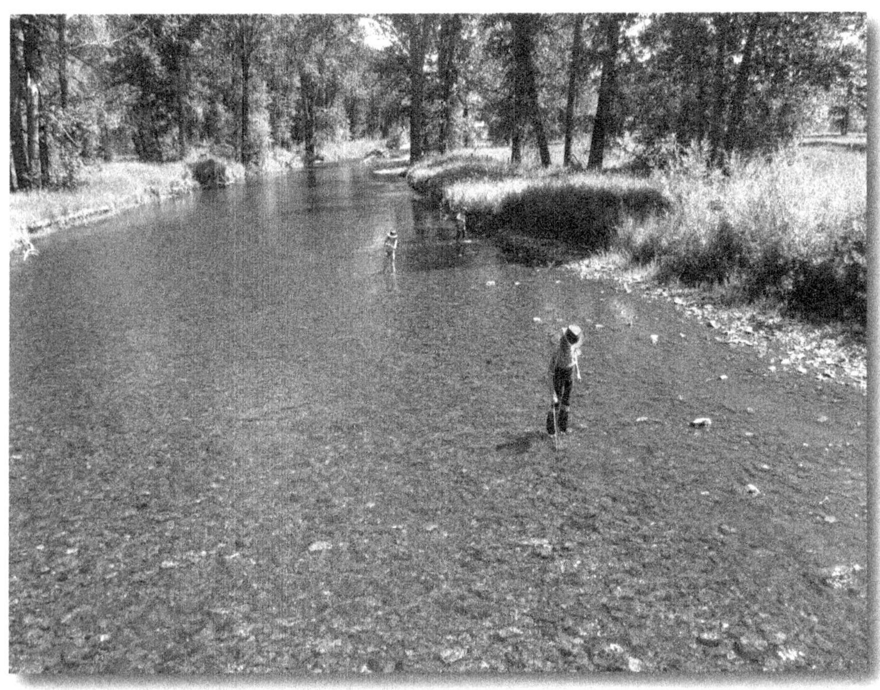

Gone fishing!

1

Go West, Young Woman!

As I GENTLY SWAYED ON MY GLIDER BY THE EDGE of our front porch, I gazed over the acres of lush green grass that rolled uninterrupted to the tree line below. Left uncut all summer, patches of it, which the horses had ignored, stood as tall as wheat and danced in the soft breeze, matching the rhythm of my own movement. The slow oscillations had a calming, almost mesmerizing effect, and soon my mind wandered back to the first time I ever saw this land.

Ten years earlier we first came west on an extended vacation, the idea being to find a permanent place to live after my husband, Bill, retired from the Air Force. This was a thrill for us; in the military you don't always get to choose where you live. You go where you are assigned, and Bill's last assignment had been a difficult one, a tour at the Pentagon. We'd only been there seven months when our world changed forever. Bill was working deep inside the bowels of the building at the Air Force Operations Center when the terrorists attacked on September 11, 2001. I remember sitting in front of the television watching a live news broadcast, while clutching my then one-year-old daughter, Sandy, close to my chest and praying my husband was still alive. Twenty minutes passed before the phone rang, and to my great relief I heard Bill's voice reassuring me he was alright.

"I won't be home for a while, Honey," he spoke calmly, "I've got to stay here and work the command center until we've got everyone relocated. I may not be able to reach you again; the phone lines are starting to jam up. Just know I'm safe and I love you."

It was the longest day of my life, but I was so thankful he was unharmed. We later learned we had been far more fortunate than his counterparts in the Navy Command Center a few hundred yards away; only two of them survived. Because of the war and the nature of his job, Bill's tour would stretch beyond six years. To help preserve our sanity during the next sixty-eight months, we began devising our plan of "escape" into retirement.

It first began as a goal Bill had set when he was a Boy Scout attending the 1969 National Jamboree in Idaho. His troop was composed of scouts from Florida and Georgia, most of whom had never been this far north or west. So following the Jamboree, they spent an extra week camping out at Glacier National Park near Kalispell, Montana, and visiting a neighboring park in Canada. He never forgot the experience, and fell in love with the mountains of the northwest at the age of fourteen, always longing to return someday to live. Despite the decades of military service that followed, he never had an opportunity to land an assignment in the region, but the desire never left him.

As for me, I'd never been west of the Mississippi, and though I wanted a country life, I wasn't sure if the wild, wild, west was the right place to raise our two young daughters. I too loved the mountains, but it seemed a bit rash to settle someplace I'd never even visited. By now we'd been living in the Maryland suburbs just outside D.C. for over three years. We had grown accustomed to the routine, which never seemed to change at its core, comprising a constant rush of people, traffic, events...none quite settled, nor fully relaxed. Always there was some degree of tension, and the pressure of this lifestyle was slowly taking its toll on me as Bill continued his long hours at the Pentagon, working projects he could never openly discuss. But as seriously as he took his work, I could tell the strain was affecting him too. In all this time we'd had only one vacation, and that had been a trip back to Florida to see our families. We desperately needed a break, and a real change of scenery. Bill had suggested we take a trip out west, but I worried out loud, "What if the west doesn't suit me?"

"Well, better to find out now, then after I retire. I've got plenty of leave time I need to burn. What say we take a month off and tour the entire northwest?"

"Where will we go? Who do we know there?" I asked.

"We'll follow the wind," he answered confidently. But my puzzled stare quickly evoked a more detailed response.

"Okay, we'll head west and see where the roads take us. Don't worry, I've got friends and family scattered across the area. We'll visit them along the way. And you'll be better able to decide if the northwest really is the right place for you."

"But the girls are so young," I protested. Our daughter, Sandy, was just four-and-a-half-years-old at the time, and had recently been joined by her new sister, Sonja, who was less than six months old.

"Well that's not a problem. They're good little travelers, and it's not like we're using oxen and a Conestoga wagon to get there. We can fly into Denver and rent a car, or better yet, a van. From there, we can cover each state by highway, stopping here and there to scout the territory."

Bill had pulled a road atlas from the shelf, and was excitedly pointing at one page with a pencil. He quickly traced a route from Colorado, through Utah, Wyoming, Montana, Idaho, Oregon, and Washington.

At first, it all seemed so ambitious and spontaneous, but I could see now he had been planning this adventure for quite some time in his mind. Then it dawned on me; for the first time in our married life, we'd be free to choose anywhere in the country to call our home. We'd already spent years designing our dream house. The large pieces of tracing paper had become permanent fixtures on our dining room table. But we'd never decided just where to build it. Here was an opportunity to finally start turning that dream into reality…if the west really was the right place for us. We planned the trip for late summer, arriving in Denver that August by plane, from which we began a large circular journey by minivan through Colorado, South Dakota, Utah, Wyoming, Montana, Idaho, Oregon, and Washington. With only a map to guide us, we visited large and small towns alike, looking for our new home, our piece of paradise. Though a month long, it seemed like a whirlwind. I remember the apprehension I felt when we departed the Denver airport on our first driving leg of the trip, headed for Colorado Springs. Would I really like the west, or was this a colossal mistake? But no sooner had we left the city and entered into the rocky country just beyond that I began notice how different it was from Michigan, Florida, and Maryland where I'd spent so many years.

Bill just smiled and said, "You ain't seen nothing yet." And so it was, as we explored a west I'd only seen in movies - flat prairies, deep gorges, tall mountains, angry rivers, and vistas that at night made one feel small in this universe when compared to all the stars around us. We visited small hamlets with names like Elk Mountain and Baker City. Along the way, I purchased an Australian Barhma hat, that I still wear to this day. It was in these places that I inhaled the freshest air I've ever known, thinking *if this is typical of the west, I'll take it.* When this first adventure was over I felt a gloomy sadness as we boarded our flight back to Maryland (on September 11, no less), and realized in my heart I was becoming a Western girl.

A year later, we didn't hesitate to take a second trip out west. We had narrowed our search down to two states, Idaho and Montana. We decided to start with Montana. Little Sonja was now eighteen months old and Sandy was five. They were good travelers and didn't mind visiting some places we'd missed the last time we were in Montana. This time we arrived in Spokane, Washington, and just as before, rented a minivan, but started heading to the west central part of Montana, specifically the Missoula and Helena areas. These were places we'd missed during our first grand tour of the northwest.

Bill had always been fascinated with Missoula, so we started there first. Unfortunately, the day we looked around the town we discovered a pungent odor that pierced the air.

"What is that smell?" I asked the realtor.

"Oh, that's the paper mill. The prevailing wind sometimes changes direction, but not more than ten days a month. You get used to it." With my hypersensitive nose I felt like a canary about to pass out in the mines. Scratch one community. What a pity, it had so much to offer.

Next on the list was Helena, the state capitol. We'd passed it up last time because one of the Generals Bill worked with, who had a home in Kalispell, assured him there were no mountains around there and it was a rather unattractive place. We were running short on time so we bypassed it on the first trip.

Later, an officer on Bill's staff, who happened to be from around there, gently offered a slightly different opinion, "Colonel, Helena is surrounded by mountains!" He also was of the opinion Helena was a nice town. Could it be Montanans were partisan about their communities?

Well, maybe, but when we arrived in Helena, we immediately liked it. It fit our entire list of criteria. It was not too big and not too small. What we liked most was that it was CLEAN. There was no trash in the streets and the downtown area was restored and well cared for. Within the city limits were several nice parks, and best of all, it was surrounded by beautiful mountains!

Even a mundane day of running errands becomes a beautiful experience when you walk out to a parking lot and see those snow covered peaks all about you. *How gorgeous; no heavy traffic jams, police sirens, or smog, just a view that belongs on a postcard.* As we left one store we saw a huge rainbow stretched from the earth to the sky. I took it as an omen.

"I like this place. It looks like a good family town," I said, as I turned my head skyward, trying to take it all in.

"I do too," Bill replied. "Let's find a hotel so we can look around some more."

After dinner that evening we decided we liked it enough to start looking for local real estate. We got out a map and circled a fifty mile radius around the city to begin our search. We also had plans to check some properties in Idaho, so we limited our stay to four days, vainly hunting for a suitable place. But as one busy realtor rather smugly informed us on the first day of our investigation, "Helena's been discovered." Translation: Don't expect too much, and be prepared to pay plenty if you do find something. On our last day we were about to give up when we were contacted by a realtor from

Lincoln, a town we had visited but rejected because of its relative remoteness. She had one more place for us to visit if we were interested. It was a half hour from Helena, just over the Continental Divide. I remembered the area from one of our scenic drives, and told Bill I wanted to see the place.

"Isn't that all national forest?" he asked.

"No, the realtor said there are a number of old family ranches and some small communities in the area. I think it's worth a look."

We met our realtor, Loraine, in Mullan, a former vital and vibrant mining community in Cheyenne County that now scarcely merited a second glance by travelers passing through. We were joined by another realtor who represented the land owner. In three vehicles we convoyed a few miles from town, turning in at a traditional log post-and-beam entrance. From there we climbed a narrow logging road. I looked out the window with both interest and trepidation, noting that occasionally my side of the trail seemed to disappear, only to be replaced by a steep ridge dropping a hundred feet or more below. We drove over a mile up the winding trail and headed directly to the back of the property for a closer view of the creek. Aside from two large pastures we passed along the way in, the entire path was beautifully surrounded by tall lodge pole pines, fur, quaking aspen, and the occasional ponderosa. I envisioned it having looked very much this way two hundred years ago when only Indians roamed the land on foot. It was like stepping back in time. Huge jagged boulders and tall trees were everywhere, and steep slopes, nearly vertical, surrounded us as we descended down a depression that brought us close to a rapidly flowing creek.

We stopped here so that Bill and the two realtors could walk along a section of the creek. I stayed with the children and took them to the creeks edge along one of the wider grassy banks. The water was clear as it bubbled and gurgled its way along to its destination below, the Arrow River. It rushed over branches and rocks, forming little waterfalls as it tumbled and turned.

We sat quietly and listened. We heard only the water. The sound was enchanting.

When he returned, Bill chatted quietly with me, "This is really nice. My only concern is I feel so closed in. There's not much of a view."

"It's pretty narrow," I agreed, "Where would we build a house? You'd have to cut into the side of the mountain."

The realtor suggested we backtrack up the hill to a clearing we'd passed coming in. We piled in our cars, climbed up the road, and rounded the corner to behold a vista we'd not been able to see on the journey in.

My eyes widened as I exclaimed, "Look at that!"

"I see it," Bill replied, smiling with delight.

"Unbelievable," I whispered, "Stop the car."

We stepped out and gazed west at the panoramic view that greeted us. It was nearly 180 degrees of mountain splendor. Huge trees, green meadows, and flowers set the foreground, with snowcapped mountains as far as we could see in the background. It took my breath away.

"Wow, you don't see this coming in; you have to turn around." I took the girls out of the car and let them have a look. Bill and the realtor went exploring and I let the girls pick wild flowers.

I also noticed that there were some cows milling around. "Who do these cows belong to?"

"I don't know," replied the local realtor, "There're ranches around here; maybe some cows got out. I don't think this land is leased."

In a little while Bill returned and I asked him to walk to the top of the hill with me. Our realtor offered to watch the girls and Bill took my hand as we strolled up the gentle slope.

"What do you think of this place?" he asked.

I looked out at the mountains and then into Bill's beautiful blue eyes, those eyes I fell in love with, nine years earlier. For a moment I could not speak and the silence hung in the air.

"I think we should make an offer on this property." My voice choked a little and I was feeling overwhelmed.

"You do?" Bill's shocked voice matched the shocked expression on his face. "You don't make quick decisions. You always have to research everything and gather all the facts." He went on in a rushed voice. "We were supposed to meet that realtor in Idaho. Do you still want to go, or do you prefer this?"

My mind whirled and I began to physically shake for some reason. "Yes, I think this is the place for us." It was about all I could say for the moment.

Bill stood looking at me, "I like it too. You've got good instincts Quinn, and I trust them. It's close to a town we like and it's hard to find a nice piece of land we can afford. We can live here year round." I could see his mind at work as he thought out loud. "In fact, I think our home should go right about here. We can call it 'Cimarron.' I looked it up in the dictionary. It means 'wild summit,' but it's also an old reference to a runaway slave."

I liked the name. It seemed appropriate, since we'd be living on the former, and we currently felt like the latter. We stood on that hillside pasture, with the sun high and bright in the blue sky, and a gentle breeze dancing through the quaking aspens beside us. I kept drinking in that magnificent view, while thinking *home…our home...Cimarron.*

Bill broke the silence, "Let's go tell the realtor we want to make an offer." He took my arm and we started to move. Tears began to stream down my face.

"Are you alright? Why are you crying?" He held me even tighter. He bent down to see my face.

"I don't know; I just need a moment. I'll be okay." I was feeling completely overwhelmed, but in a good way. We had found our home, a real home, not just a place where we lived for a few years. This wasn't a temporary interlude where I'd have to dream or worry about our next move. This was it. This is what it felt like to be home. I stood there motionless and took it all in one last time…for now.

"I want to take some photos before we leave," Bill remarked. He walked around taking snapshots from different angles. On our way down the hill we saw a train go by as cows grazed in the foreground. "I want a picture of this," he said. "How often to you see that? Doesn't that look like the west? What are the odds? Sandy, hurry up and stand right there and I'll get you in the photo too." Our little blond five-year-old stood smiling with the breeze in her hair as he snapped the shot. Bill was so proud of that photo that he hung it on his office wall to admire everyday. The funny thing about it is, now that we live here, we see the cows and trains every hour of every day. Who knew?

We told our realtor we wanted to make an offer, and asked if she knew someplace we could fill out the necessary papers. She answered, "You betcha" and gave us a big smile. I'd heard this expression before and would again many times. "You betcha" is almost always accompanied with the requisite smile. They just belong together, like salt and pepper.

We completed our paperwork in Stratford, another small community four miles west of us, then returned to our hotel in Helena to await a response. I remembered that song John Denver and Emmie Lou Harris sang together, "Oh Montana give this child a home…Give him a fire in his heart and a light in his eyes. Give him the wild wind for a brother in the wild Montana skies." It played in my mind the rest of the evening in the hotel.

It was not long before the phone rang. Loraine announced, "Congratulations, your offer was accepted. You will soon own a piece of Montana." We were so happy! We agreed to meet her the next day to go over any further details.

I was exhausted, both physically and emotionally, so I decided to get washed and go to bed. I was just finishing my shower when I heard a loud banging on the bathroom door. *Something must be wrong. Bill wouldn't pound on the door this way.* I shut off the water, grabbed my robe, and opened the door to see his alarmed face.

"Did you feel that? I put the girls on the floor next to the bed."

"Feel what?" I was confused. I had felt nothing in the shower.

"The earthquake, we just had an earthquake! We were really shaking."

I looked at Bill and my two little ones. *An earthquake! What have I done? I just bought property here and now we've had an earthquake?*

Bill must have read the look on my face because he smiled wryly, "Don't worry, Honey. It's just Montana's way of saying, 'Welcome.'"

We were waiting to meet Loraine, our realtor, the next day at the nearby Perkin's Restaurant. I was looking at the local newspaper, its headline story focusing on last night's quake. But what also caught my eye was another article titled "First Murder in Helena in Over Ten Years." *Oh great, earthquake and murder, just another Payton Place.* Of course I did put it into perspective. I had lived around cities with far higher murder rates—Detroit, Miami, Washington, D.C. The fact that such a tragedy was headlines news here was, in an odd way, reassuring. But the earthquake remained the primary talk of the day. Our realtor came in and sat down.

"How bad was the earthquake here?" she asked desperately as her brown eyes darted between us. Loraine flipped a lock of dark hair over her shoulder and continued, "I was in the epicenter over near Dillon. It really shook us all up. We had some damage. I'd just stopped at a gas station and was using the restroom when the toilet started to shake. It was so bad it threw me on the floor. I was struggling to get up and looking for something to hang onto when the next thing I know, my keys are falling out of my jacket into the commode! Thank God I'd just sat down because now I had to fish them out. I don't have an extra set and my house and office keys were on the ring too."

I was trying not to laugh, but since she was, I didn't feel so bad. By now we were all laughing. What are the odds? Welcome to Montana.

2

Green Acres We Are Here

TWO YEARS LATER, BILL FINALLY RETIRED FROM nearly thirty years of combined service in the United States Air Force and Air Force Reserve. We had completed his last assignment, still in Washington D.C. It was a great relief, as some of the past events were hard to look back on and remember.

Now we were anxious to start our new life away from the metro D.C. area. Bill had created a meticulous relocation plan which involved first driving 700 miles south to Florida to retrieve his business property and to exchange our older two-wheel-drive Ford Explorer for a new four-wheel-drive pickup truck. We would load the eight-foot bed with his tooling, protected from the elements only by the blue tarp, and hitch a rental trailer to the bumper. In it would be the other necessities we would use until our new home was finished and the rest of our household goods could be brought out of storage. With our seven and three-year-old daughters in the back seat, we began the final 2,500 mile leg of the journey to our new home. Ahead of us awaited seventy-three acres of the most beautiful mountain property I had ever seen, in our forty-first "Treasure State," Montana.

It took us several days to crisscross the country on our modern interstate highway system. Unlike the pioneer families of old, we had all the comforts of hotels and restaurants, but still encountered the frustrations of bad weather, dangerous road conditions, and wind. Our tarp flapped wildly, despite being tied down, and in time, needed several repairs. Thank goodness for duct tape. Along the way we made the obligatory stops to visit family and friends in Tennessee and South Dakota.

We were still slogging through rain, wind, and snow on the Interstate when we passed Clark Fork, one of the earliest permanent communities in Montana, and our county seat. Shortly, we would find ourselves traveling through a narrow valley that ran for over twenty miles until it was interrupted by the vast Continental Divide, which separated our small hamlets from the state capitol of Helena, nestled in a sprawling valley on the opposite side. The Divide, we would soon learn, was not just a physical barrier, but one of weather, culture, and perhaps time itself.

Snow pelted the windshield, and I remarked how unusual it was to see it in May. Bill just shrugged, "Welcome to Montana."

Soon we would approach our entrance somewhere between the twin communities of Stratford and Mullan. Did I say twin? Never had I known two towns that were so close, and yet so different. I had read a book that described the colorful histories of the twin towns; Stratford, with its focus still on ranching, and Mullan with its emphasis on mining and logging, had been rough and tumble places. But the mines played out, and timber fell by the wayside, a victim of pine beetles and eco-politics. Fire and flood had done their share of damage as well, so that neither place merited a second glance anymore unless one needed gas, a meal, or a drink. The Northern Pacific Railroad still runs through the middle of Mullan, following the meanderings of the Arrow River. One can even find the occasional angler, knee deep in the rushing waters, standing in somber reverence, genuflecting with his fly rod to the goddess of good fishing (which, according to some texts, was also the goddess of sexuality and fertility, which might explain some male anglers' passion).

To the east stands the Continental Divide. To shorten travel time between the Helena Valley, Mullan, and the many other communities further west, in 1867 a road was built over one of the mountain passes. It was managed by a French Canadian woman until her mysterious murder a year later. But Mullan, like other mining communities of the period, was a rough and tumble place back then. By 1891 it was thriving with hotels, restaurants, and thirteen saloons. It also had several stores, a blacksmith shop, livery stable, meat market, and barber shop. Sadly, most of the town was destroyed in a fire in 1926, and never recovered. Today it's a sleepy hollow, and mainly a bedroom community for those working in Helena. Gone are the saloons (save one), the bordellos, and the mining.

I was jolted back to the present about a mile from our new home when Bill asked me to watch for the log and beam entrance. Just as we neared it, the clouds broke and a shaft of light smiled on us. Of course I took it as a good omen. We had been worried because our builder, Bob, had been calling us along the way with weather updates. He was concerned we could not get our new truck and trailer up our "road."

The "road" was in reality nothing more than an old, seldom used logging trail. Thanks to the rain, it now was almost a mile of mud rising up to our home, which was still under construction. We had purchased this land in the dry summer and had not thought about the implications of the spring rains, which was the first of a series of features I soon mentally cataloged under "this was not in the brochure!"

That earlier sign of good luck proved to be true. By some miracle, we did make it all the way up, however, a dump truck bringing in a load of granite fill rock, was not so fortunate, and Bob's crew was in the process of pulling it free with a large backhoe when we rounded the last bend to see our house for the first time. "Welcome to Montana," the half finished structure seemed to say.

I remained undaunted by the rain, eager to see our new home. Bill carried Sonja in his arms, and I helped Sandy cross the thick soup of muddy clay to get to the framed dining room area of our house.

I handed her to one of the construction crew, but discovered I could not extricate myself from the oozing mud. That same hand then lifted me up to the dry floor, sans one shoe which disappeared into the muck below.

It would not have been so bad, but as he lifted me up, a rush of dirty slush slid from the roofline onto my head! There I was, an embarrassing sight standing on one foot, my long black hair dripping wet (not the best of omens), yet all I could think to say was, "It's okay; at least I'm home!" But inside my head I heard a voice sneering *Welcome to Montana.*

Go West, Young Woman!

3

*A Creek Runs through It
& a River Runs near It*

T HE DAYS PASSED QUICKLY, BUT CONSTRUCTION PROCEEDED slowly on the house. In one of the few moments I had available to ponder our future in this new land, I realized just how much we had given up to be here. The word that best sums it up is "convenience". There wasn't a whole lot of that. We were twenty-five miles from most shopping, entertainment, or dining; and communications were limited to the telephone and a few scattered radio signals. Local television reception was nonexistent, no matter how large of an aerial we placed on the house. Bill wasn't keen on the idea anyway, remembering how a decade earlier, while living on our tree farm in Florida, he periodically had to climb out of the bedroom window and onto the roof at night to manually adjust our aerial for better reception, while I hollered from downstairs when the signal looked the strongest. Nor did either of us desire to watch an endless parade of tragedy each time we turned on the set. That was just the sort of trap we were trying to escape. Instead, we'd glean our news from periodicals and internet stories, all at our own leisure.

And then there was the new dialect to master. As an example, I was looking over my front pasture and imagining wild horses running freely through it and the meadows beyond. In the past, I had always used the words *pasture, meadow,* and *field* interchangeably, but I was initially befuddled when I heard the locals refer to the parks around here. To me, a park was a public place, with well manicured grass, beds of planted flowers, rows of old oak trees, scattered benches, and a winding jogging trail. Or it might be a ball field where little league teams competed, while the parents screamed oaths about the umpire's poor eyesight. Perhaps they meant a state or national park, like Yellowstone. I hadn't seen anything around Mullan that resembled any of this, so when I asked our builder, Bob, about where all the parks were, he chuckled and explained it was a colloquialism for any open area of grass, devoid of trees. *So I guess we now owned a couple of parks and didn't even know it.*

I also learned the "correct" pronunciation of the word *creek.* I was explaining to one of Bob's construction workers that our land bordered part of Powder Creek.

He looked at me puzzled. "You mean *crick.*"

"I think it is Powder Creek," I said earnestly.

"It's a *crick,* Powder *Crick,*" he replied.

I wasn't sure what to say; where I came from, a *crick* was something you got in your neck. A *creek* was a small stream. Well, when in Rome...

4

The Refrigerator Incident

FOR THE NEXT SIX MONTHS WE LIVED IN THE WORK SHOP Bob had built for Bill's business, half of which had been converted to temporary living quarters. This allowed us to oversee and participate in the remainder of the house construction. The shop was "cozily" comfortable, complete with a small kitchen, family room, bath, storage/laundry, and two small offices we used as bedrooms. All of our furniture, bedding, and kitchenware remained in government storage, so we did have to improvise.

Some of the first items we purchased in Montana were a refrigerator, stove, washer, and dryer. I remember loading up our truck with these appliances in the Lowe's parking lot in Helena. The wind was really starting to blow, and ferocious gusts swooped in, making standing a challenge for my petite frame.

"This wind is awful; I'm worried about crossing the mountain to get home," I said, gripping my jacket close to me as my hair whipped my face. I could hear it rushing past my ears with a muffled, physical blast. I felt like it was going to lift me off the ground and set me down "somewhere over the rainbow." I hastily looked in the window of our truck and mentally checked to make sure my girls were okay. Sonja and Sandy were still young and always my first concern. Two pairs of big blue eyes under golden blond hair gazed back at me, smiling.

"You worry too much," Bill said grinning reassuringly, but the kind look from his striking blue eyes did not deter me.

"I think you should tie these boxes down, Bill; something could blow out."

"I don't have any ties; besides, these appliances are too heavy to blow out. They're packed in without an inch to spare."

"I don't agree. I don't like it."

"They're not going anywhere," he commanded, somewhat irritated. We turned to the two Lowe's employees, who nodded their agreement. I was outvoted. So we started our drive home across the "Pass," our heavy truck moaning as it fought against the headwind. For a brief time it let up and I felt some small relief, but I pulled down my sun visor to use its mirror to keep watch on our supplies in back…just in case.

We were just beginning the long, half mile high climb up the pass, when a violent gust shook the truck. My stomach tightened in fear as a split second later the refrigerator was lifted out of the bed like a rocket being launched from a silo. It rose above the truck, and then gracefully bounced down the four lane highway.

"The refrigerator blew out! Pull over! Stop the truck!" I yelled, straining my voice.

Oddly enough, my first thought was one of gratitude. Thank goodness there were no cars around to interfere with its journey. Bill quickly pulled over, jumped from the truck yelling epithets, as he ran toward the now heavily dented box lying in the middle of the road.

As Bill began to push the refrigerator from the highway, several cars approached, but easily swerved to avoid it, and kept on going. This was one time I was glad Montana only has one person per seven square miles. As Bill struggled with the refrigerator, an old white pickup pulled over and a lean, weather-beaten man got out. He trotted over to Bill and, without introduction, helped him push the heavy box into the emergency lane.

Together, they were able to move it quickly. I suppose the fear of an oncoming vehicle rounding the curve was highly motivating. Safely off the road, they smiled, shook hands and exchanged names. After thanking him, we learned he lived in Mullan. He helped us put the refrigerator back into our truck and loaned us some ties to secure it and all the other boxes safely. Bill promised to return the ties to our "good Samaritan's" house after we got home. As soon as he was finished with us he quickly drove away. We were learning that many Montanans are not a chatty lot. When Bill got back in the truck, he was smiling.

"What's so funny?" I inquired.

"He said we must not be from around here. But he added we shouldn't feel too bad, 'Unless you've lived here a while, you don't understand how powerful the wind is. Most folks lose something out the back of their truck—the first time'. This was our first. I guess we get a pass."

We shared a chuckle and some relief at this information, now that the crisis was over. No one was hurt and all we lost was a little pride and one brand new refrigerator.

As he started the truck, Bill turned to me and said, "You aren't going to let me forget this, are you?" Once again he gave me his wry look with those serious blue gray eyes.

"Not for awhile," I answered coolly.

In our family history this has become humorously known as "the refrigerator incident," the first of many new experiences that were a testament to our unpreparedness for mountain life.

Go West, Young Woman!

5

A Mouse in the House

KNOWING OUR FURNITURE WOULD ARRIVE SOON AFTER we moved into the new house, we were determined to get by in the interim on as little as possible, so a memory foam mattress on the floor served as our king-sized bed. We purchased a futon for the girls to share (yes we strapped it down in the truck). Minor sundry items were acquired at the local thrift stores, while the modern successor to the general store, the big box stores like Lowe's, Home Depot, Wal-Mart, Shopko, Target, and Costco, provided everything else.

With the shop now adequately outfitted to serve as our temporary home, we settled into our new routine for the following half year. The next adjustment would be to the regional fauna. We hadn't long to wait. That first night, while Bill snored blithely, I awakened to a noise coming from the adjoining laundry room. Always a light sleeper, I had developed "Mommy ears" long before my first child was born. It was a grinding, ticking sound emanating from the carpet edge behind the door only a foot from my own feet. My stomach tightened in a knot, and fear gripped my mind, for I recognized it at once.

Now I am not a physical coward. In my younger years I was a state duty officer in conservation law enforcement, and also taught Hunter Safety for the state of Florida. I have handled snakes as large as pythons, alligators, cougars, leopards, tigers, monkeys, iguanas, birds of prey, and various other wildlife, but I remain to this day deathly afraid of *mice.* I've been on the receiving end of many jokes as this information leaked out over the years, but it is something I have always carried with me.

"Bill, wake up," I said quietly, not wishing to disturb our intruder. He groggily asked why I woke him from a sound sleep.

"Listen!" I said "Do you hear it?"

"Hear what?" He listened, and of course, as when taking your car to a mechanic to explain that funny noise under the hood, we heard *nothing.*

"Just listen," I insisted. I could not believe I was actually *hoping* to prove I'd heard a mouse.

In a moment, there it was again, the sound of a mouse chewing on the carpet.

"I'll shut the door," Bill sleepily offered.

"You have to get him," I said. "I can't sleep on the floor with a mouse. It might jump on me."

"I can't believe you're afraid of a mouse," he announced out loud for the rodent to hear. Then he looked at me. The near panic on my white face must have been visible even in the dark, for his expression suddenly changed and appeared to say, *Oh right, I forgot we were talking about you.*

He got up from our bed on the floor and flipped on the light. I was already standing up practically on one foot, wrapping my pale blue nightgown around my legs, wishing now it was a suit of armor. He stumbled about and looked in the laundry room, but saw nothing but a small area of pulled threads where the mouse had been chewing.

"I don't see it," Bill said. Suddenly he jumped sideways and yelled, "There it is!" The mouse had scurried across the floor behind the washer and dryer.

He doesn't like them either, I thought to myself. *I'm not the only one!*

"We can't catch it tonight. Tomorrow we'll be in town and I'll buy some traps. In the meantime I'll just shut the door."

"That won't do. He's been chewing on the carpet and could come under the door."

"Honey, he can't crawl under the door, and he isn't Mighty Mouse, so he can't lift it either."

I just shook my head firmly, and soon Bill was placing duct tape along the bottom of the door and carpet.

"Satisfied?" he asked testily.

"Not really, but I suppose it will do."

He grunted and went back to bed, quickly falling asleep while I vigilantly stood guard for fear the mouse would chew through the tape and wind up caught in my hair. I'd read about such things, or was it bats? Anyway, I was so afraid I would wake up with a mouse running across my foot, or worse, my face, that I scarcely slept the rest of the night. In the morning I insisted we lay traps for the tiny demon (there could be more than one, you know). We hadn't long to wait. Within a few hours the traps were sprung but the mouse had escaped—sort of. We later found him dead in the washing machine. The lid was closed, so we never could figure out how he got in there.

To further our initiation into rural life, we were greeted with our first snowstorm two weeks after our early May arrival. We awoke that morning to find fourteen inches of snow on the ground. It had started snowing the night before and Bill had insisted on telling me "it wasn't sticking." We soon heard the rumble of builder Bob's Caterpillar tractor, plowing a path to us. When he jumped down from his "Cat," the big diesel motor still chattering, Bob chimed in, "Kind of a heavy snow for May," he said smiling. "We usually don't get this much this time of year."

Apparently, when an unexpected dump hits the area, everyone takes it in stride, as if it's just a minor inconvenience. In the D.C. area they would have shut down the roads and closed the schools. But weather is a major factor in life here. I've often heard the expression "if you don't like the weather, wait five minutes and it'll change." Never had I seen more extreme examples. The same day it snowed, I saw hail, rain, and sunshine, all within thirty minutes, in the spring! A common saying in these parts is "Montana has two seasons, winter and July." We learned quickly to check weather reports at least daily.

It would take several months longer than we anticipated before construction would be finished, with many more new experiences lying ahead, but we wanted a big change and a new lifestyle. We definitely accomplished that goal, and along the way found having a rural mountain home is not the same as living in town. I was only just beginning to grasp this idea as I went from military wife to country life.

6

The Cows Come Home

"BILL, COWS ARE LICKING OUR WINDOW!" I SHOUTED as I was awakened by the sight of a clear thick smear of saliva on the glass pane above us. Our temporary bedroom in the office of his shop, which itself was a building dug into the side of a hill, provided the cattle easy access to grazing next to the roof on the upper part of the berm. A mere two feet separated this side of the roof from the ground. From this vantage point the cows could easily reach the windows below them. Why they would want to lick them remained a mystery to me. Perhaps they were collecting the morning dew or maybe glass tastes like grass! Either way, their gooey saliva still clung there, glinting in the rays of the rising sun. At first I was horrified by the sight of a huge pink tongue moving up and down the glass, fearful it might give way at any moment, hurling 1,200 lbs of unprocessed beef on top of me. I hurried into the living area of the shop and raised the blinds on the picture window, only to discover more bovines impressing their lips on the windows. *Why do they do that?* I wondered to myself. Maybe we were under a zombie cattle attack.

Bill decided to scare this one away by opening the side door and yelling at the beast. Startled, she jumped sideways, lost her footing, and quite gracelessly rolled partway down the hill. Quickly regaining her footing, she then sauntered off to greener pastures—literally.

I guess he really did scare it away was my first thought. I took a second look just to be sure the cow was on her feet and unharmed. She was fine, and as she nonchalantly passed the corner of the house, carelessly knocked down my bird feeder and stepped on it. I just shook my head with disbelief.

I was still upset when I stepped outside and found dozens more cattle camped in our front meadow as if on some extended holiday, eating, napping, and doing those unmentionable things all cows are famous for.

"We have to call the owners and ask them to take their cows out of our front yard," I said. "Yesterday, I stepped in…well, you know, the waste they leave behind!" I could not help thinking again, *not in the brochure!*

The cattle belonged to Herman and Gail, the patriarch and matriarch of one of the oldest ranching families in the state. They leased the land next to us for their cows to graze, but a large portion of it was not fenced. The cows liked our yummy green grass, and some decided they liked our house even more as they lazily scratched themselves on the scaffolding. We called to invite our ranching neighbors to come up and meet us. Given the circumstances, at first it was a little awkward, but while Bill and Herman discussed ranching traditions, I was happy to finally meet Gail. Not petite like me, she was tall and svelte, yet physically strong from decades of hard ranch work. Outwardly a no-nonsense person, and tougher than some men I've known, I soon discovered that inside she was all heart, and possessed with a kind soul and an interest in art. I had found a kindred spirit, and within a few minutes she had offered to teach me how to drive a tractor. I felt honored.

In return, I gave her a fresh batch of my extra vanilla chocolate chip cookies. This proved to be a happy coincidence, as baking was not her favorite pastime, but eating baked goods was. And since I'm always looking for someone on whom to test my new recipes, this later evolved into a recurring practice, with her family gladly serving as my willing guinea pigs. I even acquired the nickname "Vanilla Queen" because I would use so much of it in my baking. The cookies proved to be the start of a wonderful friendship.

Herman and Gail had the cows removed, but since bovines have no interest in boundaries, they often returned. One of Gail's sons would dutifully retrieve them, but a long term solution was required. As we became more familiar with local customs and laws, we realized if we wanted the cattle permanently off our land, we would have to fence them out ourselves. Ranchers weren't required to fence them in (yet another item not mentioned in the brochure). By the time our first summer ended we had made plans to locate our property lines so we could begin fencing. Lesson number three was about to be learned.

Go West, Young Woman!

7

The Facts of Life

WILDLIFE, WEATHER, AND LIVESTOCK ANIMALS figure prominently in a country lifestyle. We were getting pretty good at dealing with all of them. My children were quickly learning the physical aspects of animal husbandry. Living in the country, there was one prime example that sticks in my mind and probably that of my daughters as well.

Bill and the girls were returning from the post office, and were driving up our logging road, when they encountered the usual crowd of bovines standing in their way. They were part of two herds belonging to some nearby ranchers who leased the properties below us. We had learned to beep the horn and drive slowly, so the cows would move aside without startling. On this particular afternoon, Bill met a large cow in the middle of the road who refused to move. She stood fast despite the truck inching forward with the horn blasting. She had attracted the attention of a large Black Angus bull. He slowly lumbered over and inspected the cow. Without a moment's hesitation, he mounted her and began to let nature take its course. It became quite a spectacle, and my daughters began a flurry of questions.

"What's he doing?" Sonja, my youngest, inquired.

Sandy, who constantly read about horses, began to explain the bull was breeding the cow, like a stallion would breed a mare to make a foal. At least that is what she thought.

29

"Do all animals do that?" Sonja queried.

"Yes," Bill broke in, "all animals breed." He inched the truck closer, pressing the horn frequently, hoping to avoid the next obvious question. The bull would not be rushed. When he was finally satisfied, the bull jumped off, and he and the cow both wandered away, freeing the road.

"So, Dad, do people breed?"

Bill responded, "Ask your mother. She'd know more about than I."

When they returned home they had to tell me all about it, in detail. Sonja concluded with, "Dad said I should ask you about it, because you know more about it than he does."

I gave Bill "the look" and said, "And just what is *that* supposed to mean?"

Later, as we sat at my dining room table enjoying some tea, I told Gail that her cows were offering free "sex education" classes. "And they didn't have the courtesy to seek parental consent before demonstrating their technique."

"Ha! My kids got a similar education on the ranch," said Gail. "I've birthed calves and foals since before they were born. One of my sons videotaped a cow giving birth as his 4H project."

"You mean his '4X' project, don't you?"

"Nancy, ranch kids learn the facts of life early. It was the same with Herman when he was working on his grandfather's ranch. Many of the cattle ranches around Stratford have been in the same families for generations. The kids all work the ranch, and inherit what the elder family members leave them in their wills. Starting out is hard. When Herman and I got married, we had nothin'. Money was hard to come by, and it paid to be self-sufficient. My children were raised on cow's milk, fresh out of the cow. I didn't buy that pasteurized milk in the cartons from the grocery store. I also used to make my own butter; and I'm still canning much of the food from my garden.

"Herman and the boys did a lot of trapping. It was just another way to supplement our income. The pelts brought in some extra cash. Chase still does it. You know, he likes to bait his trap with fermented hoof trimmings"

"You mean the toenails off your horses?"

"That's right. He soaks 'em in a water jar until they decompose. Once they get really foul smellin', he smears the stuff on his traps. The animals can't resist the odor."

"I guess it's a Montana perfume for wildlife. You should bottle it and label it 'Call of the Wild'"

"Yeah, except it's so dang putrid. Chase also likes to use dead mice, which reminds me, the next time you trap some, would you save the remains for Chase?"

"Uh, sure, Gail. Say, did you ever do any trapping?"

"Mostly it was my job to clean the pelts after they'd been skinned out. I used to wash 'em out by hand."

"It sounds like messy work; but I guess it was worth it to have that extra money."

"Oh, it was, but I didn't really like it. Although one woman I knew in Clark Fork refused to wash 'em by hand. She'd throw her coyote skins in the washing machine instead. It was gross! I told her, 'No way I'd do that.' I didn't want that disgusting stuff in my washing machine."

"You mean the same washer she did her clothes in?"

Gail nodded and took a sip of tea.

"I wouldn't do that either," I said with a grimace. "When the girls come in from the pasture, they sometimes have a little manure on the bottom of their jeans. That's bad enough. It makes me want to dump a whole bottle of detergent and stain remover on them, and throw them straight into the washer. Sometimes I think about just how hard it was to stay clean without our modern conveniences. But like you, I'd draw the line at coyotes in my washing machine, no matter how much I want to be a Western girl."

She nodded and murmured, "Um-hum."

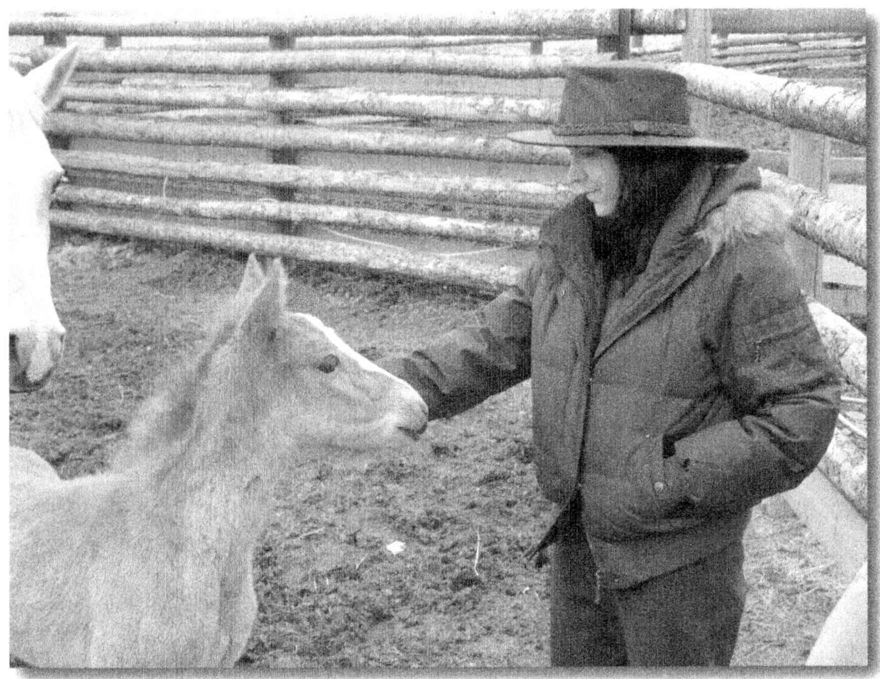

Making a new friend

8

Winter of Discontent

S IX MONTHS OF LIVING IN THE SHOP WAS FINALLY rewarded just before Halloween, when I was "carried" into our 95% complete home. I was beginning my recovery from an unexpected femoral hernia operation, made urgently necessary thanks to a dismissive lapse in medical judgment by a military doctor ten months prior.

As I was carted up the staircase, I watched our finishing carpenter, Denny, hard at work, alone in our living room with his router and saw. I was glad the work was continuing, even though the pace had greatly slowed. When I mentioned this to Denny, he stunned me with his reply.

"Everybody's gone huntin'. Bob's not around to watch over them. He's out guiding hunting parties for the next six weeks."

I feared the work might come to a complete standstill; however Bill stepped in to keep things moving forward. We soon had three painters hurrying about, rushing to complete the exterior work before the cold weather set it. Despite the chaos, I was happy just to be living in our new home. Thanksgiving came and went before the staircase was finally completed. Even Christmas found some remedial work left undone, but by the end of January we were at last free of workmen and beginning to settle into our new home on the range.

Our first winter was in full swing, and soon we realized the mile long road that snaked up to our place would be snowbound without a plow. Fortunately, one neighbor was equipped with a skidster and snow blower, so we hired him to keep the road clear. This wasn't always possible because one never quite knew when a strong wind might leave impassable drifts along the route, effectively blocking the road. When it did, we invariably discovered it at night during a return journey from town.

Our first such encounter set the pattern to follow. It was about seven in the evening, dark, and cold. The wind had been blowing while we were away, but now was still. All seemed well until the last quarter mile, at the steepest turn. Even in four-wheel drive the tires began to spin freely and the truck started to slide sideways toward the edge of the road where it drops off sharply to the bottom below.

My mind raced; were my children in the back seat strapped in? Did they have their jackets and gloves on? Could Bill stop the truck before we plunged over the side? What could I do? I felt so helpless, unable to avoid the danger. After what seemed like hours, the truck stopped at the edge of our road, one back tire nearly dangling over the steep drop off. Bill got out and inspected the situation. We discussed our options and decided it was best to leave the truck and walk home. The temperature had dropped well below freezing as we checked our cold weather gear inventory. Bill was missing his watch cap, Sandy lacked gloves, and Sonja did not have a scarf. One of our two flashlights died the moment we turned it on.

Bill was concerned I might have trouble reaching the house on foot. I was still recovering from my unplanned surgery, so he wanted to try getting the truck back onto the road one more time. I was against it. We all had to pile out of the vehicle from the drivers side, for if we tried to exit from the passenger side we risked falling down the embankment. *This was not in the brochure.* We huddled together as Bill pressed the gas peddle and the wheels once more vainly attempted to grip the slick road. The truck spun a little more sideways but otherwise stayed in the same place.

"Stop!" I shouted. "No more Bill, you're going to fall off the side." My stomach was churning and my chest was tight. Bill relented and climbed down from the cab. "I guess we'll have to walk," he shrugged.

To make matters worse, we had forgotten to turn on the outside house lights, so Bill marched quickly ahead of us to switch them on. With a child in each hand, I began our slow trudge through the snow. We had to cross the cattle guard carefully to prevent anyone catching their ankle and breaking a leg.

I wrapped my hand around Sandy's gloveless fingers and told her to put her other hand in her pocket. The wind began to pick up and blowing snow stung our eyes. Poor little Sonja, then less than four, was knee deep in it and having an especially tough time walking uphill. Sandy, being seven years old, was doing a little better but was very scared. I prayed with every step. We were struggling. I called for Bill to carry Sonja, but he couldn't hear me as he moved further ahead. A sick feeling washed over me. I called again. The cold was hurting my lungs, and with every breath was biting into my chest. This time he turned and I called to him, repeating my request, almost breathless. He came back and lifted Sonja into his arms, promising to come back and help me with Sandy. He was moving fast and in a second or two was around the corner. Sandy and I now were alone.

Bill had given me the working flashlight, so I shined it on the snow just ahead of us to see where we were stepping.

"I'm afraid of running into wild animals," I heard Sandy's small voice squeak. "What if we meet a wolf or cougar?"

The same thought had crossed my mind, but I dismissed it. "They're not out in this cold," I reassured her in a lighthearted tone, even though I was quickly getting out of breath. I squeezed her hand. "Let's save our energy and not talk. I want you to follow the light on the ground and we'll be home soon. Just try to step on the light, okay?"

One step at a time, I told myself as the pain of the wound burned inside me, *You can do this*. A blaze of light cut through the darkness as the house lit up but it still looked so very far away. "See, Daddy's home. He'll be back to help us in a moment; keep moving." In less than a minute

I saw Bill close the front door and start down the road to us. *Even the early settlers did not go out in weather this cold. Why did I move here? What was I thinking? We're all in danger. No time for this now.* I seemed to be having an argument with myself but it was interrupted by a sharp pain in my lower abdomen.

Bill took Sandy's hand. "Help her along, Bill," I said. "She needs to get in the house." He wanted to wait for me but I insisted I could make it alone. Bill continued his ferry service to the house. It was not far now, but I soon saw him coming back for me. He held my arm and together we navigated the drifts, but it took some time. Once inside, he sat me in a chair by the fire. *Thank Goodness for gas fireplaces.* I could finally rest, and so I collapsed with an ungraceful thud. I was dizzy, weak, and feeling nauseated, but otherwise okay. *I just hope I haven't torn any stitches.*

Bill nursed the tips of his ears. We checked the girls for frostbite and found they had suffered no real harm. "At least the food won't spoil," I sarcastically remarked, thinking of all the groceries we left in the truck.

"But it will freeze, so I'd better go get it," Bill unenthusiastically replied.

Before departing, he called a neighbor and explained the situation. He agreed to meet Bill later at our truck and pull it out with a tractor, if necessary. *Now I know why everyone owns a tractor.* Uncertain as to when he might show up, Bill donned a proper cap and warmer coat before setting out with the girls' sled. He made two trips loaded with perishables before help arrived. With a little effort and a lot of skill he soon had the truck out of the drifts and back on the road for us so Bill could drive it home without further incident.

Afterwards, we assessed the situation, talking at length about what could be done to make the road safer and easier to travel in winter. We decided to limit winter travel to daylight hours, and to include a rather large emergency kit in the truck, complete with tire chains and a snow suit (to wear while chaining up the tires). By the time winter was over we'd become fairly practiced at installing and removing chains. When summer came we would have Bob widen the curves, build more drainage ditches, and improve the roadbed with decomposed granite taken from a pit on the back of our land. He even built a small berm at the sharpest corners to catch our tire in the event we started to slide again.

With our first winter officially behind us, I was beginning to feel as though I was becoming more a part of the community, a seasoned and accepted Montanan. That illusion was soon crushed as I dined one evening in that same café in Stratford where we completed the initial offer on our property. The tables being very close together, I could not help but hear the waitress remark to a customer, "Oh honey, things are changing around here. We have a big shot from the Pentagon moving in and he built that big house up on the hill. I've heard some things about him, you know, one of those government types."

That remark definitely caught my attention. *Oh dear, they must be talking about Bill.* Since the waitress was practically at my elbow and smiling at me, I commented, "You must be talking about my husband, Bill. He's in the restroom right now, but I'll be glad to introduce you when he comes out. You'll like him." I pretended not to notice the shocked expression on their faces as I gave them a friendly smile.

After introductions were made, we all became acquainted and talked for a while. I realized then that many people had their minds made up about us long before we ever moved here. It would take more than a single year to convince them otherwise.

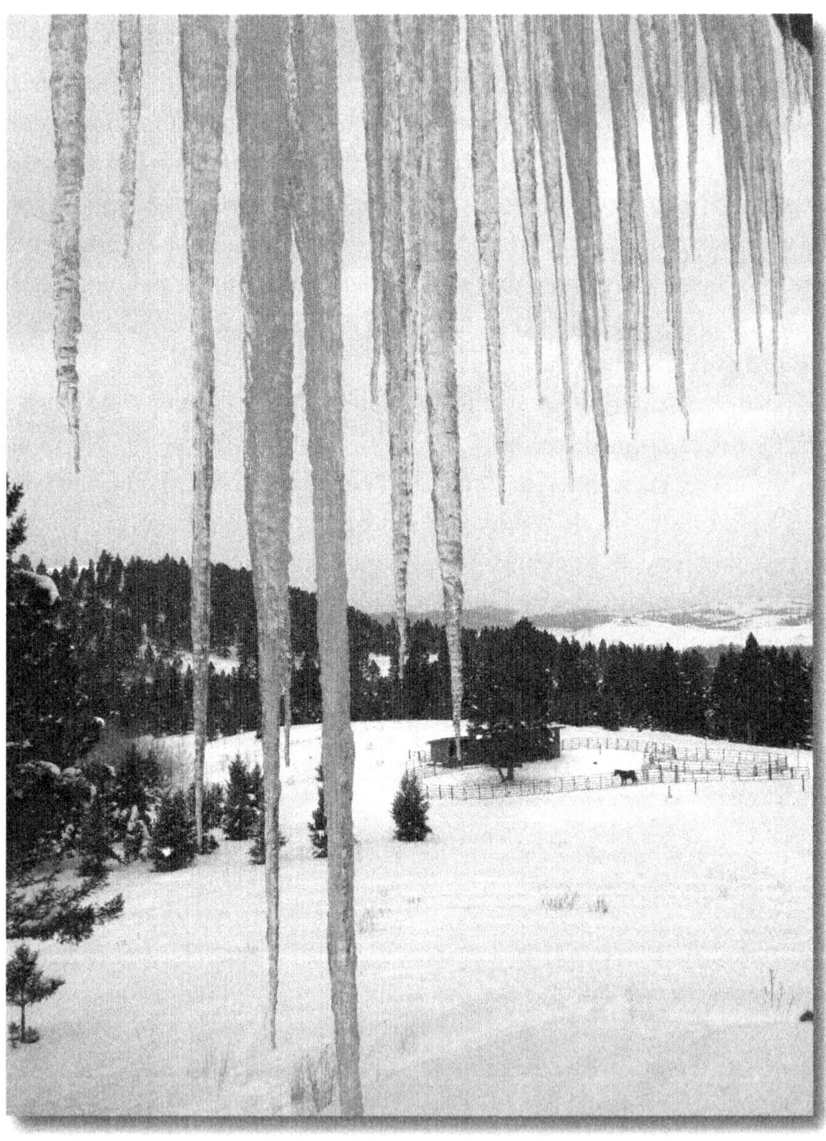

Ten foot icicles frame the view on a winter's day

9

A Dog's Life

I HAVE ALWAYS LOVED DOGS AND HAVE HAD ONE as my constant companion for as long as I can remember. From my tiny dachshund, Snoodles, who slept on my bed when I was a lonely, fatherless child, to my 100 lb yellow lab, Teal, who both hunted with me and protected me in darker days, all of them proved their worth a hundred times over. At present though, we were without a canine.

Our last wonderful dog, Sunny, had become very ill and died just six weeks before our move west. He had been a stray we found the morning after Hurricane Earl struck us while we were living in rural north Florida a decade earlier. A German shepherd/Labrador mix, he would remain with us for almost twelve years after we nursed him through heartworm, mange, starvation, physical and emotional abuse, a major jaw bone infection, and numerous open wounds. We knew he was worth saving. He had arrived with another mongrel mix we named Hannah. She was in even worse shape than Sunny, and he cared for her, often taking food from his own dish and dropping it at her feet when she was too ill to rise. It wasn't long before Hannah passed away, and Sunny then began caring for my dearest and most faithful friend, Miss Teal, my yellow Lab of fourteen years. A few months later it was Teal's turn to go and Sunny remained by her side all through her final suffering. After that last evening when the vet had ended her pain, Sunny could not accept her passing. He even removed the blanket from over her silent face as if to say she was only sleeping. We both knew better, but the gesture touched me deeply.

With the baton passed to him, Sunny proved himself a very brave and protective fellow. He always escorted me around our land and once saved me in our own front yard. I was just coming down the steps from the porch when I saw Sunny alert to something a few feet in front of me. He froze, and then leaned in as if pointing at it. I looked down from the last step and gasped. There sat a poisonous water moccasin, half hidden in the grass. It had slithered into our yard unnoticed by all but our very alert Sunny. I was very lucky. If Sunny had not seen it first, I could have been bitten.

That was not the only time Sunny protected me from danger. While I was expecting with Sandy, Sunny and I would walk down the dirt road on our land almost every day. One morning as we started our stroll, he suddenly stepped forward and blocked my path. I tried to step past him but he cut in front of me again, blocking me again. He pressed his side against my legs and would not let me by. I knew Sunny was smart and I trusted him completely.

"You don't want me to walk down the road today? What do you see boy?" I asked as I peered down the path. I construed by his face that he was telling me something was wrong. His eyes, one brown and one marbled blue, were full of concern. I decided to heed him.

"Okay, let's go home," I said, as I turned around and headed toward the front door. He followed obediently. I never did find out just what had upset him and why he wouldn't budge, but I instinctively knew he had saved me and my unborn baby from some unseen danger.

As with Miss Teal, his death those many years later was a great loss to our family. I was not even sure I wanted another dog; the emotional commitment had been so great. We had promised Sunny for the six years we were trapped in a Maryland suburb that eventually he would be free to roam the open range again once we settled in Montana. Hannah and Miss Teal rested peacefully in a field back on our old Florida tree farm. Sunny would go west with us, his cremated remains traveling in our modern day covered wagon, across the country to our new home and his final resting place. A beautiful cherry wood box in a green velvet case still sits on a shelf by our fireplace in the family room where Sunny continues to watch over us eternally.

As winter ebbed, I considered enough time had passed for us to once again acquire a dog. I was glancing through the *The Gold Standard*, our county weekly, and saw an ad from our local humane society and animal shelter. It contained a picture of a German shepherd/St. Bernard mix.

"Look at this guy," I said, showing Bill the photo. He laughed, "He is a big boy."

"I bet he could handle anything that comes his way," I retorted. Then it hung in the air.

"Do you want to go look at him?" Bill asked.

I wasn't sure. I knew we needed a dog because we had wild animals to contend with, not just annoying chipmunks, but cougars, bears, wolves, and coyotes. We had seen the tracks near the house, and it worried me enough that I had heeded Gail's suggestion to tie bells on the girls' shoes. As she had mentioned more than once, "Make all the noise you can outside. It keeps the wild animals away."

I checked the website and also saw another possibility, Kobi, a shepherd/malamute mix. "Let's just go look," I said, "I'm not making any promises." Bill just smiled.

I was disappointed to learn the dog advertised in the paper was adopted shortly before we arrived, so I inquired about Kobi. The animal control officer brought him out on a leash. He was smaller than I expected and only about eight months old. At first he acted like a nut job. *What a banana head.* As Bill walked him around the yard, I explained to the officer how I wanted a dog for protection and to warn us of any danger.

The officer shook her head, "I don't think Kobi is the dog you need. Ever since he got here he's avoided any confrontation with other dogs. He won't fight them, and he backs down whenever he's challenged. I think he'd run at the first sign of danger. If you want a constant companion, I'd suggest Dora. She's a sweetheart."

Dora was a very friendly small black lab mix, and I liked her. But she'd been living at the pound for several years and obviously considered it her home. In fact, several other owners had returned her because she kept running back to the place. I wanted an animal not so tightly bonded with other people or places.

Instead I focused on watching Kobi. As Bill approached, Kobi came up to me, a happy wiggling mass of muscle. He was a stocky guy, I would give him that. He immediately pressed against my legs and calmed down. He pushed so hard I had to brace myself to prevent falling backwards. *He wants a connection.* I felt the immediacy of his request. Here I go again. "Will you look me in the eye?" I asked him.

I know dogs do not like to be stared down. Most will not look at you, or they take it as a challenge and then, depending on the dog, you may have trouble on your hands.

I took his face in both hands and turned his chin up to me. He did not look away. For almost thirty seconds I searched his eyes, talking in a soothing voice. He never moved. I released him and knew he was mine, or was I his?

"We should think about it over lunch," I said. Bill agreed, so we thanked the officer and drove away. The girls were afraid of Kobi and did not want him.

"He's not aggressive. He just needs to be taught some manners. He jumps because he's friendly," I told the girls. If there was one thing I did not like, it was a dog that jumped and licked you in the face. It's part of their nature, but not mine. They exhibit both traits to their mothers to show respect and renew the bond of the pack. However it is something that can be trained out of them, usually within a few days.

We decided to adopt Kobi, partly because I didn't agree with the officer's assessment that Kobi's unwillingness to fight with other dogs was a sign of weakness. I also believed that the issue of bravery could not be decided until tested. A dog that loves his owners will most likely put himself in danger to protect them. It's not just a matter of love and loyalty, but also about maintaining the strength of the pack.

When I called to say I would adopt Kobi, the officer told me there was a problem. *What now?*

"The original owner wants Kobi back," she said.

"You won't return him?" I said, urgently. "Clearly this person cannot give him proper care." I felt my stomach tighten.

"I don't want to," she replied, "She can claim him, but I told her she had to pay a fine and his kennel fees for the duration of his stay. I don't think she'll do it, but I must give her a few days to comply. It's the law."

"Is there anything else I can do?"

"No, just wait. Do you really want him?"

"We do," I answered firmly.

"Let me look into it and talk to our county attorney. This owner has several violations and I'm reluctant to place the dog back with her. I'll call you in a few days."

I explained the situation to Bill and we agreed all we could do was wait to see how this played out. A few days passed and still no word about Kobi. I decided to call and inquire if there was any news.

"I've not heard anything," the officer replied, "Give me a couple of more days."

"I understand," I replied rather glumly, "I'll wait to hear from you."

I was feeling unsure about the whole prospect and a little sad for this dog. That Friday afternoon I received a call from the animal control officer, "Do you still want this dog, Kobi? If you do, you need to come get him today."

"We'll be there in an hour!"

Kobi was delighted to climb into the back of our pickup, but he wouldn't sit still. I didn't have a portable kennel, and I feared he would jump out somewhere along the road. We fastened a leash to his collar and had no sooner tied it off when he leaped over the side. In horror I saw him briefly dangle from the truck, and thought he had broken his neck. But before that fear could be realized, the link snapped and he was free on the ground, happily playing with the kids.

"This won't work. How will we get him home? We've got twenty-five miles to go."

Bill scrounged around and soon produced two pieces of rope and a spare collar. With two collars around his neck, we secured him in the middle of the truck bed. One rope stretched from the first collar to the left side of the bed, while the other stretched from the second collar to the right side of the bed. No matter which way he turned, he could not move from his central spot. Just to make sure, I had the girls keep a constant eye on him as we drove down the highway. When we reached our house he was squirming violently, trying to free himself. I cautiously attached a new leash to him before releasing the ropes and was rewarded for my efforts by nearly being dragged off the truck. *What a great sled dog he would make, if only we owned a sled.*

Our next chore was acclimating him to his new home and establishing his boundaries. Fearing he might bolt for Clark Fork the moment we took him off the leash, we only removed it when inside the house. We had been assured he was house broken, but just to be certain, we took him out every few hours on a leash to relieve himself. This he did gladly, and repeatedly, marking his new territory every few yards. It was still winter and much snow clung to the ground, but Kobi plowed through it like the snow dog he was, dragging poor Bill behind him. After a few outings like this, I decided the best course was to use a pinch collar. I generally didn't favor them, but had found them useful on particularly obstinate dogs until they learned their manners. With Kobi it took about a week before he finally understood his boundaries and relented. I never had to use it after that.

Kobi did not bark or make too many sounds at all. I thought it was perhaps some kind of arrested development. I knew he was bright, and only a couple of weeks after we brought him home he proved it. The first time I heard him bark, I could hardly believe it. It was at night when I heard a loud, deep, vicious, roaring bark like that of a lion. I called out, "I think that's our dog!"

Bill and I ran from opposite ends of the house to see what the commotion was all about. There he stood on the back porch with every hair on his back raised, and all his teeth baring. He was prepared to leap down the slope when we called him back. He stopped and returned to us. It was a good thing he did. In the shadows of the Aspen trees just off the back patio was a large fury animal moving slowly away, and apparently unafraid. Uncertain exactly what it was, we brought Kobi back inside. The next morning we let him out again. An hour later we heard that same throaty bark we'd heard the evening before. This time he was backing up slowly

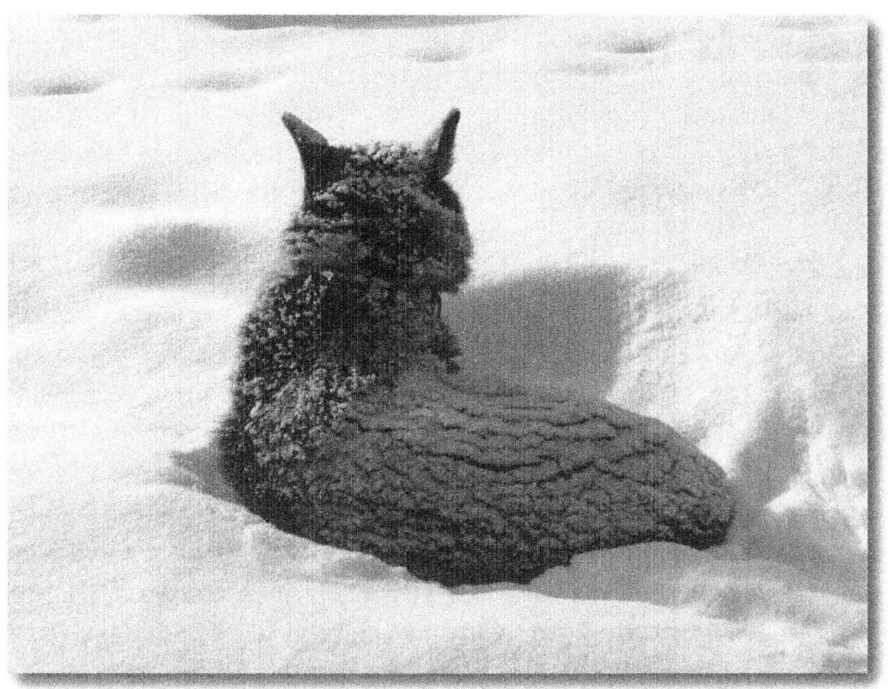

Kobi on sentry duty

towards us, but his head remained focused straight ahead, up the hill. I saw it sitting calmly behind a bush only twenty yards from the house, a lone grcy wolf. I had heard wolves would send out a member to lure dogs from their homes, only to be descended upon by the entire pack. Kobi had nearly fallen for it last night, but now appeared savvier as he continued backing toward the door, snarling all the way. Bill exited with a rifle as the wolf began to move toward the shop, a couple of shots sent him packing at full speed, never to return.

"Nice shooting, Dad," said Sonja. "You missed him."

"He left, didn't he? That's good enough," Bill snorted. Sonja just eyed him suspiciously.

I was quite proud of Kobi. He was not afraid, nor would he cower and run from danger. He was protecting his home and his family. As a reward, I gave him some macaroni and cheese for supper. To this day I have only heard Kobi bark a few times, and then only when he sensed immediate danger. After these two incidents he became much more talkative, and ever since has made constant grunts, groans, and snorts of approval or disapproval, but rarely does he bark.

When I called Gail to tell her about the incident, I mentioned we had called the Montana Fish, Wildlife, and Parks Department (FWP), to ask them about the legality of shooting predators. "They said it was okay to kill one close to the house if it was threatening your family or pets," I told her, "but they'd want to send out an investigator to recover the carcass."

Gail interrupted me with a stern warning, "Don't never call FWP if you kill a wolf, no matter how justified you think you are. They get to decide what's justified, not you. And if they've got a fly up their nose, they'll fine you, especially when ya' live south of the highway like you do."

"What's that got to do with anything?"

"Everything. Their rules say it's legal to shoot a wolf north of the highway, but not south."

"That's crazy," I insisted.

"Duh? That's why ya don't call 'em. They'll either ignore ya' or harass ya'. So what are ya gonna do? Obey dumb rules, or protect your family and livestock?"

"Well I'm going to protect my family, of course."

"Then you need to do what any sensible person would do. Follow the three S's. Shoot, shovel, and shut-up."

It was then that I remembered a photograph I'd seen in the local paper of a dead wolf draped over a stop sign along the road. I mentioned it to Gail.

"Yeah, that's what I mean. FWP had been asked to deal with a wolf that was killin' livestock, but they did nothin' about it. So somebody took matters into their own hands. Most folks have a pretty good idea who it was, but they ain't talkin'. Their only mistake was not buryin' it. Instead, they wanted to make a political statement and left it on the road sign for everyone to see."

"Wow, the code of the west," I mused.

"Somethin' like that."

After we hung up, I mulled over the disturbing information Gail had provided me. It seemed irrational that this was even an issue, but I was to learn, over time, that apex predators such as wolves, cougars, and bears, had both their supporters and detractors, not just here in Montana, but across the country. It was not simply a local matter, but a national debate, that would come back to taunt us from time to time.

I looked down at Kobi, who'd been napping by my feet the whole time. He stared back up at me when I moved, his eyes soft and hopeful. I patted his head and said, "My, what a ruckus you nearly created just by being my fearless protector." He wagged his tail, and rolled over, begging for some belly rubs.

Fearless as he was when confronting imminent danger, he was surprisingly peevish when confronted with ear medicine or the dreaded bath. It was like owning a bipolar dog, yet his native intelligence always rang through.

We had a remote outdoor sensor that read the temperature and sent a signal back into the house to a digital unit in the living room. One cold winter morning I noticed the display was not showing a reading. I assumed the battery was dead, but when Bill went out to check it, he realized it was missing. Irritated, he yelled, "Nancy, that dog took the thermometer! I can't find it!"

Assuming the wind had knocked it down, I suggested he search the ground around the porch, but that wasn't possible due to the snow everywhere. Bill was even more convinced, "Kobi took it. We'll never find it now."

"Let's ask him," I replied.

Bill stared at me with a tolerant sigh and said, "Fine, talk to the animals, Dr. Doolittle."

I called Kobi over to the windowsill and politely asked him to find the small, square, white box that was the thermometer. I pointed to where it used to be and asked him to bring it to me.

Kobi immediately turned and ran out into the yard. He began to dig in the snow, and when he returned to me, he dropped the little box in my hand!

"That's my dog!" I laughed out loud. Bill was smiling too, until he looked at the unit. Kobi had chewed it up and ruined it.

"Great," Bill groaned. "What's the point of having it back if he broke it?"

I had to speak up, "Because he did what I asked and he understood what I said. He's a smart dog." Bill would remind me of those words very soon when I became very unhappy with Kobi.

Just as rural country living is not without its problems, so it is with dog ownership. Aside from the usual chewed boots and house training accidents of puppy ownership, we had a more expensive incident.

Bill came in the house one morning with a piece of my license plate holder in his hand. "I have to tell you something," he said in a serious tone. A sinking feeling fell over me; I had only had my new car less than ten days. I was so proud of my black and shiny Toyota Highlander. It had taken me a while to convince Bill we should buy it, but being so small in stature, it was difficult for me to drive our big truck, as I could barely see over the steering wheel. Seeing the broken plastic in his hands, my anxiety only increased.

Bill went on to explain that not only was the license plate holder broken off, but the SUV was full of scratches. I was not prepared for what I saw. My beautiful new vehicle was full of deep claw marks on the hood, doors, and roof. The first thing I did was cry. Apparently the malamute side of Kobi, our great hunter, had chased a mouse all over the car, trying to catch it. There wasn't even the consolation of having dispatched the vile rodent. I was livid and ready to take him back to the pound that night.

The Ford/Toyota dealership was able to buff out most of the scratches on Mavis (the girls having named it after the black locomotive from the *Thomas the Train* series), but I remained angry with my overgrown puppy. On the one hand he was very intelligent and protective, but on the other hand equally destructive. Hats, shoes, gloves, and bicycle seats were not immune from his chronic chewing. And then there were his happy feet. While mostly a homebody, on occasion the urge to explore struck him without warning, and he would disappear all day. The struggle for dominance and control would continue unabated for years.

The car scratching incident was still bothersome enough that I had trouble sleeping for some time afterward. It was during one of these restless nights that I saw the motion lights go on in the back yard. I got up to have a look and I could hardly believe my eyes. There was some large animal about the size of a dog in our back yard.

"Bill, wake up and see this," I hissed. I did not want to wake up the children. "Look over by the girls' swing set. What is that?"

Bill stumbled to the window and crouched beside me, "I don't know; it might be a small bear. I'll go down and have a closer look. Leave the lights off."

Kobi was awake and standing by the back patio doors. By now the creature had crept over to beneath our girls' swing set, about thirty feet from our back patio door. I watched with awe as the moonlight outlined it. I now knew it was a young cougar. I could not tell if it was a male or a female, but it gracefully lowered itself into a sitting position and wrapped its tail around its back legs. I could not help but admire it; what a lovely painting it would make, a perfect study of light and shadow. *How can something be so beautiful and so dangerous at the same time?* He silently lowered himself into a crouch, and I privately wondered—BAM! The rifle shot startled me. The young cougar flipped high in the air, landed and quickly darted down the hill into the tree line in three large bounds.

Bill returned to the bedroom and flicked on the light, yelling, "I missed! With a scoped rifle no less! He was just too close. I wasn't sure where to aim. I just hope I didn't hit my shop." Then he reflected for a moment, "Well, he won't be coming back."

I had to agree; the cat needed to be discouraged from being on the girls' swings. He could not be allowed to get comfortable and feel our home was part of his territory. My family's safety came first, but now how was I ever going to get to sleep?

Go West, Young Woman!

10

Houdini Dog

KOBI HAD DEVELOPED SUCH A STRONG BOND WITH the family that he could not bear to be parted from us for a moment (except when the call of the wild beckoned). The resulting damage each time we left him in the garage was proving to be more than we could afford. Concerns about wild animals, and a fear he would follow us if left outside when we went to town without him, led us to install a ten-foot wide chain link kennel. To make it both cougar and bear proof, we overlaid the top with a latticework of 3/8" diameter iron rebar (reinforcing bar normally used in concrete foundations for added cohesion and strength). Bill even constructed a little dog house that matched the color of our house, and placed it inside the kennel. Nothing could get in, and Kobi could not get out, or so we thought. Kobi had other ideas.

The first time we locked him in the kennel, we heard him howl woefully as his pack drove away. Upon our return home we found him happily bouncing down the driveway to greet us. He was so pleased with himself you could almost hear him say, "Look what I can do!"

"At least he stayed home, and didn't run off to find us," I remarked, trying to look on the bright side. I stared down at Kobi and realized just how filthy he was.

"Oh great! He's been to the creek and is covered with mud," I sighed. "Now we'll have to bathe him."

We inspected the kennel and found he had actually unwoven some of the chain link enough to squeeze his way out.

"What kind of dog can untwist wire? This is unbelievable!" Bill said while examining the unraveled links.

"A really intelligent one," I offered, without being exactly complimentary of his skills.

"I'll have to find another way to secure this kennel," Bill responded confidently, as if the matter was settled, but again, Kobi had other ideas.

The voice of my trusty friend Gail rang in my ears, "You should keep Kobi outside in the yard; he is a dog!"

Sometimes I thought she was right. Gail had working dogs that attended her when she worked her cows. The dogs lived outside all the time, and slept in a kennel at night to protect them from predators. Kobi was our protector and companion, so I believed that if he were to fully bond with the family, he had to be with the family. That meant lying at my feet when we watched TV at night, and snoozing by the kitchen door while I cooked. He was great company for me, but Gail remained unconvinced and simply quipped, "When I die I want to come back as your dog."

Since we couldn't put him in the kennel until it was repaired, we left Kobi in the garage during our next trip to town. We wouldn't be gone long this time, as we were just picking up material to strengthen his kennel. We concluded he wouldn't be too stressed, and we even cracked a garage window an inch so he would have some fresh air. But Kobi had a severe aversion to being confined. When we rounded the corner to our house on our return, I saw a streak of black and white rush to meet our car. Kobi lifted himself up on his hind legs and looked in the window at me, all smiles and panting tongue.

"How?" Bill and I asked simultaneously.

We pulled into the garage and were greeted by the sight of an open window with its screen ripped away and hanging outside. He had pushed his portable dog kennel underneath it, climbed on top, and nosed the window up enough so he could jump through the screen. Prior to that, he had nearly clawed his way through the sheetrock wall next to the mudroom door.

"What a mess. Look at this!" I shook my head as I examined the door.

"Why would he do it? How did he do it?" Bill quizzed himself while examining the scrap of shredded window screen he found left on the sill.

"Apparently when he couldn't claw through the wall, he went out the window," I said, disgusted by the sight.

Bill sighed and started repairing the kennel. The window screen would have to wait for our next town trip. To our continued surprise, in the interim, Kobi kept escaping, easily chewing through the hardware cloth and screen mesh we had added to reinforce the chain link fence. By now, the local Lowe's Home Improvement Center employees all knew us and Kobi by name. He was a favorite visitor to their store when we occasionally brought him to town in the truck, and it was his favorite stop as well. Each time he saw us entering their parking lot, he would begin scratching excitedly on the kennel door and whine to be let out. Once free, he'd dance a jig around the lot before marching triumphantly through the sliding glass doors to announce his arrival. He became the unofficial store greeter to anyone willing to pet him. He even received a Lowe's apron to wear about the store. Customers would stop to have their photo taken with him, and he bathed in the limelight of local fame until corporate headquarters began enforcing a policy forbidding pets inside their stores. Poor Kobi, he learned early that all glory is fleeting, and sometimes was sacrificed on the altar of legal expedience (i.e., the potential threat of lawsuits against deep pockets, should a dog leave his "marker" for someone to slip on, or bite the hand that feeds him).

But that reality was still in the future, and for now, we remained determined to find a way to keep him safe at home. On our next town trip we purchased heavy gauged metal wire "hog panels" to reinforce the chain link walls of the kennel. It was about the only material he couldn't chew through, but Kobi eventually would sacrifice a tooth discovering this truth.

Success at last, no dog escapes from Kennel 13! Or so we thought again and again. The battle of wits was on, man against canine. Who would emerge triumphant? Persistence paid off—for the dog. When the direct approach failed, Kobi attempted to tunnel out, but we had placed wire mesh on the ground and connected it to the kennel when we built it, so this effort proved futile for a very long time. He next resorted to constantly chewing and pawing the gate latch until it gave. We added a clasp to the latch; he responded with brute force, pushing the tubular frame of the gate until it bent enough for him to shinny through. We bent it back and added a chain;

he just bent it someplace else and escaped. The gate became so deformed, that we finally placed a series of chains on it and secured them with several metal clasps. Kobi learned he could paw one of them free and wiggle through the door, so we replaced them with one long chain wrapped in serpentine fashion around the frame and gate, and secured it with a padlock. But the padlock didn't always work, and I was just about convinced he was hiding a lock pick in one of his paws when we figured out that if the chain wasn't pulled tight enough, he could create enough slack to wiggle between the kennel frame and door. Man's best friend, ha! We needed a bunker, not a kennel, to hold this dog. That would come in time (sort of), but for now we were losing the battle of wits, and it was becoming embarrassing each time the phone rang, and I answered to the sound of someone saying, "I think I have your dog."

We tightened the chains, and most of the time it worked, but the war of wills was not over, and would continue, unabated, for some time. In the interim, it would become a sideshow, as we became preoccupied with new and more pressing issues.

11

Logjam

I T WASN'T THE SOUND THAT AWAKENED US AT 4:00 a.m. that alarmed me; it was the vibration I felt through the bedroom walls.

"Are we having an earthquake?" I asked.

Bill got up and pulled back the drapes.

"What is it?"

"Lights, from heavy equipment moving up our road."

"Who are they?"

"Loggers heading up to Clay's property."

I cringed when I remembered the chance encounter Bill had a few weeks earlier at the Stratford Café with Clay, a neighbor who owned a parcel further up the mountain. He had contracted with a logging company to remove timber from his land while prices were stable. We had considered doing the same because of the fire hazard presented by the Japanese beetles that were destroying much of the surrounding forest, but declined when we recalled the initial devastation harvesting had done to our tree farm back in Florida a dozen years earlier. From our experience we also knew that replanting would require fifteen to twenty years for trees to reach maturity. While Clay's land was out of sight of our place, we had not expected logging trucks and bulldozers to begin work so early.

The next few weeks became very tense for us. Snow remained on the ground and the trucks arrived every morning at 4:00 a.m. Every few hours one of them would race down the mountain and cross the middle of our property on the journey out. The first trip down proved to be a frightening experience for us when a heavily laden truck suddenly appeared just as the girls had begun a run down our front slope on their sled. I screamed at Sandy and Sonja to stop, but they didn't see the oncoming vehicle. Bill ran and tried to flag the driver, but to no avail. We watched in horror as the truck and sled continued on their collision course. Kobi was running alongside the sled, always trying unsuccessfully to hitch a ride. Whether he made contact with it, or the sled hit a heavy drift, I will never know, but suddenly it veered to one side and stopped several yards short of the road. The driver barreled through, either unaware or unconcerned. I was so livid, I wanted to barricade the road or dig a deep ditch across it.

"This has got to stop," I fumed at Bill.

"I'm not sure we can stop it, Honey, but I'll contact an attorney and find out."

Not knowing where to begin, we asked several neighbors for advice and located a firm in Helena. Unfortunately, the attorney assigned to us was less than knowledgeable or aggressive, and we were left with a feeling of complete helplessness. As it turned out, providence once more stepped in, this time in the form of economics. The cutting had proved less than profitable, and the company ceased operations on the mountain within a month. At our insistence, the logging operation owner did repair most of the damage to our road that had occurred as the spring thaw set in. Bill wanted to leave matters at that, but I felt as though the sword of Damocles was hovering over us. *What if prices rebound and they start cutting again? What if other people decide to come up here?* We'd had hunters show up during deer and elk season, acting as if they owned the land. And why not, there was no sign, gate, or fence to deter them. Even Gail's cows still grazed here when the mood struck them. Something had to be done.

"Bill," I said one evening in bed, "we need to build a fence."

12

Good Fences Make Good Neighbors or Where the Buffalo Doesn't Roam

BEFORE WE CAN BUILD A FENCE, WE NEED TO FIND our exact boundary lines," Bill explained as he searched an internet site of geographical surveys. "From the description in our deed, we should own the entire northwest corner of this section." He pointed to an enlarged satellite photo which clearly showed the logging road leading to our place, but it had not yet been updated to include our home. "We'll need to hire a surveyor."

"Where will we find one?" I asked.

"Where we find everything anymore; we'll Google it on the Internet."

We didn't have much trouble locating a company in Helena to conduct the research and verify the boundaries with their GPS equipment. Bill walked the property with them, and surprisingly, they managed to find the corner markers, one of which was nothing more than a stone which had been engraved with three hash marks many decades before. Bill accompanied the survey crew over very densely wooded and rocky terrain. When he returned that evening he appeared worried.

"Why so glum? Or is it just exhaustion?" I asked.

"Well, there appears to be a problem. Our northwest corner has a dovetail in it that will have to be fenced. It's a piece too small to build on, and apparently was deeded decades ago to some family member so he wouldn't have to move his fence. But that's a minor point. The real issue is that the entire west fence another neighbor erected years ago is located almost fifty yards onto our land. It'll have to be torn down and moved, or we risk losing several acres through adverse possession."

"What's that?"

"As I understand it, anyone who openly uses your property with your knowledge can eventually claim it, or at least claim an easement on it, if you've never objected to his actions."

"That can't be legal!"

"I only know what our last attorney told us. We may have to find a new one to sort this out—someone who specializes in land rights. I don't want to begin any fencing until we've spoken with one."

A knot began forming in my stomach. It was warning me matters would only get worse before they got better. Land titles, boundaries, easements, right of ways, cows, fences, trespassers…just how convoluted was this mess?

We soon found out when we met our new lawyer, Wyatt, in Missoula. Our research led us to his firm because they specialized in property law. We quickly discovered the importance of fencing our land in order to establish concrete evidence of our boundaries and our intent to maintain them. A title search of the area was like a history lesson and genealogy study all rolled into one. We could almost feel what it must have been like to be the first permanent settlers in an area that previously had known only the occasional presence of man in the form of the transient native Indian. Aside from a few arrow heads to mark their passage, no permanent evidence remains of them, having been replaced long ago by the now rotting posts and rusting strands of barbed wire fences emplaced by the calloused hands, sinewy muscles, and gritty determination of those first

Western pioneers. Even that memory was fading and would soon disappear altogether, to be replaced again, this time by modern fencing and metal poles that some might call progress.

We drove to Missoula for our first meeting with Wyatt, a distinguished looking, silver-haired gentleman, who reminded me of the stereotypical college professor (which, it turned out he also was). We sat in his comfortable office atop one of the few "tall" buildings in Missoula, and he listened attentively as Bill explained our predicament.

"If we put the fence on line with the survey, we'll have to cross a road that one neighbor uses to access his property. We'll also be cutting off another neighbor from our creek where he's been watering some of his cattle. But I've checked; it's not his only source of water. He can access the same creek a few hundred yards back on his own land."

Wyatt leaned forward, clasping his hands on his desk, "I must emphasize the importance of establishing your ownership and use of the land. Therefore, I recommended you not enter into any easements you are not comfortable with. Since you hope to pass the land to your daughters someday, it would be imprudent to enter into any arrangements that they would have to honor, perhaps in perpetuity. I also recommend you notify each neighbor of your intent to fence your property. By law, they are responsible for maintaining their half of the fence line, but they are not necessarily responsible for erecting any new fence. You may find yourself bearing this cost alone. But it will suffice as proof of your intent to maintain your property rights. It will also allow you to control access through your property, which is not permissible under the law by anyone who does not exercise a current easement, or else a letter of access from you.

"And one other point, our review shows that such access has not been granted to anyone for anything other than traditional use."

"What does that mean, exactly?"

"It means no loggers can cross your property without your permission. Any rancher who holds an easement, can come across to check his livestock, since that is considered 'traditional use' under the law."

"What about hunters and hikers?"

"They would need an easement or your permission."

That was enough for me. Good fences make good neighbors, or so I hoped. But I was concerned how Gail might react because the fence would affect her access to our creek, or at least that portion which crossed our land. I'd seen enough Western films growing up to know water rights and land access were major concerns of ranchers. In the movies it was the hired gun who always settled matters for them. In a way this was still true, except that now the hired guns wore expensive suits and carried cards that read "attorney at law."

As it turned out, I had little to fear when I broached the matter with Gail and explained why we were fencing our property. She accepted our decision with the stoicism so common to the breed who works the land.

"It's only one small point where your land touches ours," I said. Her husband started to comment, but after a quick glance from her eyes, he refrained. I left it at that. We had three other neighbors to contact, but only one of them raised an objection because it was his fence which would have to be moved. Bill tried to reason with him, but he dismissed our claim, arguing that his grandfather had erected it in 1912, and he would not pay to have any of it relocated.

When we asked Wyatt what our next move should be, he recommended we erect the fence as planned. It would block our neighbor's access to his land. If he agreed to pay for his share of the fencing, we would agree to remove the blockade. The next few months remained tense as we proceeded with hiring a fencer. After reviewing three bids, we chose Bart and his crew. Work initially proceeded on schedule for several weeks, but as the terrain got rougher, his crew began to dwindle. Eventually nobody showed up for work (and it wasn't even hunting season), and all we had to show for it was a half mile of fence, a pile of unused metal posts and barbed wire, and an old rusty camping trailer that was left in our front meadow. All efforts to reach an accommodation with Bart failed, and soon he too evaporated along with our deposit. After some time had passed, the trailer, too, disappeared.

In Western stories it always seems a hero in a white hat shows up about this time to make matters right. In our case it was another fencer named Jarrod, who came to our aid. He was aware of our plight, and, incensed at the actions of his colleague, graciously offered to finish the job at a reduced fee. And true to his word, he did just that. By the time the cattle arrived to feed again on the surrounding hills, our property boundary was completely incased in new strands of barbed wire, and the cattle could only look longingly at our grass. But best of all, I no longer had to take such care where I stepped.

As for our neighbor, he eventually relented and paid his share of the new fence. We were far less successful with the remaining two land owners, Montana law having proven somewhat fickle in such matters. As Wyatt had warned us, one cannot compel a neighbor to erect a common fence, but they are obliged to maintain their share of it. The first neighbor had no fence; therefore the cost would be born by us alone. But the longest section of existing fence was shared with a logging company from Oregon. All efforts to negotiate with them failed, so in this case we also had to bite the bullet. But we had our fence, my new friendship with Gail remained intact; and with the help from Wyatt's law firm, we eventually resolved all title issues, receiving acceptable compensation for most of our losses and expenses.

I thought perhaps brighter days now lay ahead, or so I told Gail. She gave her typical shrug and replied, "The fence'll keep the cows out, but not the bison."

"Bison? We have bison here?"

"Not yet, but if a certain politician and his pal get their way, we will. They're pushing to open up the 'Powder Keg' for grazing. It's got all the ranchers and hunters upset."

"What's the Powder Keg?"

"It's a large wildlife management area the state just bought, and it borders you and me. Now FWP wants to put buffalo on it; and it ain't even their natural habitat."

"And my fence won't stop them, I presume."

"Heck no; you'd need the Berlin Wall to do that. But what's worse is buffalo can spread brucellosis to cattle, and ruin our herds. That would kill off the ranches and open the place to developers—like this politician's pal."

"Well, is anyone doing anything about it?"

"Herman's joined a citizen's review committee that FWP was required to set up. We're raising awareness about the seriousness of the problem if buffalo ever wind up here. And right now they want to bring in a herd of fifty. Some of my friends have already let it be known if they do that, then FWP can expect to find fifty carcasses within a week. It's that bad."

"Wow, that is serious. A range war in my neighborhood was definitely not in the brochure."

13

A Horse is a Horse

W E'D FINALLY SETTLED DOWN INTO A ROUTINE AFTER two years in Montana. My daughter, Sandy, was now nine years old. We still found small town living a tough nut to crack. There were only a couple of other girls her age in the area, and they had known each other all their lives. Sonja was now five, and there were no girls her age. Although we home-schooled our two daughters, we did get involved in our community. Bill became a member of the Stratford Volunteer Fire Department until they found out our home fell within the Mullan fire district. For insurance reasons, he couldn't stay, even though the Stratford fire chief lived directly across the highway from us. I became a local Girl Scout leader, and on the side, initiated projects within the Mullan and Stratford school system to help our soldiers deployed to Iraq and Afghanistan. An old childhood acquaintance of Bills was now a senior Army officer in Afghanistan, so for her Girl Scout Bronze Award, Sandy prepared a video of people around our community thanking his troops and wishing them a safe return. It was a very proud moment for us when she stepped up to the podium at the capitol building to describe her project and receive her award.

Having achieved her goal, Sandy yearned for something more related to her newfound interest in horses. I too wanted to get Sandy involved in something she could share with other girls her age. I often heard her fellow girl scouts talk about their involvement with 4H. In the rural west, animal husbandry and horse back riding are very popular. In fact, if you look around, most people have either cows, pigs, sheep, or a horse or two in their fields, along with the requisite backhoe or tractor. Regarding the latter, I must admit I did puzzle over this at first, but then later came to fully appreciate why. It was just another lesson I would soon learn.

The elevation and remoteness of our home was not well suited to raising most livestock, and my interest in cows was limited to the supermarket, but horses were another matter. I also believed riding might build Sandy's self-confidence, and horse care would help encourage her to learn responsibility. We decided it was worth a try, so I approached Sandy one day when she was reading in her room, and casually asked, "Do you want to learn to ride a horse?"

Her face was blank and expressionless at first, before the idea fully registered with her. Then it exploded into wild excitement as she shouted an enthusiastic, "Yes!"

I called Gail for advice, but she didn't know of anyone who taught riding lessons. I was not surprised because all the ranching families start teaching their kids to ride around three years of age. They grow up with it and are expert riders by the time they hit their teens. I decided Helena would be the logical place to find a riding instructor since it was less than thirty miles away, and we shopped their weekly for supplies. After several inquiries we found a place in the Helena Valley that seemed right for us, High Mountain Stables.

We soon found ourselves standing in a round pen with the owner, Roy. He was a middle-aged man, thin and of medium height, with graying hair. His darkly tanned face and straw hat evoked images of a man who had spent most of his life outdoors. He smiled broadly as he spoke in a gentle voice that showed he had an easy going, kindly way with children. I was glad because I did not know how Sandy was going to feel about this whole idea.

We had no real experience with horses. She had only ridden one once, and that was a pony at a fair that was hitched to a turning wheel. I had less experience than she, having seen them up close a few times myself, but otherwise knowing practically nothing of their nature or behavior. I was uncertain how Sandy would react to one. I didn't know if we would leave that day with a new hobby and a happy smile, bored indifference, or tears of terror.

The voice of my friend, Gail, went through my head, "I think riding is a good idea; you should do this for Sandy." So here we were in the round pen, waiting nervously as Roy brought out a small horse on a lead rope, an almost thirty-year-old mare named Donna. She was dark brown, with a white star on her forehead. She remained calm and quiet, as did Sandy. Sadly, Sandy stood on the other side of the pen, shoulders hunched forward, afraid to approach both man and horse. I watched with interest as Roy quietly spoke to Sandy, telling her about the horse, while rubbing Donna's neck.

"Do you want to pet the horse? She's very soft," Roy told her. "Go ahead and try; she won't hurt you."

I urged Sandy, and reluctantly she approached the two until she managed to stand next to them. But the fear flowed through her like a river, and I glanced pensively at my husband. He was also watching intently, and offered her words of encouragement. I thought to myself *I don't know if this is going to work, but at least I tried.* I shouldn't have worried. Touching the horse seemed to calm her and soon she was sitting on Donna's back. By the end of two hours, Sandy was riding on Donna, arms stretched up in the air while being led around the pen by Roy.

"She's a natural," Roy said, as he pulled a tobacco pouch from his shirt pocket and began rolling a cigarette the way old cowpokes did in the movies.

That day in the round pen led to her first two years of riding lessons, and the beginning of a love for riding horses. What I did not yet know was how that day would lead to my own love of horses, and how much that would change our lives.

Go West, Young Woman!

14

In Search of
Mr. Good Horse

"YOU SHOULD THINK ABOUT GETTING A HORSE," Gail said during a visit a few months later.

"I think riding lessons is enough for now," I replied.

"Oh come on, you can't keep taking the girls to town forever. Horses are not that much to take care of and you're wasting all your great pasture grass." I could see where this was going. "If you're not going to get a horse, then get a cow!" Gail laughed. Ever since we first arrived she'd been trying to convince me to get a couple of cows. "Oh you're going to get a horse, I'll talk you into it," Gail said confidently.

"I don't think so, Gail," I answered. "I'm a dog person, not a horse person."

"You can learn about horses."

"No, probably not," I quipped, "I just don't see it happening."

"We'll see…," she laughed as she climbed in her truck and parted.

I sat there, swaying in my front porch rocker, thinking about what she had said. Gail had managed to plant a seed in my mind yet, and had no doubt she was still smiling about it even as she pulled into her ranch four miles away. I found I too was smiling.

Each time we met after that, Gail talked as though I'd already decided to buy a horse.

"Don't get a mare," she cautioned, "I've had some bad experiences with mares. One kicked me in the leg, giving me a compound break. I couldn't work for weeks after that. Herman and the boys had to carry my load."

I knew it must have been a painful experience, and losing a worker, even for a few weeks, is a hardship on a family run cattle ranch.

"Besides, mares are moody and difficult. Well, some are alright, but most are a handful—hormones, you know."

I sipped my tea warily, "You still want me to get a horse after hearing this story?"

Gail was not deterred, "Of course; you just have to be careful."

"How can we be careful, wear full body armor?"

Gail just laughed at my remark. She really would have laughed if she had known only part of me was joking! Honestly, a horse had been on my mind too. The riding lessons were getting expensive, and we were in town at least twice a week now just for them. Sandy had shown no signs of tiring of horseback riding and my youngest child, Sonja, had begun riding Donna. Sandy had been asking me for some time if we could get a horse, but I was very reluctant to make such a commitment. Part of me worried that if she got tired of riding, I would have a horse in my front yard, and we'd end up taking care of it and the over eight tons of manure it would produce each year. A huge effort and expense would go to waste, and more importantly than that, I was worried my girls might get hurt. What I had seen of horses so far, I liked; I loved meeting them. Seeing all the different breeds, and getting to know their personalities, was something I looked forward to every week. However, there was a fear I kept secret. Horses are big! I felt some apprehension because of their physical size. What if my girls got thrown off or stepped on? What if a horse fell on them or bit them? What if a horse ran away with my child? I had heard of the numerous injuries and several local horror stories, including one death.

"It's not *if* they get hurt; It's *when* they get hurt," Gail replied when I finally told her how I felt. She then snorted and added, "I've been thrown some twenty times in my life."

I couldn't believe it, and replied incredulously, "You got back on each time?"

"Eh, it's no big deal. I've fallen off, my kids have fallen off. It's all a part of riding."

The idea made me shudder. It was only three days later that my fear would be reinforced.

Sandy was enjoying an informal ride under Roy's tutelage at a riding stable in town. A local group had been formed to give underprivileged children an opportunity to learn basic horsemanship. Roy had just volunteered to serve as an instructor, but the horses were not his. They were a collection of donated equines of uncertain lineage and training. Sandy was riding a large quarter horse named Trooper, who had once been a forest service mount.

Despite his size, he proved easy to control, that is until an unbroken horse in a nearby round pen began bucking. This seemed to excite him, and he started to trot around the arena. The trot became a lope, which quickly turned into a gallop. Sandy was not familiar with how to slow an unwilling animal down, and she quickly reverted to simply hanging onto the saddle horn. Free of his reins, Trooper made a dash for the wide low gate that straddled the open doors of the arena. I stood behind the safety wall that encompassed the arena, watching helplessly, knowing at any moment he would either crash into it or attempt to jump over it. Sandy was unprepared to handle either disaster, and clung tightly to the saddle. Roy, who had been standing in the center of the arena, ran to intercept them. Bill started climbing over the safety wall to assist, and had just cleared the top when Trooper suddenly turned and ran toward him. Bill leaned over and extended his arms in a desperate attempt to grab Sandy as she galloped by. But when Trooper turned, he came near enough to Roy, that he was able to grab his halter and stop the horse in his tracks.

Sandy was none the worse for the experience, but I was a nervous wreck, and Roy was livid after discovering that none of the horses had been properly vetted before children were allowed to ride them. Had Trooper not turned at the last moment, in all likelihood, Sandy would have been thrown. Following Gail's logic, that would have been the first of many more to come. Were we really doing the right thing, letting her ride? I was beginning to have serious doubts.

I wasn't sure what Bill was thinking, so I decided not to broach the subject with him until I had calmed down and could think rationally instead of emotionally. Later, back at home, we discussed the merits and risks. I first approached the issue from the standpoint of cost.

It was going to be quite an investment. Purchasing a horse is a small expense compared to the infrastructure needed to keep one at home.

We looked out the window to our front meadow. The grass was getting tall. "*A fire hazard, if you don't get something to eat that grass—I know, how about a cow?*" I could plainly hear Gail saying in my mind.

She was right; we needed a horse. Without realizing it, I blurted out, "We could keep it down there, just below the road." Instead of questioning me, Bill stared at the small field below the house just across the logging road. I could see the wheels turning as he too thought aloud.

"It's over 100 yards from the house. We'd have to lay a water line all the way down there—and maybe electricity." His face winced, and he added, "It'll be expensive. We'll need some kind of a shelter…and a tack room…and a corral."

He was right. There was so much to accomplish even before we could think about buying a horse. A couple of more months passed when I casually mentioned, "Sandy is still asking me about a horse." It was evening, and for once we had a few moments alone.

"Then let's talk about it," he said, "What do you suggest we do?"

"I have mixed feelings about it," I confessed.

Bill replied, "She really enjoys riding; it makes her happier and more content than anything else I've seen her do. And it calms her."

"I agree. I've noticed a difference in her attitude and I think she needs a friend." I took a deep breath. "Her happiness is worth the time and money invested. If having a horse in our front yard will help her spirit, then she should have one. She can work with it every day. It's not an indulgence, but a true need on her part."

Bill agreed completely. Even though he had no interest in them, in some ways he was more committed to this horse endeavor than I was. We had sparked Sandy's interest in horses and it showed no sign of abatement. Our decision filled me with both excitement and apprehension. *WHERE DO I BEGIN?* We needed a plan.

"It has to be her responsibility; I'm not taking care of a horse," I told Gail firmly on the phone one bright spring morning.

"I knew it!" her triumphant voice shouted at me, "You finally decided to get Sandy a horse. How exciting! Okay, a cow is next!"

"No cows, Gail"

"Yes cows; I talked you into a horse didn't I?"

Go West, Young Woman!

15

A Cunning Plan

WE HAD NO HORSE, YET IT DID NOT TAKE LONG BEFORE we set to work on the plan for our little stable and corral. It would be a simple affair containing a hay storage area, a stall with a water source, and a tack room for all the gear and tools we envisioned needing.

We collected material and labor estimates from professional builders, but determined the cost was too high. Since we both had done much of our own home construction in the past, we decided to do most of the work ourselves. The only "extravagance" we allowed was related to the external appearance, thus the green metal roof and caramel colored siding closely matched our house and shop.

In the meantime, we talked with Roy, who had been training Sandy for some time now. He believed she could handle a horse of her own, but he did not know of anyone with a suitable mount for sale, and suggested I start checking local advertisements. We didn't subscribe to any paper, so I searched the Internet, particularly Craigslist. *Suitable* was the word which kept crossing my mind. I knew I needed a kid-safe horse, something unflappable or "bomb proof." This meant finding an equine with a calm temperament, or so much experience that it was not nervous or easily scared. Such a horse had to be tolerant of anyone who made a lot of mistakes, lacked advanced riding skills, or maybe used poor judgment while handling the horse on the ground. I was about to embark on a search for such an animal, but felt more like I was looking for a used car. As with automobiles, I found out some sellers were not exactly honest in their advertisements. I discovered this fact when I made my first call about a pretty palomino.

The mare was advertised as having a gentle, sweet nature, had been ridden by children for years, and was a horse anyone could ride. When I spoke with the owner and explained my situation, she listened intently and assured me her horse would be a good choice. I looked over the list of questions that I'd written down earlier that day. I quickly learned the last question I asked should have been my first question.

"When was the last time someone rode the horse?"

"Seven years ago."

"Seven years?" I replied incredulously, the shock on my face no doubt reverberating in my voice.

"Yes," the woman replied nonchalantly.

What in the world do I say now? My mind groped for a reply.

"Why has it been so long since someone has ridden her?"

"My children have gone off to college and there's no one to ride her."

My next question led me closer to the truth. "Does anyone handle her on the ground?" It seemed like the most logical question to ask next.

"No, but she's such a good horse and really safe."

Maybe seven years ago, I thought.

"I think I need a horse that has some recent riding experience. My girls are still very young," I said, trying to sound interested, but my mind was filling with darker thoughts. *Too much time has passed. How can anyone advertise this mare as child-safe when no one has even touched her in seven years? This horse just sits in the pasture without human contact? She doesn't even qualify as a pet. This has to affect her attitude. Maybe she no longer wants anyone to climb on her back and tell her what to do.*

Sensing my waning interest, the woman tried to convince me to come see the mare, and suggested I pay to get the horse a tune-up. I assured her it might be a nice horse, but my children first needed some more experience in the saddle. I wished her good luck in finding a new family for her mare, that with her good qualities, it would not take long before someone would snap her up. I hung up the phone and let out a long sigh, feeling absolute dismay. *This is going to be harder than I thought.*

"Experienced rider," "intermediate rider," and "not for a beginner" were phrases that were becoming all too familiar. I scanned through hundreds of ads on numerous websites.

"We don't need a horse yet, we don't even have the barn area started," Bill reminded me.

He was right, but I was on a mission. I believed that this summer was the best time to find a horse for Sandy because I wanted her to have time to bond with it and enjoy it before the winter cold set in. I did find a couple of promising advertisements, but when I looked into them further, I found they were in towns too far away. I wanted something local. I even expanded my search to a fifty mile radius from our home, but nothing appeared.

"I am surprised there aren't more horses available around Helena," I remarked one night at dinner. "I had found a single candidate, but the owner wanted $4,000 for his gelding." I thought Bill would choke on his supper when he heard that.

Weeks passed, and I started to consider this search as part of my daily routine. One afternoon, as I began clicking through Internet ads, I saw one which read, "TWH for sale." I didn't know what "TWH" meant, so I read further. It described a fourteen-year-old mare that was fourteen hands high. I knew a "hand" was the typical unit of measure for a horse and equated to four inches. I also knew a horse was measured from the ground to the top of its withers, that being the "highest non-variable point of the skeleton." A fourteen-hand horse was fairly small. So far it sounded good; and age was in her favor. It went on to describe her as being "used to dogs, chickens, goats, and other distractions." Children were currently riding her, and, best of all, she was priced at $750. It showed promise.

But I remained curious to know what a "TWH" meant. *It must be some breed of horse, but which one?* I soon found out it meant "Tennessee Walking Horse." *Good, at least I know what it is; now to find out more about it.* So I began reading about Tennessee Walkers and discovered the horse had some very good qualities. It was gentle by nature and used a smooth four-beat gait, the gait being a gliding motion that a horse is born with, rather than something it can be taught.

I was looking over the ad again when an unusual thought popped into my head. *This is your horse.* I wasn't sure if I consciously thought those words, or if it was just a strong feeling, but it was real enough that it startled me. I only knew I had to pursue this, whatever the outcome, and I did.

I called our trainer, Roy, and told him about the ad. He agreed the horse was worth seeing, and he offered to inspect it and make his recommendation. It was fortunate that the horse we were going to see was only a few miles from Roy's house, since this would count as a lesson for Sandy.

I responded to the email address, but the seller had not provided a phone number. Periodically, I checked to see if I had any reply. Within an hour a message appeared in my inbox; it was an email rejection notice. Apparently the server had decided my email was unsolicited and unwanted, and had not delivered it to the seller. I tried several more times, always with the same outcome.

"Let's just forget it," Bill said, "If it's this hard to contact the seller, maybe it's not meant to be. Take it as is a sign, Quinn."

Oh dear. How can I tell him about the feeling I had? That vibe, that intuition, maybe I'm wrong, but I'm not ready to give up.

"I am not ready to give up," I looked Bill in the eye. "Is there any other way to send this email?"

He thought for a minute, "Let's forward the email to someone and have them send it."

"Great idea," I chirped, "I suggest Grace." Grace, and her husband Russell, had been my friends for over twenty years so I knew they would help me with this idea. I called to tell her the email was on its way to her inbox, but all I got was her answering machine. *How frustrating. Maybe Bill is right. Maybe I should give up.*

Just then Bill remarked, "Call her cell phone; they may be out for the evening."

"No, I don't want to bother her if she's out. I think they may be celebrating their anniversary."

I heard the frustration in Bill's voice when he said, "She won't mind. You're her friend."

I stood there thinking of the time difference between us and the east coast, while Bill became increasingly impatient. "I'll call her. It's no big deal to me." He dialed their cell phone number and Russell answered. Bill explained our dilemma, and he agreed to forward the email as soon as they returned home.

"You see, Honey, no problem."

"What about their anniversary dinner?"

"I didn't ask; he didn't comment." *Men!*

Good to his word, Russell later wrote he had forwarded our email to the seller. I responded with a big "thank you" and promised to let them know if anything came of it. *Okay, now we wait.* Then I began to wonder if the seller would think it strange that my email was being forwarded by a friend in Florida, asking if we could see the horse tomorrow.

What if they misunderstood who the interested party was? What if they didn't send me a phone number? What if Roy couldn't make it? What if the horse had been sold? What if…stop it! This was ridiculous. Why was I getting so worked up over a horse I knew practically nothing about? I didn't even have a photo of her. Maybe she was some poor, worn-out nag. Maybe she had the mange. Alright, stop it again. Just wait and see.

Around nine the next morning the phone rang. When I picked it up, an energetic female voice rapidly introduced herself as Linda, explained she was the broker of the horse, and she had just seen my email. Her very pronounced New York accent indicated to me she was not a typical Montanan, so at least we had one thing in common. We were both outsiders—strangers in a strange land. I figured this alone created a bond and put me more at ease. We quickly set a time to meet for later in the afternoon at her place.

I gave Roy the directions, and he agreed to meet us there; but as soon as I hung up the phone I experienced the mixed emotions of both excitement and trepidation. *Was I getting in over my head?*

"I'm going to see a man about a horse," I joked with Gail on the phone. "Did you ever think I would say that out loud?" I told her about the upcoming appointment with glee and was pleased when I heard the happiness in her voice mixed with a little shock. She had thought I would require more convincing. I had to admit that I was actually enjoying the idea.

I read the directions to Bill as we drove down a long dirt road in blustery weather, towards the address Linda had provided. After several false tries, we finally located the stable among a series of ranchettes in the middle of Helena Valley, a largely underdeveloped tract outside the city. We pulled into a driveway beside a large corral containing numerous horses of all sizes and colors, wandering around. Some of them looked up in interest as we approached, while others ignored us completely.

I wonder which one is for sale? My heart began beating just a little faster until I saw an old, rather tattered looking white horse being led on a lead rope across the drive to a large round pen. Bill and I looked at each other. *I hope that's not the horse we're coming to see.* I could tell from his expression that Bill shared my concern.

We parked the car, and as everyone got out, we were met by Linda and her husband Scott. Linda was a pretty, dark-haired woman in her late twenties. She was confident and polite. Scott offered his hand as we made our introductions, and judging from his fitness and military haircut, I correctly assumed he was a state police officer. The patrol car in the background was also a dead giveaway. He reminded me of the many officers I had worked with during my time in conservation law enforcement, and together they formed a handsome couple.

As we waited for Roy to arrive, we made small talk about the weather. It was uncomfortable standing there in a spitting cold rain. Luckily, as Roy pulled up, the rain began to slow down. We again made introductions while Linda asked her stepdaughter, Terri, who looked about twelve, to bring out "Shammie." I held my breath for a moment wondering what I was about to see when Shammie rounded the corner. Bill and I exchanged glances with a smile.

"She's beautiful," I whispered to Bill, and he agreed. Shammie was a paint, mostly black in color, with some white patches on her body. Her face was black with a white diamond on her forehead, and her body was sleek and shiny, with slim legs. Overall, she was elegant and graceful in appearance, though fairly small in stature, but this only added to her appeal. I felt a little spark of hope.

Don't get too excited, I said to myself. *She still has to pass a lot of tests. She still may not be suitable.* I turned to Roy and told him to take over. I had plenty of questions, but wanted to listen and learn first.

Roy asked Terri to walk and trot her on the lead rope down the driveway so he could assess her gait. He was looking for any sign of lameness, or hip or foot problems. He also wanted to judge her general conformation. They came toward us while Roy watched intently.

"Good," he reassuringly announced.

I did not realize until that moment that I had been holding my breath, and suddenly I let out a small sigh. Bill and I, along with our two daughters, stood in a little gaggle off to one side of the round pen and watched as the assessment continued. Roy now took Shammie and held the lead rope loosely in his hand while he turned and spoke with Linda. Just then Shammie turned and took several steps, heading in my direction. She stopped, facing me squarely, only a foot or so away. I was little startled; even though she was considered a small horse, she still looked big to me. Not really knowing what to do with this horse who was looking me calmly in the eye, I awkwardly said, "Apparently we have not been formally introduced. I am Nancy."

I reached up to touch her head and she just stood there. I rubbed her head until I heard Roy's now stern voice, "We have no time for that."

He tugged at her rope and led her away. *That was interesting; I wonder if she likes me?*

Linda asked Terri to lift and clean the horse's hooves so we could see her feet, as well as her reaction to the process.

"She has shoes," I remarked. "Are they necessary?"

We really didn't want to shoe a horse every six weeks, and considered it an extra expense, as well as an unhealthy choice for an animal that would not have strenuous chores or difficult riding terrain.

Linda replied, "No, in fact, this is the first time she's ever had shoes; they were only put on two weeks ago. My farrier had planned to buy her, but his wife wouldn't agree to another horse. The shoes can be taken off without a problem, and she can be a barefoot horse."

Pleased to hear this news, I next asked why she was for sale. Linda explained the owner needed a pack horse for long hunting trips into the Elkhorn range. Linda convinced him Shammie was simply too small to pack through the mountains.

Next, Roy ran his hands along the horse's spine to feel for any abnormalities or painful areas. He remarked, "She does get enough to eat."

He was grinning, so I assumed he thought she was a little plump. Linda told him she liked her horses a little fat, rather than too thin. Honestly, I had not seen enough horses to make the comparison, but I liked what I heard. Roy asked Linda to saddle the horse while he continued to rattle off one question after another concerning her health and disposition. He voiced our concerns about needing a horse for a child. Linda responded positively to all queries, and then with the saddle on, she led Shammie to a large fenced arena. Roy asked permission to aggravate Shammie, reminding Linda that sometimes children do awkward things around horses. Roy waved his hat over Shammie's head and tapped her on the ears with it. She didn't spook, but looked rather bored and turned her head away. He pulled on the saddle and crinkled a plastic bag around her face. She just turned her face the other direction, but remained in one place.

Now it was time to ride Shammie. Terri and all of her twelve years jumped on Shammie and rode in a large circle around the arena. I watched with interest as the horse moved along the fence line, bored and indifferent to the chickens and goats who roamed in and out of the corral. *No wonder this horse is not afraid of barn animals.* An unnamed orange cat and a fluffy dog named Remi raced into the yard, but Shammie paid them no heed. I turned my attention back to the young girl riding Shammie as Bill talked with Scott. I stood near the gate with Sandy and Sonja, both of whom were entranced by the horse. It was now Roy's turn to ride.

He mounted Shammie and moved her off in a rapid gait. He wanted to see how well she could transition from a standing position to a trot. She did not disappoint him as she smoothly entered her gait with ease. Meanwhile, Linda was explaining to me that Shammie was registered with lineage papers, and I inquired if that held any special significance.

She shrugged and replied, "Only if you plan to breed her. Otherwise, there's plenty of good horses available who are 'grade'—I mean unregistered."

I moved away from the group to process all the information I was being bombarded with at once. While I contemplated, Bill and Scott swapped war stories, and the girls entertained each other. Roy had stopped riding Shammie, and was now sitting on her back. Again, she suddenly turned and took several quick steps, stopping in front of me. I was about to reach for her when Roy announced it was time for Sandy to try her, and he moved her off to the small round pen. *This has to mean something, I wish I understood, twice she's come to me.* I turned my attention to Sandy and asked if she wanted to try riding Shammie. Roy believed she was safe enough, so without hesitation Sandy agreed.

She mounted Shammie, and after two turns in the round pen, proudly announced, "She is so smooth!"

"How do you like her?" I asked, finally starting to relax a little.

"I love her," Sandy exclaimed with a huge smile.

There was one last test. I offered Sonja, my youngest, a chance to ride Shammie. We set her up on the horse's back and I led her about the round pen with a lead rope. Shammie behaved fine with a little one on her back. Even though it was not our plan for Sonja to ride while still so young, I didn't want her left out of the experience. For now, we only wanted a horse for Sandy.

I asked Linda if it was okay to bring our dog, Kobi, out to meet Shammie. I did not think it would be a problem because this horse had been around a lot of animals, but I did want to see Kobi's reaction to Shammie. Bill brought him out on a leash and Shammie looked him over. They were both unconcerned about each other, and Kobi did not seem the least interested in the horse after his first curious sniff. *That went okay, so this was a non-issue.* I marked it off my mental check list.

I took Roy aside and asked him what he thought of this horse. He believed she was not for a beginner, but he also believed Sandy could handle her well enough. In fact, Roy liked her so well, he told me not to make an offer because he thought she was worth the asking price.

I was hesitant, and could hear Gail reminding me, "Don't ever pay full price for a horse." Although I was still learning about horses, I was in complete agreement with her warning. I rarely paid full price for anything if I could avoid it. I was a bargain hunter at heart.

Bill was still talking with Scott on the other side of the pen. Scott was currently in the Montana Army National Guard, so he and Bill were both enjoying the conversation as they discussed their respective military service.

Not wanting to interfere with their male bonding, I chose this moment to get a better look at this horse. I didn't ride, so I had to rely on my own judgment regarding the spirit of this animal. As I approached her, she did not move away. I spoke to her gently and rubbed her head and face. I then touched her all over her body. It was truly amazing. I could feel the power of her dense muscles just under the surface of her soft coat. I could feel the wildness of her ancestors, along with the domesticated side of her personality. It was all there under my fingertips.

How can she be so soft and so strong at the same time? It is almost a contradiction. I should look her in the eye; hopefully, it will not make her uncomfortable. I leaned in and moved my face close to hers. Although horses are not dogs, this is how I assessed any animal or person. If you look them in the eye, you will find what you need to know about them. My thoughts died down as I gazed into her left eye and laid my hand on her neck.

What do you want to tell me? I am listening.

I waited for a moment and we stood together. Her eye was big and brown, but relaxed. I could feel she possessed a tremendous amount of pride and dignity. She seemed to enjoy my touch, and I felt her head lower a little as she gave into the moment. I sensed nothing wrong or disturbing, just a willing acceptance. A thread of a connection was born. Based on these feelings and Roy's recommendation, I had to speak with Bill.

"I hate to interrupt your conversation," I said, "can we talk about this horse?" I repeated everything Roy had said, and explained my perception of Shammie. He trusted both our opinions and we decided to make an offer of $500. I knew Roy thought we were playing a dicey game, but we considered it worth trying to bring the price down. Our barn area was not even started yet, and we would have to pay Roy to board Shammie at his facility for a couple of months. Any saving would be helpful.

I explained our situation to Linda, and she believed it was reasonable. She would contact the owner, and promised to call us as soon as she had spoken with him. Finished for the day, we followed Roy out the driveway and turned onto the long dirt road. Less than a mile from Linda's home I could see Roy in his car ahead talking on the cell phone. *I wonder if he is speaking to Linda? No, it's too soon. She didn't have time to contact the owner. A quick phone call could mean yes or no. Maybe Roy is just talking to a friend.* Thoughts continued to run wildly in my head as we bumped our way down the dirt road.

In just a short time we were pulling into Roy's driveway. As we exited our car, we heard Roy say, "Congratulations, you have a horse!"

It was Linda on the phone! A huge smile crossed my face as I threw my arms around Sandy and cried, "You have a horse, how exciting!"

I was laughing and holding her at the same time. She looked a little shocked as she replied, "Wow, really? I am so happy!"

We made arrangements to have Linda deliver the horse to Roy's place the next day. We wanted to be there when Shammie arrived at her new temporary home, so we planned to come back to town the next afternoon. That night over dinner I asked the family what would be a good new name for her. The comments began to fly like a migration of birds going south. We all agreed "Shammie" was the wrong name for such a beautiful ladylike horse.

Shammie sounded like an old rag you used to clean your car. *Who could pick such a name?* I later learned that Shammie was a nickname and her registered name was Shazam Winter Magic. Winter and Magic were the sire and the dame. Shazam was her given name by a previous owner, but it still didn't fit her.

"How about *Lady?*" I suggested, thinking of her majestic beauty.

"Too common," Sandy replied.

"Well, she is beautiful, how about *Belle?*" I offered.

Belle means "beauty" in French and it did not hurt that it was my favorite Disney heroine. The girls really liked it, so we agreed it was a good name. Tomorrow we would give her a new life and a new name. None of us girls could sleep that night because of all the excitement. Bill snored away.

We arrived early at Roy's stable the following morning, and after a short time we heard the low moan of an engine pulling a trailer. We walked to the front drive and watched as Linda's truck and trailer approached, coming to a full stop in front of the house.

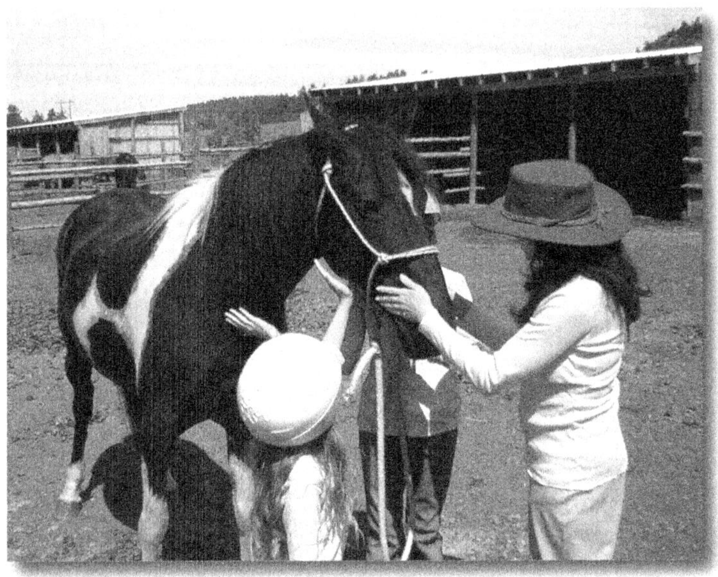

Meeting Belle

Linda jumped out with a smile, announcing, "Here we are!"

The girls squirmed impatiently in one spot, anxiously waiting as Linda and Terri opened the heavy metal doors.

"I forgot to ask how she does in a trailer. How does she load?"

"I'll show you, she does fine," Linda replied.

Terri brought her in and out of the trailer three times without Belle showing any concern or skittish behavior. *Thank goodness.* It was one of the questions I had forgotten to ask the day prior. Linda led Belle to her new corral and Belle walked in like she owned the place. I soon found out this was typical behavior for a lead mare. We all brushed and fussed over her as she stood like a queen deserving every moment of adulation.

"Goodbye Shammie," Linda said giving the horse a final pat, "Enjoy your new family."

Linda bid final farewell to all of us and drove off. But this would not be the last I would see of her; I just did not know it at the time.

16

Saddle Up

A S MUCH AS POSSIBLE, WE WANTED SANDY TO RIDE Belle at Roy's stable, even though it was a ninety-mile round trip drive to his place on the other side of Helena. But eventually we'd be moving her to our place, and needed to acquire the necessary gear. I'd heard about a place nearby that sold used tack. Roy knew the owner and suggested I take the horse in to be fitted for a saddle. I'd never thought about it, but it made sense that not all saddles fit all horses, so I arranged for Roy to meet us at the store with Belle a few days later.

I'd already learned that trying to get directions from Montanans is a bit challenging. Where we live there are no street signs and people give you directions by landmarks such as, "You know the big rock?" or "The house with the black roof," or my favorite, "Look for the big tree." In town the directions are just as vague. Everyone who has grown up around here knows where the stores are, but they rarely remember all the street names. I can't tell you how many people have offered me directions to anywhere in town that started with, "Do you know where the taco place is?"

This time we were looking for a place outside of town, in the "Valley" When I think of a store, I usually envision something with a large parking lot and big signs. I was relieved to find this store was really more of a small shop next to the owner's house. His yard was filled with a wonderful assortment of antique farm and ranching implements. Inside, the shop was crowded with an array of second-hand saddles, harnesses, halters, bridles, bits, and assorted tools, along with brand new tack. In back, the owner, Ben, was busy crafting beautiful handmade saddles. Ben walked over to greet us with a limp, a souvenir from his years spent as a bronco rider.

Just then, Roy drove up, and Belle's head popped out the side window for a look around. Roy brought her out on a lead rope while Ben assessed her girth, withers, and head. A moment later, a delivery truck backed away from the front of the store, and roared close by, showering gravel on our horse. Belle never moved. She just stood there, acting as though nothing had happened.

"That is one good horse," commented Ben as he plopped a small saddle on her back.

I had previously watched Roy teach Sandy about the parts of a saddle and tack, and I was beginning to learn quite a bit of horse lingo. This day I was receiving a lesson on how to fit a saddle to a horse and to a person. To the rider, it's mostly a matter of comfort and the size of the seat. To a horse it is much more. If the saddle is a poor fit, it may cause a sore. That would be painful to the horse and perhaps cause a safety issue for the rider. I did not want Sandy to get bucked off because a saddle was uncomfortable for Belle.

After trying a few saddles, we found a good fit with a used small black Western style, inlaid with silver engraved plates. Sandy liked it and Bill was delighted with the price. It was also light enough so Sandy could carry it herself and place it on the horse. We had already purchased a thick grey wool pad, because my research had determined it was the most comfortable type for a horse.

Next we looked at bridles, bits, and reins. I asked Ben to pick out an inexpensive leather setup for us. Looking through all the choices, I could see what an investment this could turn into. There were so many beautiful examples of his workmanship, but this was for a beginner child. There would be plenty of time in the future to save up for the next level. We decided on a nice dark burgundy leather headstall and matching reins. Meanwhile, Sonja was busy picking out brushes and other grooming aids.

We girls looked through all the hoof picks and colored brushes. Of course, we chose one pink brush that was Sonja's size. We also chose a finishing brush and a curry comb, as well as several other tools we thought would come in handy. Bill just stood there and groaned, realizing we were to become steady customers of Ben's little shop. With all our new tack and saddle loaded in the car, I felt like a real Western girl all the way home.

Go West, Young Woman!

17

A Stable Environment

BELLE WAS SETTLED IN NICELY AT ROY'S STABLE. However that only increased our urgency to build a place for her to live in. Roy had come across some used metal panels for a round pen and offered to sell them to us at a reasonable price. They were a little banged up and in a mix of colors, black and green.

"It doesn't bother you they are two different colors?" Bill teased me. He thought it might offend my artist sensibilities.

I rolled my eyes at him, "At this price it doesn't bother me one bit."

We had priced round pens, and I knew what kind of investment we were facing. These were the kind of panels that fit together with steel pegs. We did not have to chain them or install any posts for support. The panels just hooked together in a circle to support each other. When Roy delivered them, we chose a flat area in the meadow just across from our little road. There we could have a clear view from the house. The panels went up in about fifteen minutes. It was a start.

Before any construction could begin, we had to install water and electric lines. We had decided to purchase an automatic watering system for Belle. It operated like a commode and consisted of a tank that held a constant reservoir of water, refilling each time the level got to low from drinking. A heat chain wrapped around the pipe kept the water from freezing. We also wanted a frost-free hydrant above ground for access to water for other purposes. I had watched other folks struggle to manually fill water troughs in the winter, and was determined we would not be lugging bucket after bucket over a hundred yards downhill in the snow, ice, and sub-zero temperatures of the coming winter. So we contracted with our old builder, Bob, to dig additional electric and water lines. A six-foot deep trench soon stretched across the meadow from our well, converging with a shallower electric cable trench from our electric box. The whole scene looked reminiscent of the frontlines during the First World War. How men ever endured such horrors was beyond my comprehension. Just standing in the dirt for a few minute left me feeling completely claustrophobic.

Regrettably, one of the trenches went right through a bed of fifty new purple irises I had just planted, part of a gift of 130 bulbs Gail had cheerfully provided me from her garden, remarking, "They spread like weeds and overrun everything; please take them."

It sounded good to me at the time. Much to Bill's dismay, I asked for his help in planting them around the house. I found they were the one thing I could grow in this climate. Every other plant I tried, died, or was eaten by the local fauna. Had I ever known I would buy a horse and need a stable, I would never have planted them near the electric box.

With the trenches now laid, Bob poured a small cement foundation for a little tack room, and then tied in our waterlines. In order to save some money, we enlisted Sandy's trainer, Roy, to assist Bill with framing and finishing the tack room and double horse stalls. The girls and I pitched in, helping with the siding and staining work. Roy and Bill installed a green metal roof to match our house. Later, Bill assisted by Gail's son, Chase, added cedar planks as an exterior finish, which we then stained to match our house. Now everything matched - house, shop, playhouse, and stable. It satisfied my artistic needs, except for those mismatched corral panels. Well, we could deal with that later.

Initially, we thought the second stall would suffice for hay storage, but Belle proved far too ingenious at finding ways in, so eventually we added a third stall, really an extension to the far end of the building which she could not quite reach.

Everyone who saw our stable teased us about it, remarking how overbuilt it was. Some neighbors said it was nice enough to move into, others said, "I wish I was your horse."

We just wanted it to blend in nicely and last a lifetime, so we wouldn't be building one again in the future. Before we finished the work, Gail presented me with a metal sign to hang above the door. It read "Home on the Range." with a small "barn star" under it. No Montana home is complete without one.

It was true. I was feeling at home. I had never lived in one place for more than six years at a time, and usually less than that. Moving and starting over had always been my way of life, all I had ever known. Now I was setting down roots at an alarming rate. With every nail that we drove into the wood frame, my life here seemed more permanent and solid. I loved the idea of belonging to this land and our homestead on the mountain. Understand, rural living sounds romantic, but it is not without difficulties and problems. We definitely remained classified under "greenhorn" status. But we were savvy enough to realize we were now in the middle of summer, and though the heat did slow us down, useful outdoor time was getting away from us.

We discussed the possibility of bringing Belle home before we were completely finished with the construction. I was concerned that living in the round pen without any shade to retreat to would be too hard on Belle's health. The sun was blistering hot.

"If it's only for a couple'ah weeks, it'll be okay," Gail offered as she continued spouting her sage advice. "I wouldn't do it all summer, but a short time won't hurt her at all. Just have plenty of water available for her to drink."

We were near the end of August and I did not want to pay for another month of boarding, so it was decided, Belle would come home.

18

Belle and the Beast

"HOW DO YOU FEEL ABOUT BELLE COMING HOME TO LIVE WITH US?" I asked excitedly one sunny morning.

The girls talked about how long they had been waiting, and were hopeful that day would be very soon. What they did not know was we had made arrangements for Roy to bring Belle today. He would be arriving within the hour and we wanted to surprise them. The stable work was not completed, so they had no idea what was in store.

"Well, I need your help at the barn today. Let's get down there now. It'll be worth it," I assured them, when I saw their disappointed expressions.

I knew the girls were getting tired of working everyday on it, but we had to be prepared before the snow began to fly. We didn't have hay yet, and until the stalls were completed, there was no safe place to store any. Without the shelter, our local elk and deer herds would eat a winter's supply in only a few days.

We made our way down the path from the house that was, in actuality, the filled in ditch of the electric line. It was not long before Roy arrived with the trailer. I could see Belle's head pop out of the side window as she took in her new surroundings. Kobi looked on, but did not seem overly interested. He ran a couple of times around the trailer to investigate, but then came over to stand with me. I saw no reason to put him on the leash because he had met the horse before, and she was not afraid of him.

Roy swung open the trailer doors and led Belle out onto the grass and into the round pen. Without any warning, Kobi jumped from my side and raced toward her, his deep throaty bark roaring like a lion. Every hair on his back stood up straight, and he angrily flashed his teeth as he drove straight for Belle.

"Kobi!" I futilely shouted. "It's okay. Kobi, come to me!"

He wouldn't listen. He was in full protection mode against this horrendous beast that had arrived in *his* front yard, convinced it meant us harm. He was determined to protect his family, even at the cost of his own life. His bark communicated his thoughts to us as if speaking real words out loud. *Shoot it! Shoot it now!*

Without realizing it, I was replying, "It's okay, Kobi, she won't' hurt us."

I looked at him and moved closer to the pen. *She will, she will! Get your gun, hurry! I'll hold her at bay!* Poor Kobi looked at me in complete confusion. *We shoot at wild animals when they come to the back patio, so what are you waiting for?* He was clearly explaining the threat to me, so why wasn't I reacting accordingly?

He ran around the horse and lunged several times at her throat. He kept turning to look over his shoulder at me. *Do it, Do it now! If you're not going to shoot this monster, at least run away! Take the girls! Why are you just standing there? She could attack at any moment!*

I could see his eyes pleading with my own. I called to him again, willing him to hear me, but his instincts remained on full alert.

During the entire fray Belle appeared quite bored. She was not the least bit afraid and simply stood there looking at Kobi, watching him dance around her feet, a mere pest, one best to ignore. *Be a good chap and run along now before somebody steps on you.* She soon wearied of his game and decided to lay down in the grass for a rest.

Oh no, I thought, *if she lies down, Kobi might hurt her!* He was now fearless, and had already proven his "killer instinct" to us on previous occasions, though the threats then were so much smaller.

Belle began to roll on her back from side to side in the warm grass. She was completely oblivious of this snarling and threatening dog. Kobi lunged at her neck and Belle just turned her head away. No one was going to interrupt the good feeling she was having rolling in this tall grass, enjoying the warm sunlight.

When Belle stood back up, Kobi, realized we were all still alive, and began to calm down. He finally responded to my voice, and stopped barking. Instead, he emitted a low growl. It took a few minutes, but he did return to my side and gave me his hurt look. *Why didn't you listen to me? I don't understand. I was only doing my job.* His facial expression was not lost on me either. It was a mix of puzzlement and irritation.

I rubbed his face and praised him for being such a good protector. I tried to explain to him that Belle would be part of our family now, and that in time he should protect her like any other member of the pack. He was not convinced, and was having none of it.

After a little while, Roy packed up this trailer to get ready to leave. He stated his belief that Sandy would do fine with Belle and did not need any further lessons.

"I've taught her everything she needs to know," Roy said. He looked around at the new stall, tack room, and hay storage area he helped build. He patted Belle on the head and with a smile said, "You lucky girl, you're going to have a good life here."

And so we thought as well, but every time we let Kobi out of the house, he would make a beeline for the round pen and bark at Belle. He was still telling her she was not welcome here. It was obvious she did not value his opinion and soon she began to pin her ears back and thrust her head at him, telling him to go away. He thought it was a game and would jump around her feet, running in circles. I watched them communicate their feelings to each other.

"Come back Kobi, here Boy," I would call.

He would stop, look back towards the house, and race as fast as could up the hill to give me the latest news. His face said it all: *She's not so bad, but I put her in her place.* And I am sure this is what he really believed. He followed through with this self-assigned responsibility for nearly a week until something changed.

We were still in the process of finishing the stable and installing electric fence, but because there was a large area left unfinished, we tied Belle to a picket line. The picket was comprised of a swivel attached to a steel rod that was hammered into the ground and connected to a long rope. At the end of the rope a steel clasp snapped onto the horse's halter to prevent the animal from wandering off. We took the precaution of sliding an old garden hose over the rope to provide some stiffness and lessen the chance of the horse tripping over it. This way she was free to eat grass in about a fifty-foot radius. Although we had fenced the perimeter of our property, it was too hilly and wooded to allow her to have free roam of it. Kobi was left to watch over her while I worked inside, and caught up with Gail on the phone.

"There is a horse in my front yard," I joked.

"I know; isn't it great?" she replied with joy in her voice. She was quite pleased with herself and for us too.

"It is," I agreed. "I think this is only the beginning of the changes in our daily routine. I find myself looking for her every time I pass a window. In fact, the other day I went outside and talked with her because I didn't want her to be lonely. I know horses are herd animals, and I have concerns about her being alone so much of the time. I was hoping she'd bond with the dog. But, so far it doesn't look like that's going to happen."

I was in our dining room, clearing the table for the family lunch, as we chatted. The girls had left a few school books and papers out, so, while I was collecting them, I glanced out the window at a sight which gave me a sudden cold, sickening feeling. Belle was on the ground, lying flat on her right side, motionless, while Kobi stood atop her stomach on all four feet, proudly looking around the meadow as if he were king of all he surveyed.

"Oh no, he's finally done it! He's killed my horse!" I yelled into the phone.

I dropped everything on the table, deaf to Gail's voice. My mind flew into a near panic. *I must get out there right away. Maybe she's still alive, or just fell and hurt her leg. Maybe she's sick—colic or some other disease.* I was desperately searching for plausible explanations as I grabbed my coat, while hopping on one leg, trying to pull on a boot. All the while I kept thinking *Hurry, hurry!*

I ran down the hill as fast as I could without falling and breaking a leg on the ice. As I approached, Kobi turned to look at me and jumped off Belle, wagging his tail and looking quite pleased. Belle stood up immediately, and faced me with a quizzical expression, as if to say *Hi, why are you running? Is there a problem?* I was stunned.

"You're fine?" I blurted out. "Why, you aren't hurt at all?"

I scanned her body and assessed her posture. She certainly did not seem upset in anyway. *What a relief!* My muscles relaxed as Kobi walked over to Belle and sat down beside her.

Then it dawned on me. "You've become friends? Belle, you're okay with this?" I asked her. "I didn't think you'd ever let Kobi stand on your back. Is this even normal?"

Belle continued to gaze steadily at me, showing no sign of concern.

"Okay...," I muttered under my breath, "if you're unharmed, I guess I'll go back to the house."

I was still talking to them as if I expected an answer in return. Turning away, I felt like a total idiot. How embarrassing! I started my way up the hill to the house, this time, at a much slower pace. *At least I am a conscientious owner.* I tried to console myself. Slowly, a smile spread over my face and my mood brightened. Now that I was calmer, I had to admit it was incredibly funny, hilarious really.

It was true. Belle and Kobi had become friends, but it was an odd friendship. She accepted him into the herd as long as she was lead mare, and he accepted her as a pack member, as long as he was the alpha male. Then I remembered I'd left Gail dangling on the phone, but I was too exhausted to run. I struggled up the hill and called her back with the good news. I no longer had to fear for my animals. We were all one big happy family...well, sort of.

After that, Kobi often felt the need to constantly prove his leadership. A day later, when Belle somehow escaped her picket, and began roaming down the road toward the creek, I decided to send Kobi to retrieve her. I called to him, "Kobi, Belle is off the line. Go get her and bring her back home."

He jumped up from his perch on our front patio and raced down the slope, rounding the corner out of sight, while I stood upstairs on our bedroom balcony admiring our new stable. Less than a minute passed before I saw Belle coming back up the road with Kobi trailing behind. He herded her through the open gate of the corral while I proudly congratulated him.

He'd keep her safe, at least during the day. Nighttime was another matter because Kobi was kept inside so he would not fall prey to the wolves. Belle would be on her own, alone in the dark. It was an unsettling feeling, made all the more real when tracks began appearing in the soft dirt along the road in front of the corral.

"Look at these, Bill," I said nervously, pointing to the prints in the wet mud. "It's a cougar. Based on the size of the tracks, it must be an adult."

I knew a fair amount about cougars from my past experience working with them in conservation law enforcement. Later, as a professional wildlife artist, I had been hired to draw them for the Florida Panther Project, so I was well acquainted with the big cats.

We showed them to the girls and again gave them the appropriate safety lectures. I decided not to let this opportunity go to waste. Because we home schooled, we liked to incorporate any opportunistic learning experience into the girls' curricula, so I had them bring down my casting box. I had learned the technique from a biologist friend many years before, and with the girls' help, we made a few good molds as a science project. In a couple of hours they hardened and we measured one of them at four inches across, which indicated an eighty- to one-hundred-pound cat. This served to heighten my concerns for Belle's safety at night. The last thing I wanted was for Belle to face a cat threat when she was still adjusting to her new home. She was a cocky girl, but a cat could do serious bodily damage, or even take her life if it was desperate enough. Still, this one seemed young enough that, in all probability, it would not chance injuring itself attacking an adult horse, especially when there were plenty of deer and smaller animals to prey upon.

Now that we owned a horse, we had the compounded problem of simultaneously protecting her, the children, and our dog. The stable was 100 yards from the house, so I began leaving a bedroom window cracked in case she ever called for help. Two nights passed before I awoke with a start. I was certain I'd heard a loud cry and Belle whinnying. I shook Bill from his usual deep slumber, and yelled, "Get up! A cougar's attacking Belle!"

Bill stumbled out of bed, fumbled with the balcony door and searched the stable with a flashlight. He returned a minute later, grumbling, "She's fine."

"Are you sure? I thought I heard a cat scream."

"She's standing in the middle of the round pen, as calm as can be."

"I was certain I heard her call out for help."

"You must have dreamed it, Honey. I didn't hear anything."

"You can't hear anything with your snoring."

"I heard *you.*"

I was starting to get mad, but after checking her status myself, I decided it must have been a bad dream, or else my imagination. But the fear was legitimate enough that the next day I asked our electrician about the possibility of wiring remotely activated lights around the barnyard. He was quite sympathetic to my concern because his own horse had been mauled by a cougar several years earlier. The fact that it had happened in California did not reduce my anxiety; it only reinforced my desire to protect our newest family/pack/herd member. Before long we had the remote flood lights in place and I rested a bit easier at night.

Go West, Young Woman!

19

Sybil

A BOUT THIS SAME TIME, I STARTED TO SEE A CHANGE in Belle's behavior; she was beginning to express her own opinions. I was very perplexed at her new ways of asserting herself. She had always been so well behaved at the stable and when she first came home to us. I couldn't understand what was going on.

Whenever Sandy put the lead rope on her, she would then rush past her and practically drag her behind, protesting. Our well-mannered horse had developed a bad behavior pattern, and I had no idea how to stop it. These issues had never come up before, and I had no information on how to deal with them. So I started reading books and searching the Internet for advice, but could find no clear explanations.

The last straw broke the morning I sent Sandy outside to place the horse on a picket. Minutes later I heard her screaming at Belle in tears of frustration. Belle had broken free from her grasp and was wandering about, dragging the lead rope, and showing not the slightest intention of obeying her commands. I decided to call Gail.

"This happens sometimes with mares," Gail said in her matter-of-fact tone. "I don't know why, but they can change when you take them from an environment they're used to and bring 'em to a new home."

"Oh great," I sighed, thinking again how this was *not in the brochure.* "What do I do now?"

"Let her know you're in charge," Gail replied. "Push her back when she tries to get ahead of you."

"She's over a thousand pounds. How do I do that?"

"Pull back on her lead rope and shout 'back up.'"

The next morning I put the halter on Belle. So far so good, she seemed to be cooperating. We walked out the gate to the meadow. I started to lead her up the slope when, suddenly, she decided to go another direction. Before I could react, she had shoved passed me to get to a clump of grass, knocking me to the ground. I could not believe it! I jumped to my feet and pulled back on the lead rope, shouting at her to back up and move her feet. She was slow and reluctant, but eventually did what I demanded. Bill saw what was happening and came over to help me.

"Let me take her the rest of the way," he said. He took Belle and led her away. That was my first mistake and it was a big one. I had just gone down a notch in her pecking order, and didn't even know it.

Another problem was beginning to develop when we tried to saddle Belle. She had always been so calm and quiet when it was time for the saddle. She would stand still and often doze during the process. Now she was swishing her tail and stamping her foot.

"What's wrong with Belle?" Sandy asked me with great concern.

I wasn't' sure, so I checked her saddle pad and cinch. Nothing seemed to be pinching her or was out of place. I didn't know what to think, but I was able to finish saddling her.

"She took the bit okay," I said. "Try to mount up."

When Sandy put her foot in the stirrup, Belle flung her tail along side and hit Sandy square in the back as if she were swatting a fly.

"She hit me!" Sandy called out in surprise.

"Belle! Stop it!" I yelled as I swatted the horse's shoulder. We struggled with her until Sandy was able to mount the saddle. *What is going on with this horse?*

"Take her into the round pen; you'll have more control there."

Belle's attitude did not improve, and her reaction was to remain completely still. Sandy squeezed her knees around Belle with no effect.

Belle was well trained and normally only required a light touch to move her feet. Sandy tried several more times with no response.

"Walk on, Belle," I commanded, but she just stared straight ahead. I was unsure of what to do next. We had not encountered this problem before.

"Tap her on the backside," I suggested, "Not too hard - just enough to get her going."

Sandy took her hand and gave Belle a little pop on the backside and she finally moved her feet.

"There you go," I said elated. Belle moved all of three steps and stopped again. *What is wrong with you, horse?* By now Sandy was frustrated almost to tears and I was just plain angry.

After a few more attempts, Sandy managed to get Belle to barely move with a light kick in the side. I did not like the way this was going, but we were both tired and ended our riding for the day. After we put the tack and saddle away, we set out for home. The walk up the hill seemed longer than usual. With each step I tried to encourage Sandy by telling her tomorrow would be better; we would figure this out. In truth, I was not feeling too confident in my own words. I felt so bad for her as I watched those little shoulders droop as she shuffled along. *All I can do is try again tomorrow.* Those were my only thoughts as we entered the house and closed the door behind us.

Belle was still grumpy the next day and for several days after, as we experienced the same poor behavior. Her tail kept flailing and swishing as though we were flies to be swatted away. I was feeling very discouraged. *Did I make a huge mistake buying this horse? Did I misjudge her personality?*

By the end of the week I was back to my books, still searching for an explanation. All I could find was information on vices, things like biting and cribbing. These were not my horse's problems. So I resorted to plan B—call Gail again. I really did not want to look like I had made a huge error in judgment, but I knew Gail would understand. I explained the problem in great detail, perhaps with more emotion than it warranted, but I was feeling really low.

Gail curtly responded to my two minute spiel, "She's testing you, kid, or she may be in her cycle."

"Her cycle?" I repeated. "I know mares have a breeding cycle, but I didn't think it would make them act like stubborn mules."

"Even worse," Gail answered.

"You know, Gail, this was not in the brochure." It was the first time I had said this out loud and she laughed.

"Don't put up with her crap; this horse can't push you around. She's a dominant mare and she wants full control. She doesn't have any herd to push around now, so she's telling you what to do. Have you even ever put a sweat on that horse?"

"I don't know what you mean."

"You need to run her in the round pen till she gets good and tired. That'll give her the what-for. If I have some time next week I'll come up and help you."

I felt better after talking to Gail. It was true; I was on the low end of a behavioral learning curve. However, I wanted to keep a positive attitude and wasn't about to give up and admit defeat. This was not too late to fix I told myself. I just need a little help.

The next day Bill joined us at the corral. Again Belle was giving Sandy a hard time. She wouldn't stand still long enough for Sandy to tighten the cinch. Bill offered to help. He walked over to Belle and started to work. He pulled the cinch in an upward motion and Belle swung her head around to Bill's left leg. She hesitated for just a moment, and then bit him hard on the thigh. I heard Bill curse and call out, "She bit me!"

"Smack her on the nose now!" I shouted across the yard to him in the pen. He did, and then I yelled, "Did you smack her hard?"

"What constitutes hard?"

I rushed over and came through the round pen gate. "Are you bleeding? How bad is it? How bad does it hurt?"

Bill was calm. "No, she didn't break the skin," he replied, "but I'll have a nasty bruise. I'm glad I had on my heavy cargo pants. I think it offered some protection."

Protection! Now we needed protection from our own horse! What if it had been one of the girls? I felt sick, Bill was irritated, Sandy was frightened, and Belle acted like nothing ever happened, and just looked straight ahead, unfazed.

Sandy no longer wanted to get on Belle. Who could blame her? We talked it over with her, and she reluctantly decided to give it another try. I agreed, as long as they stayed in the round pen. Belle seemed calm and Sandy was soon in the saddle without a problem. Strange as it sounds, Belle did not give us any more trouble, and the ride went smoothly. Both Bill and I stayed in the pen during the ride, and kept a close watch on Belle, but she showed no other aggressive behavior.

I looked at Bill's leg later that evening. The bruise was as wide as my outstretched hand. It was huge. "I'm sorry," I said.

"It's not your fault," he replied with compassion.

Even though we had made this decision to get a horse together, I felt incredibly guilty. After all, I had chosen her, but I never suspected she'd do anything like this. She certainly hadn't struck me as the type to be so mean. Why would she do such a thing? I couldn't understand it, and I was starting to worry about the future. I voiced my apprehension regarding Belle, but Bill was unconcerned. He said they were just animals and we'd learn how to deal with this problem in time. It was all going to work out. He thought I was putting too much emotion into it. Well that emotion had to come out somewhere, so I called Gail the next morning.

"I have a horse that bites!" I announced on the phone almost as soon as she said hello.

"What?" she answered, her voice strained. "What happened?"

"It was awful," I replied, and went on to describe the gory details.

There was a momentary pause before Gail responded, "If she is in her cycle, then tightening the cinch may have hurt her abdomen. The only other reason I can think of is she is testing Bill to see if she can be in charge of him. She's trying to find out if she can be the leader. You did the right thing telling him to swat her on the nose. I hope this is over."

She mentioned again that mares could be more trouble than geldings. I think she felt sorry for me because she offered to come up and see Belle sooner rather than later.

"She needs a good workout in the pen. She doesn't have to work too hard for anything, and right now she thinks she's queen of the mountain. She's beginning to figure out you guys don't have a lot of confidence or experience in handling horses and she's taking advantage of you. What she needs is an attitude adjustment."

I was confused, "I thought once a horse was trained, it knew how to behave."

Gail snorted, "Oh no! They treat each person differently. A lead mare in particular will always test you a little at a time. I'll be up tomorrow afternoon and I'm bringing my big, heavy saddle. That child's saddle she carries around is too easy. I want her sweaty and tired when I'm done with her."

"Are cows this much trouble?" I asked trying to keep my sense of humor.

"Oh yes," Gail said laughing.

I was really looking forward to the next day and wanted to learn everything I could about handling this horse before she became even more belligerent. I started reading again and learned that every herd has a hierarchy or pecking order. The stronger personalities want to make the decisions and take charge. Stallions and lead mares eat and drink first, and generally boss the others around to make sure they understand the rules. Sometimes "middle class" horses bite or kick each other to make their point, while the rest fall into a lower rank order. The last horse in line is the one with the weakest personality. It does not mean they are not a good horse or would not make a good companion; they are just the most submissive of the group.

It all sounded rather brutal to me but I did not question the facts. This as important information that could help me in the future. I was embarrassed by how little I really knew about horses. There was so much more to ownership than just how to ride or put on a saddle. Having a horse live on your land, and handling them everyday, was so much different than showing up for a two-hour lesson twice a week. I was up to my neck in it now and I had to make it work. Belle was simply seeing us as her new herd within her new home. She was testing each of us, one at a time, to see where we belonged in the hierarchy. How could I let her know we were the leaders and she was the lowest ranking member?

Gail was good to her word and arrived the next afternoon. Summer was ending, but we were blessed with a warm and sunny day. The location of our round pen presented a post card view of the mountains and wide, blue open sky above. Each day like this reminded me of why we moved to Montana, its breathtaking beauty, tall evergreen trees, lush meadows, fresh air, clear running creeks, and that magnificent sky. As Gail worked the horse, I daydreamed, but soon her voice rang out sharply, and I turned my attention back to her instruction.

"Now watch everything I do," Gail cautioned me. "You wait out here while I take Belle into the round pen."

I watched intently as she placed the halter on Belle, and simultaneously voiced stern warnings for her to mind her manners and obey the commands given. Once in the round pen, she continued her lecture.

"I teach my horses to swing around and face me so that I can close the gate."

Gail slapped her hand hard against Belle's hind end and the horse moved over. She did this three more times. "I want to show Belle I mean what I say. You have to be firm with her."

I looked into Gail's stone face and could tell she meant business. Belle was beginning to believe it too, for she stood respectfully, without offering any resistance. Gail picked up her eighty pound saddle and with a big heave-ho, tossed it onto Belle's back. Within thirty seconds the horse was saddled and ready to ride.

"Wow, you did that super fast," I said, amazed at how quickly it was accomplished.

"We don't have time to fool around when we're working. We have cows to move."

Gail picked up a whip with an orange flag on its tip and walked to the center of the round pen. She pointed the tip in Belle's direction and, with a flip of her wrist, she sent Belle to the edge of the round pen. She then began flipping the whip low to the ground behind the horse, and Belle responded by walking along the corral panels in one large circle.

"Move a little faster, Belle," Gail commanded as she increased pressure on the horse by raising the volume and authority in her voice. She snapped the whip hard against the ground and Belle responded by

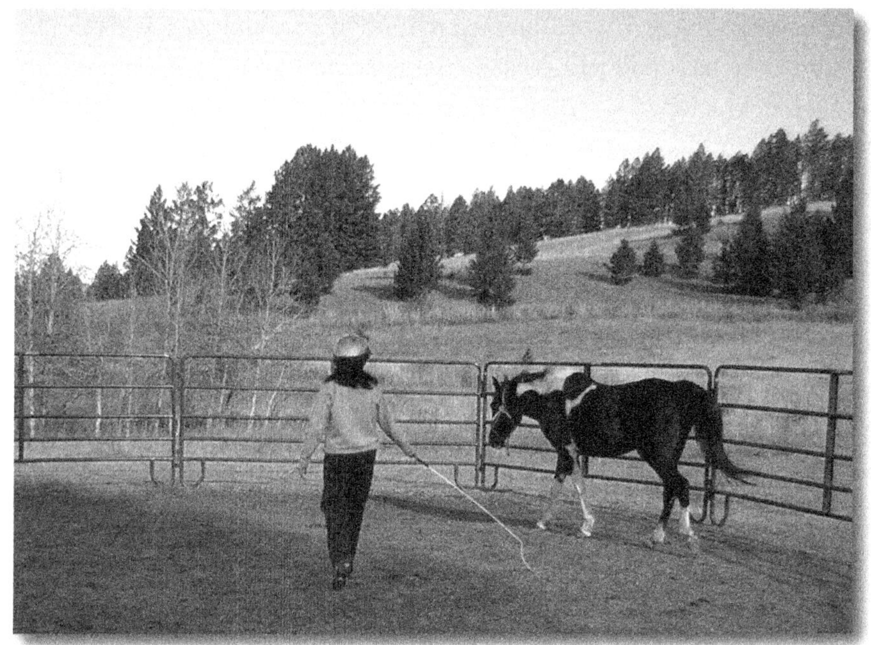

Training day in the round pen with Belle

increasing her pace. Gail whipped the ground more frequently, increasing the pressure still further until Belle lurched into a gaited run around the pen. Her eyes never left Belle as she rotated in the center of the pen, and continued to encourage her to run.

"You're fat and out of shape, Belle. Keep moving," Gail bellowed in her best imitation of an unsympathetic Army drill sergeant. "You have to keep her going for several minutes. Look at her sides pushing in and out. She's breathing heavily now, so I'll bring her in to me for a moment. Besides, I'm getting a bit dizzy myself!"

Gail lowered her arm and Belle turned, taking a couple of steps toward her. Belle faced her, breathing hard. "She hasn't been out of breath since you brought her home. This is good for her."

Poor Belle, I thought with a hint of sarcasm because I was not very happy with her personality change. I had bought a sweet obedient mare, but within a few weeks of living with us she had turned into Sybil, the horse with sixteen personalities. You never knew what you were getting. Sometimes she was nice and sometimes she was a devil. I was beginning to understand part of it was our fault for not knowing how to handle her on the ground, and part of it was just her strong personality. I could see now that I would have to develop an even stronger personality to be a leader in her eyes. In time, I hoped she would follow my lead.

After Belle had rested for a few minutes, she began breathing easier, so Gail sent her out for a few more exercises. After a few minutes, she brought her in again and pointed out a white patch between her back legs. "I bet you've never seen that before. That's horse sweat."

I leaned through the rails to get a better look, and sure enough, I saw a wet, almost foamy substance on her legs. It was true; Belle was working hard and looked tired. Gail soon ended the training session and let her stand a while before removing the heavy saddle from her back.

"Do you think this will take some of the vinegar out of her?" I teased Gail.

"It should help," she shrugged with a smile. "Come out and do this every day and see what happens."

Before she headed home, I gave her my profuse thanks and hugs. I had a growing respect for her, and through our friendship, began to learn much more about cows and horses. After that, I could not purchase a pack of hamburger without thinking about how hard she and her family worked to make a living by supplying the public with meat.

Later that night I hit the books again; I wanted to know more about this round pen business. I read about something called a "join up," an exercise in gaining trust and respect. The idea was to send the horse out into the pen and make them trot around you. From the horse's view you are casting them out alone. This is uncomfortable for them, but you stay connected by looking them in the eye. Then you search for cues from the horse's body language to see if they are going to give in to your leadership or stay emotionally distant. When you see the proper behavior, you release them from running and see if they come to you of their own free will. If they do, you have achieved some success. I thought it was worth trying. I followed the advice of my friend, and the next afternoon took Belle out to the round pen, intrigued to try the join up.

I stood in the center and sent Belle out as Gail had done. Belle moved away and then turned back and tried to come to me. *It is not supposed to go this way.* We stood facing each other. My lack of confidence must have shown. She snorted and looked a little angry that I would ask her to do such a thing. Apparently it was okay for Gail to ask her to do this, but not for me. I remembered how Belle had bitten Bill, and I instantly felt afraid. She was a thousand pounds of muscle and I was only a petite, 107 pound mass of quivering flesh. She was well experienced at being a horse, but I had no experience at being a herd leader. I stood there looking at her for a few moments.

I have to do something. I took a breath and sent her out again. She turned and went to the side of the pen. She started moving and I looked her in the eye. I desperately wanted to know what she was thinking. She went around the first lap as I watched her. It was as if we were engaging in some kind of a dance. She was so beautiful with her head and tail raised high, that she reminded me of one of those elegant movie horses. I waited to see if her ear would turn to me. According to the book, this would be a good sign. No, not yet, she was just going through the motions, or should I say emotions. She snorted again and came a little too close to me. I did not like that; I wanted her to stay nearer to the edge of the ring. *I think I just lost another point. I can't let that happen again.* It did not take long before I noticed her ear was turned my way. She was finally paying attention to me. I gave her a few more laps and turned away from her, my hands to my side, as I gazed down at the ground with my shoulders relaxed. If the book was right, Belle should come to me in the center of the circle and stand next to me.

I didn't have long to wait; she immediately walked towards me and stood patiently next to me. I looked up at her and she began a licking and chewing motion with her mouth. It was just like the book said; all of it was a sign of acceptance. Awkward as it was, I had earned some respect

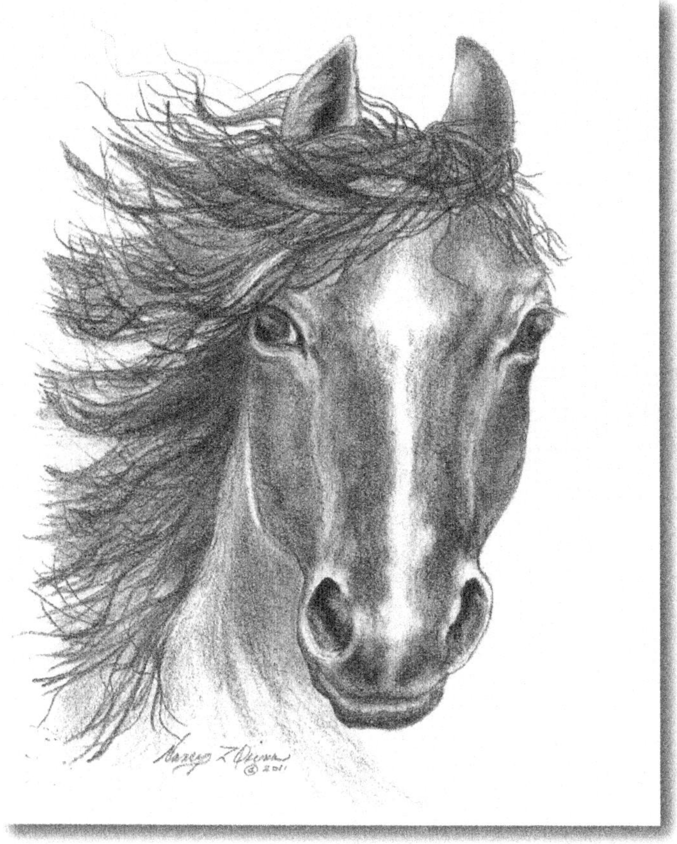

The author's graphite drawing inspired by Belle

from her. We were on our way to forming a new relationship, and I was elated that another small thread had woven itself into the connection we were building. I rubbed her head and spoke gently in her ear.

"What a good girl," I said softly to her. As I began to step away, I noticed she followed me. I turned to the right, then the left, and she continued to follow me. We walked around the pen for a few minutes. *I wish I knew what to do now.*

I connected the lead rope to the halter and led her out to the corral area. I patted her again and tied her to the hitching post. After she had stood quietly for a few moments, I released her with a rub on her head, and let her walk out to the field to eat some grass. As I closed the corral gate, I was smiling. I felt both happiness and relief as I hurried up the hill to the house.

I was anxious to report to everyone about my progress with her; for once I had a positive topic of conversation for the dinner table. Over the next couple of weeks Belle's conduct improved dramatically, and we were beginning to have some good days together. Sandy was a happier rider and I felt better about horse ownership. I still watched Belle closely, as I did not yet completely trust her with my girls. I must have had good intuition because she was not through testing us yet.

20

Misstep

"TALK TO HER, SANDY," I SAID THE FOLLOWING afternoon as we were brushing Belle. "She should learn to recognize the sound of your voice when she's enjoying a pleasant experience."

I knew we were struggling with our new horse adventure, and I desperately wanted this to work out for all of us, but especially for Sandy because she rode Belle. This was a lot to learn for a ten-year-old girl who had not grown up with horses, and who was unsure of herself. She needed more confidence handling a thousand pound horse that was used to being a herd leader. But being firm was difficult for a girl with a gentle hand and lack of practical ground skills. She did well in the saddle, but all the rest of it was not so easy, including little tasks like taking Belle out to the field where she could be left in peace to eat the grass she dearly desired. Bill often took Belle in and out of the pasture area, thinking she'd give Sandy trouble, but this only moved her further down in Belle's pecking order.

It finally came to a head the next Saturday morning when I asked Sandy to bring Belle in from grazing. I stood on our deck and looked out as Sandy made her way to the little tack room to get a halter. It was drizzling rain and I was pleased to see that Sandy had on a rain coat with the hood up to cover her head. She entered the meadow and approached Belle, who did not even look up. Belle was too busy eating and did not wish to be disturbed. Sandy approached her and tried to slip the halter past her nose, but Belle turned away, and the dance of frustration began. With each attempt, Belle turned and walked away, increasing Sandy's frustration as she desperately followed her around the meadow.

"Toss the lead rope over her neck," I called. "She usually gives up when she feels it there."

Sandy stepped closer and gently tossed the rope as Belle moved away, but the rope missed its intended target.

"I'm about to quit!" she yelled in desperation.

"You can't stop," I shouted back. "This is your horse, and she can't stay out any longer. We have to go to town and she can't eat wet grass all day."

I was firm with her, but I understood how she felt. Part of me wanted to go down there and finish the job for her, and another part wanted her to do it on her own. "Slowly approach her and try again," I said, trying to sound encouraging. "You can do it."

The rain was now increasing, and so was Sandy's frustration. She moved over to Belle and tried again. Belle walked away, tugging grass out by the roots, chewing it as fast as she could. I had a feeling Belle knew her grazing time this morning was coming to an end, as was Sandy's patience. She began to cry, and the tears mixed with the rain on her face.

"One more try, honey girl," I called to her. "I have faith in you."

She stomped her feet in anger as she trudged over to Belle's side, and with a determined hand slipped the halter over her head and tied it. "I did it!" Sandy shouted with gleeful happiness.

"Great job!" I called out with relief.

They began to walk towards the corral, when Belle decided not to pass up a lovely, enticing clump of grass, and stopped, bending her head to the ground. Sandy tugged at the rope, which Belle ignored. I offered more advice, but this time Sandy ignored me. While she struggled with the lead rope, I suddenly heard a sharp piercing scream from Sandy. I called to her, but she kept on screaming. Through her tears I heard her cry, "My foot!"

"Push her off!" I yelled, nearly ready to climb off the upper deck and jump to the ground.

Sandy gave Belle a hard shove on the shoulder and she moved, releasing Sandy's foot.

"Are you okay?" I shouted to her.

A weepy voice answered, "Yes."

Sandy put Belle into the corral without any further incident, but as I watched her climb the hill it was evident from her slumped posture she felt defeated. I could see it in her face when she trudged into the house. Immediately I inspected her foot and to my surprise discovered she was wearing nothing but flip-flop sandals.

"Where are your boots?" I angrily snapped, incredulous at the thought she would have been so careless. "You could have lost a toe or broken your foot. You know the rules! You must wear your boots around the horse. This time you were lucky."

Sandy stood mute, then meekly replied, "I was in a hurry."

"Let me help you off with your coat," I said firmly. I reached for her shoulder and slid the coat off of one arm, only to discover she was in her pajamas.

"Why didn't you dress first?"

Sandy glanced away, replying, "I was in a hurry to put Belle away, and I didn't want to get my clothes dirty."

I made her look me straight in the eyes as I ordered, "Never again! You must be properly dressed before you go outside. Well, at least you wore a rain coat. Now go and get cleaned up; we'll talk about this more, later."

I was becoming completely frustrated with both Sandy and Belle. I was still in the middle of a steep learning curve and seeking help anywhere I could find it. Feedback and advice varied and were sometimes conflicted. The more I inquired, the more I felt I was a fool asking stupid questions. Why did I buy a horse when I clearly did not understand the psychology of the beast? Slowly it dawned on me that not all the information I was receiving could be accurate because it simply did not match my limited, but growing, experience. Some people, whom I initially believed to be skilled equestrians, responded with advice that did not address my issues.

A couple of people took pity on me and offered to come out and help. But when one such experienced rider suggested Belle was too difficult to handle and should be sold, my heart sank.

Discouraging as that was, I did give it careful consideration. I did not want any of us to get hurt, but was this really a case of a bad match between horse and rider? Was I a poor horse handler and in over my head? If Belle had been unmanageable from the beginning, I might have agreed with this advice and sold her off. But she was well mannered and easy going early in our relationship. That told me we were doing something wrong as a result of our inexperience, rather than Belle being too difficult. What we needed was more education, time, and experience. But who could I turn to for help? Gail was busy haying, and I didn't want to waste the good summer weather.

I needed somebody who fully grasped horsemanship, horse care, and horse psychology. I knew enough by now to avoid self-proclaimed experts like the one who said, "You talk your horse to death. It can't understand you. A horse doesn't give a thought about what you are saying anyway, so don't bother talking to it unless you're giving it one-word commands."

This was one piece of advice I refused to accept completely. While there was some truth in the remark that an animal didn't understand all your words, their meanings, or the context in which they were being used, that did not mean it could not distinguish the intent in your voice. The meaning of one's tone of voice and loudness, with all its emotion and inflection, could be understood if it were repeated often enough in the same context. At the psychological level, an animal behaviorist might explain that you were building connections in the animal's brain, and shaping its behavior. Hence, simple word commands would suffice. But I didn't want a clinical association with my horse; I wanted an emotional connection. I didn't just want to own animals; I wanted a bond with them that transcended a cause-and-effect relationship. Kobi always understood me, so why shouldn't my horse? She might never know what my words meant, but she'd know what I intended, if only by the feeling in my voice.

At the same time I decided I should be learning her language, and how to communicate with her. I was sure she was trying to figure out such things about me as well, so I reasoned it was only logical that talking with a horse helped build those necessary bonds. All we needed was someone to translate for us, or better still, teach me how to think and speak like a horse.

As I brushed Belle's coat with a curry comb, I pondered where to find such a person. I thought, perhaps a horse training video would suffice, or maybe I needed to attend a training clinic. My thoughts were rudely interrupted by a sudden blast of arctic wind. Fall was upon us, and if that breeze was any indicator, winter would quickly follow. The problem would have to wait until spring for resolution.

21

Winter World

WE BEGAN PREPARATIONS EARLY FOR THE COMING WINTER. We had learned to conform to the earth's rhythms, so in summer we collected wood for our fireplace, and stored hay for Belle. By late fall the tack room was emptied of anything that could freeze, and all containers were tightly sealed. I set out my favorite candles, and took warm fluffy blankets from storage and placed them about the family room and loft. I soon started my favorite seasonal ritual, baking cookies, pumpkin bread, and apple cake. As expected, Gail's family dutifully volunteered to serve as test tasters for any new concoctions I had a mind to invent.

We had not quite finished siding our stable by the time the weather turned decidedly cold and the first heavy snows fell, but we had sheltered plenty of hay for the winter, and the automatic watering system was working in the protected stall. Belle was as comfortably quartered as any horse, and did not seem fazed by the colder temperatures.

I was satisfied we were as ready for the long darkness as could be expected. And though I admit winter is my least favorite season, there remained something strangely satisfying in knowing we were better prepared this time around. We had accomplished every task that was essential to our new way of life, and I looked forward to just enjoying a

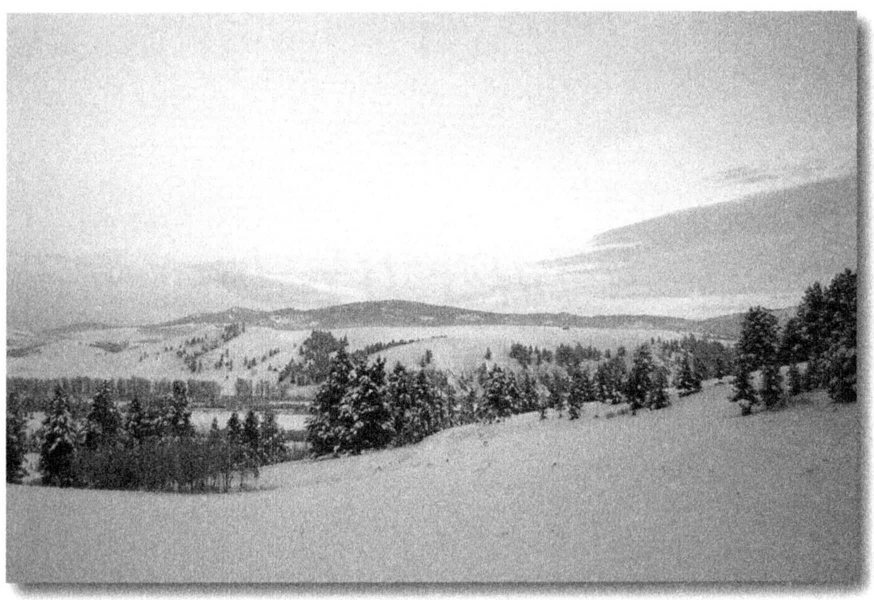

Winter sunrise

few quiet moments with a cup of hot tea by the fireplace, while watching the snow silently descend and collect everywhere. On those rare days when the sun was still out, I would be mesmerized by all the glitter in the sky as each flake swirled up and down, dancing in the air, before settling to the ground. Once there, the crystallized flakes glinted like a million tiny diamonds. It had a way of making one feel rich, not with the value of gold and jewels, but with the simple natural pleasures of life.

One of the greatest of those pleasures remained the beautiful sunsets we enjoyed most evenings. First came the growing shadows that turned the sky and ground to softer hues. Next came the changing colors, as though God were preparing a great canvas upon which were painted broad strokes of pink, blue, yellow, and orange. The clouds, most striking of all, faded from one pigment to the next as the sun dipped further below the horizon, its last rays casting purple shadows that spread like a blanket, first over the valley below, and then the mountains above. When the wind was strong, the dark shapes of low clouds moved rapidly across the flats and peaks of the terrain, as if trying to reach a new destination before darkness engulfed all. It was truly a magical gift for the eyes.

The only downside to it all was having to feed Belle in the blustery, sub-zero temperatures. We gave her a handful of sweet molasses corn with her food to ensure she had extra calories to burn for warmth. Our consolation was the knowledge that these freezing chores would be followed by an offer of hot chocolate or tea by a warm fireplace.

"Don't use your hay supply until it's absolutely necessary," Gail had warned me. "Put Belle on the picket and let her dig for grass. Not only will it keep her busy, it's good for her health, mentally and physically. Don't just keep her in the round pen and let her get bored. She needs something constructive to do in order to stay warm and keep herself occupied."

I agreed, so everyday we took Belle to a new spot in our field and pounded in the picket stake. She would happily dig, causing snow and ice to fly up in the air. She reminded me of a snow globe with the flakes swirling around her fourteen-hand figure. *Too bad I couldn't hook the plow to her and let her clear our driveway. Just think how quickly she'd finish!*

Since it was now frigid outside, we couldn't continue our rides, so Belle had plenty of extra time on her hands after coming in from picket duty each evening. Her hay stores interested her greatly, being located just behind the gate. She believed if she could just get that pin out, the gate would magically fly open, and she'd no longer have to work for her food.

I had not given the notion any serious thought until I was eating lunch one afternoon, when Sandy looked out the bay window and exclaimed, "Look! Belle's in the hay!"

I peeked through the dining room window, and sure enough, there she was, happily munching the hay bales, the gate having mysteriously swung open. Later, upon closer examination, we determined she had pulled out the retaining pin by gnawing on the retaining wire attached to it, until she was able to pull the pin out. It hung there, almost completely chewed through. *What a clever animal.* We secured the pin in a new location, out of reach, and thought the problem solved, but a few days later I again looked out and saw Belle's head fast to the ground as she tried to wiggle under the hay gate. She was bowing with one leg stretched out in front of her, and her other legs bending low. I never thought a horse could get into such contortions, but she had. She did not succeed, but she was no quitter.

The next day as I sat down by the dining room fireplace to enjoy a cup of hot tea, I saw Belle on the ground, lying flat on her side in front of the hay gate. *What is she doing now?* Her head slid sideways under the gate, and she snatched a mouthful of hay. She jumped to her feet, triumphantly, and began happily munching.

"Unbelievable," I said, shaking my head. I let her enjoy her small victory while I finished my tea.

It bothered me that such an intelligent horse was left so alone outside all the time, but at least her antics kept her mind occupied. Kobi occasionally kept her company, but often I found myself obliged to bundle up and make my way through the snow for a visit. The cold did not bother Belle, but it bothered me immensely, so I could only stay for a short time before becoming chilled to the bone. When I could no longer feel my own nose, I'd start for home. I often wondered how she could bury her face full in the snow searching for some thin blade of grass, while my face froze even when covered.

Once, I mistakenly decided to bring her a treat, and upon pulling the apple snack from my coat pocket, she became quite excited. I thought I had done something nice for her, but the next day when I arrived, instead of being grateful for my company, she rudely began searching my pockets with her nose. I told her to stop and pushed her face away, but she was determined to find a pellet in there. I again shoved her face and scolded her. She just turned her head away and took a few steps to her right. *This is the last time I give you one of those treats.* I was still learning horses were not dogs. Feeding them did not earn their respect or acceptance. They just viewed you as another source of food.

The rest of that second winter was not particularly eventful. We continued with school and looked forward to the upcoming holidays. The day after Thanksgiving we walked around our property looking for a Christmas tree.

"We can't have one as big as last year." I reminded my husband with a smile and raised eyebrows. For our first Montana Christmas he had cut down a tree so huge, it had to be chained to the back of the truck and dragged home. It measured twenty-two feet high. Our friend, Mark, was visiting us from Florida, and between their collective grunts and groans, he and Bill managed to get that monster into the house. We had ample ceiling height in the living room, but erecting and stabilizing the brute presented a real challenge, after cutting it down to seventeen feet, it became more manageable. Eventually, we secured it by tying it between the stairway and loft railings. Once decorated, it was beautiful, I had to admit. I called it our "Griswold" family Christmas tree. Luckily, no squirrels jumped out of it like in the movie *Christmas Vacation,* but Mark has not returned to celebrate another Thanksgiving, preferring instead, to now come at Christmas, after the tree is already in place and decorated.

I always enjoyed making homemade cookies and candies as Christmas presents. In the past I'd even tried my hand at Kahlua and biscotti, but judging from the lukewarm responses I usually received, I concluded that many folks are conditioned to expect a store-bought gift. It was, therefore, with some trepidation that I prepared my Christmas surprises for Gail and her family. When we met to exchange gifts, I could see the concern written on her face, but it wasn't over my homemade presents. It was her fear we might not appreciate the basket full of canned jam, honey, and cookies she had made for us. We both laughed in relief, and after that, enjoyed many phone calls back and forth, talking about the latest recipes we had created.

I also make stockings for our animals. It may be silly, but our pets are part of our family, so that second year we hung Belle's stocking next to the one I had sewn for Kobi. Santa came on his appointed night and filled them. Kobi received some treats and a new leash. In honor of her first Christmas with us, Belle received a new hot pink lead rope. While Gail and I were discussing our Christmas day events, the news about the stockings came out.

"You have a stocking for your horse?" she asked incredulously.

"Yes, and she got a pink lead rope in it," I replied.

I was beginning to think she had never met anyone like me. I was eager to change the subject, so I inquired about her Christmas dinner. We talked about our menus and I asked if she had a big crowd. I knew Gail's husband had a big family. I described how I set a pretty table for the four of us, with colored dishes, and seasonal table cloths and napkins. I always enjoyed such rituals, probably because I am a party planner at heart.

Gail laughed and joked with me, "Honey, I'm so busy cooking that I don't set a fancy table with napkins. You're lucky if I throw a paper towel at you when you come through the door."

"Very funny; I'll be sure to inform Martha Stewart."

22

Trespassers

URING DAYLIGHT HOURS I WAS MUCH LESS CONCERNED about Belle's safety. She was forming a tight bond with Kobi, or perhaps it would be accurate to say he was forming a tight bond with her. When winter finally came, he demonstrated my faith in him one afternoon by showing his willingness to protect Belle when a coyote came into the front meadow. Kobi watched it from a sitting position on the front patio. Bill saw it too and fired a couple of shots at it from the upstairs deck with a rifle we now kept by the balcony door for just such occasions. I watched the snow spray from the ground as the bullets hit the fresh powder. They surrounded the coyote as he high-tailed it away, zigzagging from left to right. Our daughter Sonja watched the combat with interest, and when it was all over, her little face turned to her father and she wryly said with a smile, "Dad, you're king of the misses."

Bill laughed as he retorted, "That's my plan—to scare them away."

When Kobi heard the shots, he took off after the coyote. He followed it to the edge of the road, pivoted 180 degrees, ran to Belle, turned again, and stood protectively in front of her with all four feet planted firmly in the snow. He sternly surveyed the yard, his body language clear. No way, no how, was anyone going to prey upon a member of *his* pack. The time had finally come when he recognized Belle as one of his own, and deserving of all the protection and privileges that goes with it.

A few days later the Christmas tree came down, we entered the new year, and the holidays were over. I finally felt I could relax and enjoy the slower pace of deep winter. But I had forgotten this was Montana where nothing should be taken for granted. I was reminded of this fact the morning I saw Belle acting strangely. I had glanced out the second floor window as I was descending the stairs. She had alerted to something, and was jumping away from the temporary electric fence. *Had it shocked her?* No, Belle turned and ran in a circle, this time blowing out her nose and stamping her feet.

I looked out, squinting through the bright sun reflecting off the snow, but could see nothing. I called Bill, but neither of us could discern the reason for her behavior.

"It might be wolves," I said. Belle had now run to the opposite side of the round pen, away from the pasture. Suddenly Bill saw it.

"It's a moose! He's in the driveway, down by the tree line," he called out. "Look at this big fellow!"

He was huge, as moose tend to be, and he was obviously scaring Belle. I was afraid he would run her into the hot wire on her electric fence.

"Where's my camera?" Bill exclaimed, as Belle continued to jump, snort, and stamp.

I had to do something and a camera wasn't going to frighten a moose.

"Maybe you should fire a shot in the air to scare it away."

"No, he's not close enough to threaten her."

While Bill was searching for his camera, I decided to try to calm Belle before she panicked and hurt herself. I stepped outside and called to her.

"Belle, you're fine." She stopped running at the sound of my voice and looked up at me, expectantly. With as much authority as I could muster, I lifted my head, squared my shoulders, and announced, "Moose! Go home! Leave now and go home, moose!" To my absolute surprise, the moose turned and began walking down into the tree line. I couldn't believe it.

"I missed him. I didn't get the picture," Bill complained in exasperation. He started walking down the driveway, hoping to catch a glimpse, but the moose was gone. We would see him again even closer to the house, but we never did get that picture.

23

Wait Until Dark

I HAD ABSOLUTE PROOF THAT SPRING WAS ON THE WAY when I saw the first lavender crocus blossom through the remains of the last snow. Purple is Sonja's favorite color, and whenever we came up the driveway she'd point and say, "Look, a crocus! Does this mean we can ride?"

"Not until the ice is all gone and the manure's been hauled off," I said. This statement was immediately followed by collective moans, groans, and, "Oh, why must this happen every year?"

As much as I enjoy the companionship of horses, there is one aspect on which they cannot favorably compare with dogs, that being their amazing ability to continuously manufacture copious quantities of manure. It has to be their single most undesirable characteristic, and in this regard they are amazingly indefatigable. Let me be clear, I have absolutely no interest in the subject of scatology. I do not want to see it, smell it, or, heaven forbid, step in it. However, it is a large part of horse ownership, and one must take the good with the bad. The girls initially complained about cleaning up after the horse, but I explained why it was a non-negotiable point. If they did not keep her corral area clean, Belle would become ill, so it was either muck it or find her a new home.

"Spring here really means the thaw, mud, and muck," I told Gail.

She just shrugged and replied, "That's Montana weather for you."

127

The corrals got the worst of it, mushy ground, heavily festooned with defrosting manure; each pitchfork full lifting more mud than horse droppings. Those we could not pick up, remained frozen in the ground like so many landmines awaiting detonation by some unsuspecting foot. Without a tractor to scrape it away, our only option was to wait for the rest to thaw. Once it does, it sticks like glue to everything that comes in contact with it. In the meantime I worried about its effect on Belle's health. I am a clean freak, and the thought of her standing, eating, drinking, and sleeping in it was an image I could not abide.

To make matters worse, I awoke one morning to find a new pond had formed in the corral. *Oh no! Where is all this water coming from?* My shoulders drooped when I saw the glossy puddles and thick, shiny muck as the sun broke through the clouds to soften up the ground even more. The source was the frost free water hydrant by the tack room. The handle was partially up, allowing a continuous flow of water to stream to the ground. By the looks of it, Belle must have rubbed against the handle and raised it enough to flood the corral during the night.

As we surveyed the mess, we knew we had to come up with a way to prevent this from happening again, so we wired the handle to the base and were pleased with our ingenuity until we discovered the hydrant had a built-in lock on the handle that we could have used. Another lesson learned that should have been mentioned in the brochure?

I now was reading everything I could about horses. I knew a clean barn area was essential if I didn't want Belle to get a foot infection from constantly stepping in her own excrement. Once the girls understood these facts, they decided it was worth pulling the little green wagon full of each day's duty behind them. To make it more fun, I bought them their own pretty red manure forks. Both took it in stride and knuckled down to the daily routine of scat removal, even to the point of inventing several amusing games regarding the whole process. And they would have a respite each winter, at least until the first thaw revealed the discharges left behind. But once spring came and the ground softened, that minefield of scat was not my only renewed concern. Again we saw the telltale signs of various predators, fresh from their long winter fasting.

We had been spared any further encounters since the young mountain lion by the playhouse episode, but my senses now were on alert. I hadn't long to wait. Bill and I were sitting in our bedroom talking, I on the bed and he in the blue recliner beside the rear window. As I inquired about our next town-day, he suddenly sat up with an incredulous expression on his face, his focus entirely on something in the backyard.

"Look, a cougar!" he shouted.

I jumped from the bed and ran to the window. It was early evening, and a mountain lion had causally strolled up to the side of his shop, and perched himself on the ledge of the retaining wall, near our woodpile.

"He's huge!" I whispered in shock. I'd never seen one so big, and we judged him at almost two hundred pounds. Both his head and body were imposing, yet he sat casually, looking in our general direction, only twenty-five yards away. As I called to the girls from their rooms to come see him, I remembered Belle was still out front on her picket.

"If he spots Belle, she'll be trapped."

Bill was already rummaging through the closet for his rifle. He emerged with it, pulling a shirt off the barrel, and ran down the stairs, calling back to me, "You watch the cat. I'm going out the front door; I'll try not to spook him."

Bill was halfway down the stairs when the cat turned and started walking up the hill into the tree line. He paused for a moment and turned to reveal his full profile, which only confirmed my estimation of his size. Strangely, he showed no interest in the horse only fifty yards away, trapped by her picket line. Perhaps he had not picked up her scent. Bill and Kobi rounded the side of the house just in time to catch a fleeting glance of the feline as it disappeared into the brush. The cat was gone and Belle showed no signs of distress. Apparently she had not sensed his presence either. The only ones adversely affected by the experience were us mortals.

It was still on my mind when I went to bed that night. Bill fell asleep right away as usual, while I lay awake thinking about it until finally drifting off into a fitful sleep. At two-thirty in the morning I was awakened by a loud cry. Still half asleep, my mind searched to make sense of that high-pitched scream. My eyes flew open wide when my thoughts turned to Belle.

"Bill! Wake up now!" I shrieked in alarm. "I think Belle's calling for help."

Bill stumbled out of bed and fumbled once more for his rifle, while I groped in the dark for the small remote control that activated our barn lights. The lights did not illuminate the entire corral, so I followed Bill out onto our small balcony with my flashlight, clutching my flannel nightgown. He had taken the precaution of mounting a powerful light on his rifle and was scanning the barnyard with it. We both searched desperately for Belle in the beam of our lights, but at first we could not locate her. Then Bill moved his light to the far corner of the round pen, and there she stood, calm as ever.

"She's alright," Bill commented with a mix of confusion and relief. "What were you dreaming about this time?"

Before I could fume and reply, the air was pierced by a loud scream, this time followed by an eruption of eerie howling.

"Coyotes," we said in unison.

"I thought it was the cougar attacking Belle," I replied sheepishly. I brushed a long strand of black hair from my face and shivered as I realized the cold breeze outside had easily penetrated my nightgown.

"Let's go in," Bill said tiredly. "Belle is safe. If they get any closer, I'll fire a warning shot to scare them away."

"It must have been on my mind when I went to sleep," I said. "I heard the scream and thought it was the horse. I'm glad she's unharmed."

"It does bring up the issue of security for her," Bill yawned as we climbed back into bed. "We probably need more security lights down at the barn. Or maybe I should pick up a night scope. I need to see better in those blind spots where we don't have lights. I'll check on it tomorrow."

Before I could reply, he was snoring again. The next day we called our electrician to install more flood lights. And Bill did order a Russian night vision scope, though we later found out it only worked satisfactorily when there were outside lights illuminating the area as well!

I told Gail we were slowly developing a plan for dealing with "night critters." She understood all too well, as it was common for ranchers to lose livestock to predators at night. Several ranchers in our area had lost their pet dogs and some of their livestock to wolves, cougars, or bears. She marveled at the measures we were taking, but I now planned to be ready for the next predator that came our way. "They need to know not to mess with a military family," I said, only half joking.

Ranching families weren't the only ones who had reason to fear for their pets. Even those who lived in towns or along the highway had cause to be concerned. One spring day while we were out delivering Girl Scout cookies only a few miles from our house, we stopped to drop off some boxes to an acquaintance of ours who lived along the highway. As I sat down at their kitchen table, the largest, fattest, gray-and-white tabby cat I had ever seen in my life strolled into the room. He flopped down on the floor, and lay on his side for a nap. Admiring his paunch, I secretly thought he looked as though he had eaten two large footballs. His sides bulged from a ribcage that must have strained with effort to avoid snapping. He looked lazily at us without lifting his head; only his eyes made any effort to move.

Our hostess, Amy, remarked, "Have you ever seen a cat that big?"

I grinned, "No, I don't think I have."

The girls were rather fascinated with the cat until they were distracted by a yellow parakeet sitting in his white wire cage on a side table near the kitchen. Amy took the bird from the cage for the girls to see. It walked on the owner's hand, and within a few moments flew up to one of the kitchen cabinets where it began chirping. It sat for a moment and then flew across the room over the cat's body to perch on the cage.

Everyone else was watching the bird, but I was watching the cat. He was looking at the bird with one eye, following its movements. *He's too fat to even try for that bird.* Oh, but he wanted it. I just believe he thought it was too much effort.

"Funny story about that cat," Amy said, chuckling. "One night after I had let him out, I heard a loud cry. I ran out front and found him lying on the ground with his side ripped open. By the looks of it, I figured he'd been attacked by a mountain lion. I rushed him to the emergency care vet, absolutely fearing the worst. The vet took him into surgery and repaired his side. Other than a scar from the wound, you wouldn't know anything had happened to him. The vet said there was no internal damage because he was SO INCREDIBLY FAT!"

The mountain lion didn't have time to get through all that fat before Amy inadvertently scared it away. I had read about fat layered mammals, such as seals, surviving what appeared to be horrendous shark bites for the same reason. Looking at him stretched out on the floor, I knew this assessment was correct. So here in the Northwest, fat can be a good thing if you're ever attacked by a wild animal. Welcome to Montana.

24

I Am NOT the Grass

AFTER THE FIRST YEAR OF HORSE OWNERSHIP, we learned the importance of pasture maintenance from Gail.

"If you don't want a bunch of unwanted weeds like thistle, you better do some meadow dragging."

"What's that?" I quizzed.

"Oh, you get something big and heavy to pull behind a tractor to break up the cow patties and horse dung. The drag will spread the stuff around like fertilizer—great for the grass. If you don't do it, then the dung clods may kill the grass underneath 'em. Then you'll likely get thistles and other weeds in those spots."

"We don't have a tractor. We've got a four-wheeler."

"That'll do. You can make a drag out of a piece of heavy steel, like a railway tie or wire box springs from a bed."

"We don't have anything like that."

"Well, you could always buy one I suppose." The idea of spending money on something you could make yourself, or do without, did not appeal to most ranchers, and Gail was no exception.

At the local ranch supply store we bought a metal field drag. It was 3' x 4' mat made of overlapping, interlocking steel hooks. We attached it to the back of the four-wheeler, and Bill started driving it across the meadow, spreading out the horse manure into small pieces that quickly dried in the sun and sank into the earth, adding nutrients back into the soil. He only got about twenty feet before the drag began bouncing off the ground and fell on top of itself, tangling into a big knot of metal links. It was an extremely discouraging start. After some time, we worked out the tangled knots and started again, only slower. The drag twisted again.

Next, we tried fashioning a metal frame and wired it to the outside of drag. This time the whole assembly flipped over. We then tried harrowing the field this way, with the forks upside down so they would not catch in the ground. We tried adding some weight on top to keep the harrow from bouncing, but the large rocks and concrete blocks just flipped off. We reinforced the frame to keep it from flexing, and finally met with some marginal success.

In time, I received all kinds of advice on meadow dragging. Some people did use old wire bed box springs, while others piled wooden pallets on top of their drags and wired them down. If I had kept asking, I'm sure I would have found other suggestions as well. There was no end to the ingenuity of ranchers. With meadow dragging over, I sat back and surveyed my new, clean looking pasture. Not a "pie" in sight.

The wet spring weather, like the winter before, had really cut into our riding time. Without an indoor arena, Belle had several months off, which made it difficult to get back into riding for both horse and rider.

"You need a tune-up," Gail cautioned me once the weather had warmed up enough.

"I need what?" I said, knowing my car was in perfect working order.

"Your horse," she explained. "You just can't saddle up again and ride after Belle has had so much time off. She needs to get used to the idea that it's time to get back to work. Start handling her and doing some ground work such as practicing putting on the saddle."

"Oh, that kind of tune-up. Now I follow you." It seemed like good advice, so I started with the girls brushing her and cleaning her tack, but she was fussy and began swishing her tail in annoyance. It was going to take some time to get her motivated to return to her job. Bill and I were discussing her peculiar behavior when I inquired, "Do you think she's lonely?"

"Probably, I think she needs a companion other than the dog. I always figured we'd get another horse sooner or later."

I wondered if it would help Belle's unpleasant attitude to have a stablemate. It had been a long winter for her and I did not want to put her through it again, alone. Horses are herd animals and very social with their own kind. I didn't want to deprive her of companionship, and I had noticed Sonja was becoming interested in riding as well. Although Belle was very good with Sonja, she was no beginner's horse. I also considered the idea of two girls at different levels of riding sharing one horse as being very impractical. So we began talking about the idea of finding a horse for Sonja and expanding our herd.

Meanwhile, Belle remained as grumpy as ever, but we continued working through it. She honored my requests, but she was not respectful to Sandy. When she tried to saddle her, Belle would nip at her, and Sandy was forced to give her a smack on the nose. But Belle did not give up easily. None of us could understand her negative change of attitude towards my daughter. But she was not the only one. While Sandy was tying the latigo, Belle tried to bite my hand. I scolded her with a loud "No!" and smacked her hard on the nose. She never tried that again, but I knew we couldn't let our guard down for a moment.

About the only time she didn't give us much trouble was when we led her out to graze. Yet, as spring progressed, I began noticing our pastures this year were producing more thistles than grass, especially anywhere we had dug up the ground to lay water lines and power to the stable. After some research, we decided to buy grass seed and plant it in our bare areas so the weeds would not take over the pasture. I was becoming protective over my grass like any good rancher, for grass equaled food for livestock, or in our case, oversized pets. I was beginning to understand how Gail felt when it came to making hay.

I had no idea there were so many types of grass seed. I must have had the "deer in the headlights" look when the man behind the counter at the feed and grain store asked me what kind of grass seed I wanted.

"I don't know. What kind of grass would be good for horses to eat?"

The clerk glanced at me as if I was from Mars, or maybe Washington, D.C. He was clearly sizing me up, and finally with a sigh, he peered over his reading glasses and asked, "Do you want clover in it?"

I felt a slight panic; I didn't know how to respond. Clover had not shown up in my research, and I wondered, *Can horses eat clover?* I couldn't decide, so instead I stood there mutely while he stared at me, but whether it was from boredom or irritation I could not tell. Then his imposing rotund frame began displaying additional signs of impatience as I pondered the gravity of my decision. In desperation I replied, "What do you recommend?"

His expression quickly changed to a frown. *Yep, it was irritation, not boredom.*

I quickly added, "I need to seed bare areas of my pasture because the weeds are beginning to spread. I was hoping you could make a recommendation."

"I can't help you," he interrupted, "we don't carry any pasture seed you'd want. Better try somewhere else."

As I thanked him, he turned to attend to some other chore, not wishing to engage me any further. Stung by his behavior, I was reluctant to enter the next feed store, as it had all the hallmarks of the first one. I walked in, a little bruised from my first experience, and wondered what kind of reception I was going to receive this time. Although this man looked like a younger, trimmer version of the other attendant, his attitude was totally different. He listened to my request and confidently proclaimed, "You want dry land pasture seed. You just spread it on the ground after a rain or snow while the ground is damp. You don't have to till it in. How much area do you plan to cover?"

We discussed the details, and he soon walked out with a large bag of seed, enough to cover about two acres. By the time we got home I was feeling much better. We hadn't long to wait for the right conditions, and soon the ground was muddy from a light rain. We divided the seed between the four of us and began tossing it out on the bare ground. Remembering the joke about Montana's weather changing every five minutes, I was blissfully sowing my seeds like a good frontier woman, when, within a few short minutes, the clouds formed into a dark mass and the wind began to howl. We worked faster as Bill urged us on.

Soon a light snow flurry began, accompanied by huge gusts of wind that made me wish I had rocks in my pocket to hold me down. Next came the hail. It stung my face and beat my wide brimmed leather hat. My poor hat, I was so proud of it. I'd gotten it in Wyoming on our first trip out here, and it was my symbol of Western independence. It wasn't a typical cowboy style, instead having a flat Spanish crown, which was so popular among Australian drovers. Now it was in danger of ruin, and it was this one thought which occupied my mind. Of course, I was far from the house on the other side of the pasture.

I quickened my pace, and soon tried running up the hill toward the house. There was a reason I had not done this before. I still ran out of breath quickly at higher altitudes. Slowing to a walk, I climbed up, holding my now empty sack. Bill stayed at the barn until the weather blew over, and used the time to clean up the hay stall. When I reached the door, with my face half frozen, all I wanted was a cup of hot tea. The girls had bounded up ahead of me, none the worse for wear. What a poor example of a Western woman I was becoming; I couldn't even handle a little hail and a short sprint. Now, where did I put my tea…?

Even without seeding, the spring weather always brought much new lush grass. It was all Belle could think about.

"Don't let her stuff herself silly on fresh green grass," Gail warned me. "She'll get a bad attitude and possibly founder."

"What's that?"

"It's an illness caused by the high amount of water in rich green grass. If she eats too much of it, it'll disrupt her digestive system and cause swelling. And that can lead to colic. That's why you always introduce her to new grass slowly. She's been eating dry hay all winter, and lots of new grass isn't good for her. So let her have a few hours a day at first. Then gradually increase her feed time, and you shouldn't have a problem."

So until the right time came, Belle would stand with her head over the fence and stare at all the yummy "green horsey chocolate" blowing in the wind. I felt sorry for her, but explaining to her that I was simply protecting her, held no merit with Belle. She looked at me as being the cause of all her unrequited grass desire.

I had noticed that, once she finally got to eat some fresh grass, she became quite frisky, with more energy and emotional responses. I commented about this to Gail one morning, "I swear Belle acts like she's had too much coffee. She's often fidgety and wants her own way, and she's been having lots of opinions lately."

"It's that green grass, I tell you," Gail replied, "It's practically caffeine to a horse."

All I could do was wait patiently. Once summer weather came to pass, the grass would dry out and I would worry less about the effects of the spring green grass on Belle. In the meantime, we rode and handled Belle whenever the weather allowed. For the most part, when I was around, Belle was respectful and seemed to enjoy my company, greeting me when I came into the corral and standing next to me, gently resting her face below my shoulder for a few moments. I felt like we were building a relationship. I did enjoy her very much, and she was more connected to me than anyone else in the family. I loved to groom her, partly because she'd stand so very still and doze with her head down. It was our time together, and I felt great satisfaction seeing her clean and shiny in the sun.

Another great quality she had was that she would remain still for insect spraying, completely trusting me during the process. I think she understood the repellent would give her relief from the stinging fly bites. After I sprayed some fluid into my gloved hand, she allowed me to rub her ears and face with it. I always spoke softly to her during these times, and she responded calmly to the sound of my voice.

25

Finding Linda

S ONJA WAS BECOMING MORE AND MORE INTERESTED in riding, showing enough promise with her skills that I even let her ride Belle in the round pen with me walking beside her. I knew how badly she wanted a horse of her own, and I considered riding as an activity the girls could do together, something that would be fun for them both. I also wanted Sonja to have the same opportunities her older sister had, so I could not deny her sweet little heart. She had worked hard taking care of Belle and keeping the stable clean, thus proving she was mature enough to handle the responsibility. Bill and I also knew Belle needed a buddy. It wasn't good to have one horse spend so much time alone. We weren't in a hurry, but we started looking into the idea of another horse for the sake of both Sonja and Belle.

Once again I found myself scanning through the local Internet advertisements, searching the now familiar terms for just the right equine. Of course, I convinced myself I was much savvier this time. But I knew that without the aid of a good advisor, I might be fooled into purchasing a less than suitable animal. Horses for beginners are hard to find, and my first few calls left me with the same discouraging feelings I had experienced the last time around. Many of the horses I inquired about were not meant for children at all, despite the glowing ads. Then one evening I saw an online advertisement for an older stud. The ad read: "Horse has a docile personality and people friendly skills." I thought this one was worth further inquiry, so I emailed the owner to ask if this horse would be a good candidate for a child just learning to ride. I had my doubts because I'd repeatedly heard most stallions were a handful, but I was becoming desperate.

When the phone later rang, I was momentarily surprised when I heard a familiar voice, "Hello Nancy, this is Linda. How's Shammie doing?"

It took me a moment to comprehend it was the woman who had sold us Belle, formerly known as Shazam, or Shammie, as Linda called her.

"Oh Linda, what a surprise, Belle is doing fine. What about you?"

She laughed and replied with her brassy New York accent, "Doing great. I see you went ahead and renamed Shammie. Don't you know it's bad luck to change a horse's name?"

"Well Shazam Winter Magic is a mouthful, and Belle just seems to suit her better."

"Okay, but don't say I didn't warn you. So how are Belle and your daughter getting along?"

"Well, at first they were going great, but since then it's been a bit of a struggle."

"That's typical; most horses are going to challenge you to establish their dominance if they can. She just needs regular groundwork so she knows her place in the pecking order."

This was the first time anyone had discussed the importance of continuous groundwork with me.

Linda continued adamantly, "Nancy, horses have their own language and unless you understand how to communicate better with them, you'll have problems with Belle or any other horse."

"I didn't realize they needed continuous training. Do you offer anything like that?"

"Oh sure, I train both horses and owners, but here's how I do it. I start the whole family with instruction on the ground—not riding in the saddle. In your case I suggest booking five lessons at first to see how much progress we all make with Belle."

"I don't have a trailer."

"That's alright. I can plan on coming to your place once a week and giving you basic skills to practice until the next lesson. Everyone in the family should participate so they can earn Belle's respect. It's good for your own safety if everyone can speak horse."

"That makes sense to me, but let me discuss it with Bill and get back with you."

"No problem. Hey, I almost forgot why I called. It's about your email on my stud."

"Your stud?" I replied, not knowing what she meant.

"He's not for sale; I'm offering him out for stud services only."

My face blushed with embarrassment, so much for my horse savvy. Then I laughed out loud, "I'm sorry Linda. I misunderstood the ad."

"You know," she said, pausing, "if it had been anyone else asking me that, I would have thought it was a dumb question, but knowing it was you and you're still new to horses, it made sense. Usually an ad will say if a horse is a gelding. If not, figure it's likely a stallion. So, I take it you're looking for another horse."

"Yes, for my younger daughter, Sonja."

"Well, you're gonna want someone with a gentle disposition. Let me do some checking around and see what I can find out."

We discussed the idea in greater detail, and when I got off the phone I felt a wave of relief. Linda completely understood what we needed, and I greatly trusted her judgment of horses. I'd also learned something useful. If an advertisement did not state "gelding," I would skip it altogether. No more inquires from me about intact males.

Linda soon wrote to me about several leads, and asked for more information about Belle, and how well we were all getting along. I did not go into great detail, but made some general comments about Belle's attitude. From this she gathered we were starting to have serious problems with her, so she offered to come out to our place for a lesson, and to see if she could help improve Sandy's confidence, as well as my knowledge.

I called Gail for her input, "I didn't know there was so much involved with owning a horse."

"I'm just glad you found someone to help you out," Gail replied. "You'll learn a lot from Linda, and in time it'll become second nature to you."

"I don't know. Right now I feel like a fish out of water. I'm very excited about our ground lessons starting, but I feel a little intimidated too. It's becoming less Sandy's pony and more 'our' horse, maybe even mine."

"Well, whoever cares for a horse should know how to handle one."

"Gail, when you met me, did you ever think I would ever talk about my stable, or discuss my livestock?"

"No, probably not at first, but I knew you had it in you," she replied. There was a pause as she collected her thoughts, then continued, "You know, I'm proud of you."

"Why?"

"Because you moved out here not knowing anything about Montana rural life; but you stuck it out and learned everything you could about becoming independent. Most people hire anyone they can find to do the work for them, or they just complain about it. If it gets too hard, they quit and move. You guys are here to stay. That takes real guts. Pretty soon you'll have a stable full of horses, and maybe some cows too."

"No cows, Gail," I sternly injected.

Later I thought about what she had said. We had accomplished a great deal in the past three years, even though we had made plenty of mistakes along the way. At least we learned from them, and no doubt had more lessons to learn, but that was in the future. The here-and-now was enough to contend with.

It was a cold spring morning when Linda arrived at our front door. We talked for awhile about the goals we wanted to accomplish today. I admitted I was leery of our own horse, and that we lacked the kind of relationship we wanted with Belle. Mostly, we were frustrated with her bossy, disrespectful ways, and I did not want to engage in a constant power struggle with her.

Linda told me, "I know Belle, and that mare will always challenge you at times because she wants to be the leader. That's just her dominant personality. If I'd known you had so little experience with horses, I wouldn't have recommended Belle. I believe she isn't for first-time horse owners."

I couldn't fault Linda; we had shown up with our own trainer when we first considered buying Belle. However, we had not learned all we needed to know about managing and adjusting horse behavior. But Linda believed, with proper handling, Belle would comply and not be so troublesome anymore. She also believed it was fate that brought us together again. Once more she remarked, "Why did you change her name? It's bad luck you know!"

I knew she was only joking, but I replied, "I think it suits her better."

"Nancy, it may suit her looks, but not her personality."

We bundled up in coats and hats and began the familiar walk down to the corral, the melting snow crunching under our feet. With the sun coming out, it had the promise of becoming a nice day, but the wind gusts were a reminder that the last biting cold of winter was still clinging on.

"Remember to put on your helmets," I cautioned the girls as we got closer to the barn area. I saw Sandy's face frown. I had decided when we bought the horse that we had to use ASTM Troxel helmets, especially made for horseback riding, and twice as tough as bicycle helmets. Even though I did not ride, I used a helmet when working with Belle, just to be safe. I had purchased a lovely pink one, and the girls chose the same style. Sonja was very excited about it, but Sandy loathed the idea of wearing one, and announced that when she was eighteen she'd ride without one because she considered Troxel helmets to be "the most uncomfortable helmet in the world."

She had made up her mind that since not all girls wore them, she shouldn't have to wear one. I would not negotiate on this point. We still had much to learn about horses, and accidents happen so fast you rarely realized it until after it was over. My two mottos were "No helmet, no ride" and "My barn, my rules."

We walked through the corral gate, and Linda spoke as I haltered Belle. "I want to see you walk her on the lead rope," she said. "Take her over there." She pointed to the meadow in front of us, still covered in snow. I began walking with Belle, but I was feeling really awkward and self-conscious of my technique.

Linda bellowed, "You're acting like you hope that horse won't give you any trouble, as if you were saying, 'Please walk with me.' Be one hundred percent confident every time you take the lead rope."

She was right, but I didn't know any alternative technique.

"Look at where you are going, not at Belle. Have a commanding presence. She reads your body language. You *must* be the leader."

I responded quizzically, "How can I be totally confident all the time when I'm still learning?"

For a moment Linda contemplated my question. It was an honest one on my part. "Well," she paused, "I guess you can't be confident all the time; it'll take a while, but you must try to present confidence even if you don't always feel it inside."

I walked Belle again with a little more determination, trying to stand a little straighter, despite my recurring back pain.

"Better," Linda chirped. "Bill, you're next."

Bill walked Belle without issue and seemed to be a bit more at ease than the rest of us. I privately wondered why Belle often challenged me more than anyone else in the family. Then the girls each took turns as Linda watched.

"If she gets too close to you or rushes in front of you, back her up with a few tugs on the lead rope," Linda instructed Sonja. She then took the lead rope from her and began demonstrating the proper technique by tugging down, then gently bumping Belle under the chin with it. Belle, somewhat surprised, showed her respect by taking two steps backward and standing quietly. I could not believe it. It seemed so simple. Why hadn't anyone told me about this? I had been struggling for months without a proper tool, and this was like waving a magic wand.

"If she doesn't do what you ask, back her up; it will get her thinking again," Linda said earnestly. "When she's thinking about a task you've given her, she isn't thinking about what she wants to do. This puts you in control and is a way of earning her respect.

"Now let's get to work on this crowding issue you're having. For your own safety, and to teach the horse you are the leader, you must keep her about three feet away from you, unless you invite her in closer. Imagine you have a thirty-six-inch-wide bubble around you at all times. Belle must remain outside that area of your personal space. If she crowds you, she is showing disrespect and competing with you for the leadership role. If she comes into your space without you asking her to do so, back her up. Always make the wrong choice uncomfortable, and the right choice comfortable. That's the best way to train a horse."

We practiced walking Belle around the corral. Every time she tried to get too close to me, I immediately backed her up. One time she refused, and Linda told me to put a little more force in my request. I could see the look in Belle's eye; it was telling me she was tired of me telling her what to do. I pulled down a little harder and faster on the rope and bumped her under the chin. She stepped back and waited.

I was amazed at how well this simple act worked. What a feeling of power it gave me—and a degree of confidence. It would make my life with Belle so much easier. Soon she began to understand where I liked her to walk while I was leading her on the rope. Three feet away, just behind my right shoulder was where I was comfortable, and Belle complied.

After that first lesson, Linda and I began a horse and family training notebook. I wrote down the techniques she described, along with our assignments for the week. One note I entered in bold lettering was BELLE MAY NOT TAKE ONE STEP ON THE LEAD ROPE WITHOUT YOU ASKING HER TO MOVE HER FEET. I had not realized I was letting her break the rules when she moved around on the lead rope. I also had not understood I had an action I could take when she was not listening to my instructions. Backing her up, and making her work when she did not comply, was an important part of establishing me as the herd leader. The next lesson was a week away, so I had plenty of time to practice walking with Belle.

"For the first time I feel like I have some real tools I can use with Belle," I told Bill that evening after dinner. "Did you notice how well my asking her to back up worked?"

"Yeah, it really did the trick," he replied. "Just keep practicing and you'll continue to improve. You can do this, Nancy; I have every confidence in you. And the extra instruction will be good for the girls."

Bill was very supportive of our efforts to own a horse. I knew he was not particularly interested in working with them, but he understood how important it was to us girls. As time passed, it became more important to me as well. It was something I had—and wanted—to learn. I could hardly wait for our next lesson.

Linda had advised me to get a solid pair of good work boots, even if I was not planning to ride, to protect my feet when working with Belle. So we headed for the local ranch supply store, but I wasn't sure which type to buy. I asked the pretty young salesgirl what was best for working around horses. She brought me several styles to look at, and I saw a particular pair I wanted to try on first. They were rubber soled cowgirl boots with the lower vamps and outsoles made of brown suede, stitched in a scallop pattern, while the shafts were a contrasting beautiful pale pink with decorative stitching in a large swirl design.

"These Justin boots are meant to work in, plus they're waterproof, so it won't be a problem if you get mud on them," she informed me.

"They seem too pretty for that," I replied, admiring the salmon pink embroidery.

"They just make them that color for the women," she smiled.

I walked around in them for awhile and found they were a little stiff, but, overall, I really liked them. Unlike many women, I will only buy a shoe if it's really comfortable. After a few minutes of consideration, I bought them. I was pleased to find out they were ten dollars off, because I'm a sale rack shopper.

My daughters were excited. "You look like a cowgirl, Mom!" they said together.

I beamed as I looked in the mirror at home. I had not worn suits, nylons, or high heels since we moved to Montana. My wardrobe had changed greatly, but my sense of style had not. I loved the fact that my boots were fun, yet stylish. It would be my secret. As long as I did not tuck my jeans into them, no one would know they were girly. They were like a rite of passage.

When Linda arrived for our next lesson, I showed her my new footwear straight away.

"Wow! You got boots!" she exclaimed. "I love the pink!"

I smiled, and half laughing, I said, "Well, that proves you're not from around here. You really *are* from New York." Even Gail didn't wear pink cowgirl boots, and I wondered what she'd think of them. I slipped them on and we made our way down to the corral.

The learning continued. "You can't train a horse like that, she's not a canine." I heard Linda's mild frustration as she saw me scold Belle when she got in my space. I had worked with many dogs, and trained them very well. I had even helped other people correct the troublesome behavior of their pets. I supposed I spoke their language, since I always communicated with them easily and understood what they were telling me. Putting a little pressure on, knowing how much to apply, and when to release it, was a basic technique of dog training. I was finding out horses were trained in the opposite way. It was the release of pressure that taught them, not the application of it. I was finding out that predators and prey animals learned differently.

During the five weeks that we had our ground lessons, Linda taught us many exercises. One of them, the shoulder turn, involved getting the horse to turn her shoulder and head while crossing one front foot over the other one.

"Remember," Linda began, "the herd leader makes the other horses move their feet."

Belle was not fond of this one, and took an almost passive-aggressive stance. So I began by placing one hand on her shoulder and the other on her face, with my fingers spread out below and down to her cheek. I began to walk into her space, hoping she would turn and take a step sideways. But Belle had braced herself.

"She's not moving," I told Linda, as I strained in frustration.

"Keep walking; think about moving a heavy piece of furniture," she called back.

I was throwing all my 107 pounds on Belle and she completely ignored me. *Maybe Linda's right, I shouldn't have changed her name. The bad luck's working!*

"Keep walking; you *cannot* give up. That tells her she's the boss," Linda said encouragingly.

Belle's eye was looking at me incredulously, as if to say, "What are you doing to me?"

I kept thinking *I'm the leader around here. Just do as I tell you.* But her hooves were planted firmly in the dirt. She had no intention of letting me move her feet. I could feel her silently saying, *"No, I won't do it."* I focused all my energy into this one task. I thought about a bright light inside me, moving from me to her like a physical force. In a moment I could feel Belle begin to relent. Her muscles softened as she gave in and took a step, crossing her right leg over her left.

"Stop!" Linda snapped. "One step is enough at first. Your goal, in time, is to move her in a circle, pivoting her on her back feet. You did it. I want everyone to practice this, try it for only one step at first and then try for a few more."

I knew the purpose of these exercises was to help us become more comfortable handling Belle by first learning to recognize specific horse behavior, and then responding in their language. Since Belle treated us as she would any other horse, we had to behave in a way she understood. It was all about knowing the right moves to make, much like learning to dance when the music was going too fast. There was always the danger of someone stepping on your toes.

I was now learning how to move Belle's hind end away from me. Using a training whip, I could gently shake it and she would move her back feet away from it a few steps. The whip became an extension of my arm, not for striking the horse, but for guiding it.

In time, I was able to move her away with my hands, just by shaking them and looking directly at the part of her body I wished to move. The more I worked daily with her, the more I understood this practice. It was another way to become familiar with her and have her accept me and my family as the new leaders.

"Let's ride today," Linda announced at our next lesson. She began looking over our tack, and then reached for a bridle, saying, "You need to get slobber straps."

I stared at her, one eyebrow raised, and smiled, "You know, that sounds disgusting. Exactly what is that?"

"It's a leather strap that attaches to the ring on the bridle and connects to the reins. It helps open the bit to cue the horse to turn, and it protects the mouth a little if you pull too hard."

"So it really doesn't have anything to do with drool?" I asked with a twinkle in my eye.

"Not really," was Linda's deadpan reply.

We saddled Belle, and Sandy's lesson began. Overall, the lesson went pretty well. Clearly there still were some respect issues to deal with, and at times Linda had to get on Belle to give Sandy a demonstration. Belle did not want to follow her instructions at all times, only when she felt like it. Since Sandy was the primary rider, Belle began to know just how much or how little she could get away with for the day.

"You should learn how to ride Belle," Linda suggested to me after Sandy's lesson had ended.

I looked at her, somewhat surprised. "Me, *ride*? I don't know..."

"You should think about it. It would help teach Belle to respect you more. I think you could handle her, Nancy."

"I'll think it over. I'm concerned it might hurt my back. Besides, Sandy's the rider, not me." With two ruptured disks in my back, I had lived with chronic back pain for many years. And recently I had been unable to walk for several weeks. My biggest fear was what might happen if I fell.

"Belle is a Walker," Linda continued. "They have a smooth gait and are recommended for people with back problems."

I smiled and promised to think it over, but my mind was screaming *No thank you!*

So we settled into our training routine that summer. Sandy rode nearly every day, and we had lessons with Linda once a week. I was feeling much more confident about owning a horse, and Sandy was gaining valuable handling experience with Belle. And best of all, the horse became more willing and agreeable as Sandy's riding skills improved.

26

Yard Wars

W E HAD EXPERIENCED MANY NEW CONCEPTS since leaving city life behind and moving out west. Conversations now focused on matters that I never thought would cross my lips—horses, cows, horseshoes, supplements, small farm animals, and wild animals. Weather also was a big topic, as well as how to protect yourself and your homestead from it. We learned about growing fruits and vegetables and, of course, we experimented with various means of dealing with the dreaded varmints, especially the chipmunks and squirrels who regularly threatened them.

The wildlife that lived on my place loved me. Each time they saw a new plant in the yard or in a pot, they assumed the buffet line was open. Deer, chipmunks, squirrels, and rabbits relished every flower I set out. It was so frustrating. They should have been satisfied with the bird seed they raided out of the feeder everyday, but no, they were glutinous to a fault.

One particular chipmunk, a rather industrious fellow, climbed inside the long plastic tube of the bird feeder, and ate so much seed, he became too fat to climb out again. I discovered his plight when I went to refill the feeder and saw one eye smashed against the plastic cylinder, blinking at me. I was so startled I nearly dropped the feeder on the ground. I shook it vigorously upside down, trying to get him out, but he barely budged. Kobi stood by, anxiously licking his chops in anticipation. I removed the top from the feeder and gave it one last huge fling. A furry torpedo flew past the dog and plopped to the ground, rolling. As soon as he stopped rolling, he righted himself and scurried to the shelter of a nearby tree. He was too fat to run very fast, and though Kobi pursued him, he managed to dodge safely about, and made good his escape. I thought that was the end it of until a few days later I found him again stuck in the feeder. Apparently he had to lose some weight before he was thin enough to climb back into the tube. Some chipmunks never learn.

I later set out silk flowers in a couple of my planters just to have some color around the patio. The chipmunks threw outrageous tantrums when they tasted them, and in anger, shredded every silk flower, spreading the remains all over the patio as a warning to the others. I had no idea they were such emotional little creatures. It was clearly a declaration a war, but being of a peaceable nature myself, I declined to retaliate.

With summer rolling in, I decided to try again with my flower garden. Sonja and I worked hard, planting over eighty giant sunflowers. We painstakingly placed each one according to the directions, about an inch deep in neatly tilled soil. We knew for sure at least some of them would grow, and we were hopeful we'd see a field of them by midsummer. All went well the first two days, until we came face-to-face with a new threat that we soon dubbed the "demented squirrel."

I had seen a striped squirrel running around the yard that I first thought was a chipmunk on steroids. He looked like a chipmunk, but was much larger, and had a black stripe running from his eye across the side of his face. He would hang around the bird feeder and eat the seeds that dropped to the ground. At the time I was unconcerned about him, until I saw what his twisted personality was truly capable of. Sonja came through the patio doors with a mixture of anger and dismay on her face.

"Mom, come look outside at our sunflower garden. All the seeds are dug up! They're gone."

I ran across the patio to find rows of little dirt mounds and the shells of sunflower seeds littering the garden. Sonja was right; our seeds had been taken and enjoyed by some pesky little creature. It was so disappointing

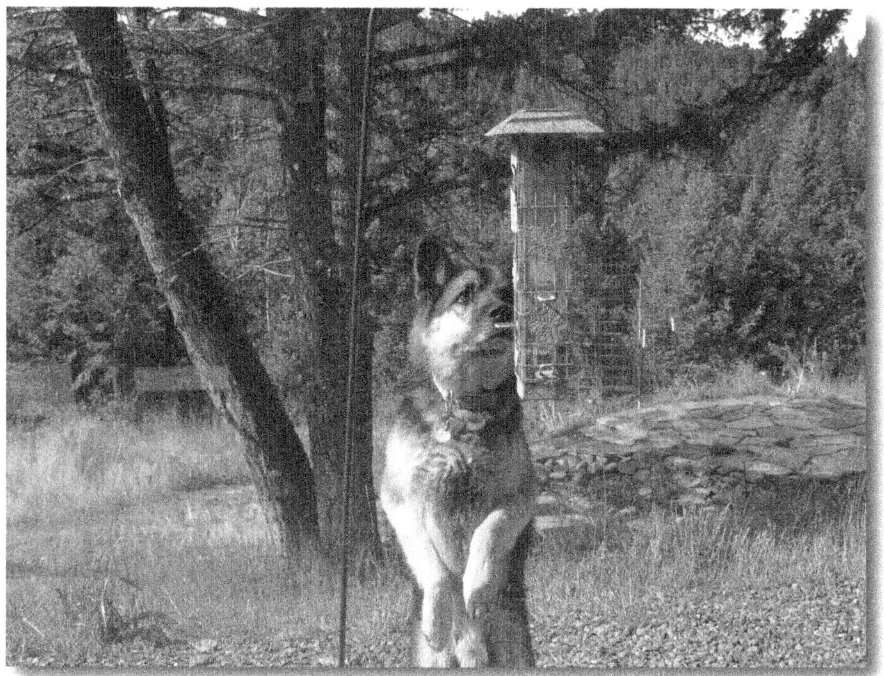

"I see a fat chipmunk!"

that we both just stood there looking at the garden, feeling like victims of a miniature bombing raid. Eventually we returned to the house and sat down at the dining room table, staring out the glass patio doors, depressed by the sight of what would have been our sunflower garden. Just then the striped squirrel ran right up the patio doors and peered inside. In his hand he was holding one of the sunflower seeds. He raised it to his mouth, cracked open the shell, splitting it in half, and then ate the seed while staring directly at us.

"That squirrel has my sunflower seed!" Sonja shouted. "I'm going to get him!"

In a flash, Sonja was out the door, chasing the squirrel across the patio. It ran into the tall grass and Sonja came back inside looking defeated. She

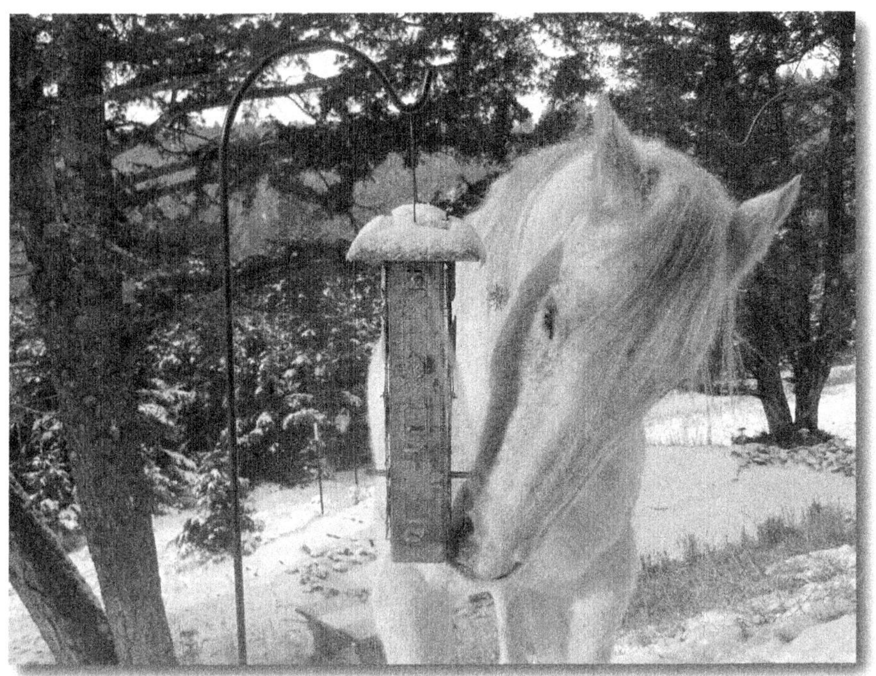

Wilson wonders, "Is there any food in here or just a fat chipmunk?"

plopped down next to me with a thump, her sense of defeat and frustration clearly evident in her dour expression.

"What would you do if you had caught it?" I asked.

"I would step on its tail," she announced very firmly, her little eyebrows knitted together and her arms crossed.

We talked it over and I tried to console her, admitting I was frustrated too. But no sooner had I spoken the words, when the squirrel was back again, waving another sunflower seed in our faces. Taunting us through the glass doors, he stood calmly eating it in front of us.

"He is demented," I announced. I could not believe he was taking such great pleasure in proving to us he could steal and eat our seeds at will.

"Kobi, get him!" Sonja shouted as she opened the door.

Kobi did not hesitate, and immediately raced outside, jumping across the patio furniture, and chasing the demented squirrel under some rocks. It squealed loud irritating chirps as it repeatedly peeked out to see if Kobi was still present. Kobi could not get to the squirrel, and the squirrel soon realized this fact to his advantage. He darted between the larger rocks, purposely teasing Kobi, and then poked out his head, laughing at him with his squeaky voice. Sonja and I watched in disbelief.

"I told you, demented, this squirrel is mentally ill with serious emotional problems. Maybe he didn't get enough attention at home," I said, exasperated. Sonja just nodded in agreement, her lips tightly pursed.

Over the next few days demented squirrel continued to torment us all. He teased the dog, and when there were no more sunflowers to dig up and eat, he decided to dine on my last pot of petunias. He did not even wait until I was inside. I was sitting in a chair at the patio table enjoying a sunny morning when I saw him dart across the grass and jump on the bubbling fountain. Less than ten feet from me, he climbed up the fountain edge and plucked a beautiful pink petunia bloom from a pot, defiantly stuffing it in his mouth while staring me right in the eye without blinking.

"That does it!" I shouted. "Get out!"

Remembering my days as an elementary school softball pitcher, I threw a small rock at him as hard as I could. It barely missed, but was enough for him to jump sideways and run back into the trees. I was fuming and let everyone know it. Bill, eventually tiring of my constant rants about demented squirrel, suggested he try to eliminate the little pest for us. *Why not bring out the heavy artillery? A career Air Force officer should be able to deal with this problem easily enough.*

As expected, Bill developed and implemented a tactical plan of action. He removed a screen from our bedroom window which overlooked the courtyard, slid back the glass, and propped a small .22 caliber rifle on the sill. Like some great shikari of India, he sat patiently, in silent anticipation of the tiger's return to the site of its last kill. It didn't take long for demented squirrel's next appearance, and when the fat fellow began scampering across the backyard, Bill opened fire. Unfortunately, our backyard was filled with crushed granite rock, and the bullets began ricocheting in different directions as the devil rodent darted between each shot.

"Be careful Bill, you're going to hit the shop or the playhouse," I warned him. After several valiant attempts, Bill quit firing.

"Blast it, he moves too fast," he replied.

Sonja just grunted, "Dad, you're still king of the misses."

Bill didn't reply, but he didn't have to. His expression said it all. However, the incident was not without some reward, for it proved to be the last time we ever saw demented squirrel. Either he ate everything he could and moved on, or else something ate him. Perhaps he feared being shot, or maybe the pair of golden eagles who nested near our house saw a "golden" opportunity. Whatever the reason, demented squirrel was gone, but not forgotten.

27

Spoils of War

DURING THE CHIPMUNK WARS, I KNEW FOR SURE I would be unable to
have a vegetable garden. Of course the rabbits and deer had joined
forces with the chipmunks, and they were all allies. I would see them out
on their daily reconnaissance patrols, looking for some tasty flower or
seed to attack.

To defend our food from their constant raids, Bill surprised me one year
with a birthday gift, a greenhouse from Costco. It was delivered in kit form,
and the surprise was on us when we tried to assemble it. It turned into the
most tedious two weeks of our lives, but we finally finished fitting every
last nut, bolt, gasket, green metal frame, and polycarbonate panel together,
and admired our handiwork. At last, we thought, a fortification to protect
our home grown edibles. I filled it with trays of lettuce, onion, broccoli,
mint, squash, zucchini, and red peppers. All the vegetables grew quickly,
and I was so pleased. It was like all my projects, well thought out,
organized, and clean. Bill even rigged up a watering system comprised of
a series of patio water misters connected to a garden hose.

All seemed right with our world until I came into my little greenhouse
one day to harvest some lettuce for lunch. What I saw almost made me cry.
The vegetables had torn leaves; some were bitten through, and on the
ground, others were chewed and spit out. Small containers were knocked

over, and many of the vegetables were devoured, or just gnawed through and left half eaten. I was sickened by the sight of all this food and hard work gone to waste. I stood in the leaf litter, and snarled *chipmunks* to myself. They had breached my security and gotten inside the perimeter.

Bill's sister, Kate, and her husband, Brad, were visiting us from Chicago at the time. I went inside to tell everyone what had happened, and we all piled outside to see the carnage. As Bill started to arrange the disheveled trays, something caught his eye. Like Goldilocks and the Three Bears, "something" was still sleeping in "our bed" of lettuce.

"There's something in here. It's the biggest mouse I've ever seen!" Bill exclaimed.

It was huge, white, ugly, furry, and had a long, skinny, pink tail. But that was not the worst part. The worst part was it had been in the green house while I was in there, sleeping only a few inches from me! Oh, how that thought gave me the willies. "Get it out!!" I cried.

The creature awoke and quickly ran behind two trays. Bill, just as quickly, slammed both trays into him, pinning his face against one of the polycarbonate panels. I could see it through the glaze, its eyes squeezed closed and its whiskers pressed against its face. It sent a shudder down my spine. Bill pushed the two trays together and trapped him, but he couldn't grab him with his bare hands. I gave him our long arm gripper claw that we used to pick up laundry when it fell between the washer and dryer. Bill grabbed his body tightly with the claw, grasped the long hideous tail with his free hand, and pulled him out.

He proudly produced him outside to the awaiting throng of onlookers. "It has to be a rat, look how big he is!" I said, grimacing, as I watched it squirm and twist in Bill's grasp.

"Well, we'll give him a fighting chance," Bill said, and then he tossed the rodent into the grass. Kobi, ever alert, took two giant leaps, and chased it into the tree line. I think he got it, but I did not want to look.

How the rat had gotten in was a bit of a mystery, but we concluded he must have climbed up the garden hose and entered through the vent in the roof. We promptly buried the waterline under the greenhouse wall, and our rat problem went away. With Kate's help, we managed to take out all the potting trays, then washed and salvaged what we could of the vegetables. We also used bleach to disinfect the inside of the greenhouse and remove the droppings it left behind. Most of the vegetables that were shredded and ruined, I left outside for the chipmunks and their allies—their spoils of war.

Go West, Young Woman!

28

Uptown Cowgirl

I ADMIT BEING A BIT OF A CITY GIRL. I ENJOY live theater, museums, and good dining. I always try to look my best in public, so I take the time necessary to apply my makeup and pick the right outfit to wear for our weekly "town day." In my spare time I search the clothing websites for sales and closeout bargains, especially Kohl's and Coldwater Creek, the latter sadly closed (a fact I still lament). I was even a dedicated QVC shopper until we moved here and lost all television reception. I really missed my daily get-together with the QVC personalities. During those long periods back east when Bill was away and I was left alone with my young girls, they became my surrogate companions. But once we came to Montana, I discovered other things that interested most local women, often out of necessity. I never thought I'd find myself looking at farm catalogs with tractors, trailers, riding gear, mud boots, and heavy work wear. It still amuses me whenever I see a woman who could pass for an East Coast catwalk model, thumbing through ranch and horse magazines at the local farm supply store. If my friends could see me now in the rural west living like this, they would not believe it.

You can't take all of the city out of a girl, and there are some metropolitan features about me that have not changed. I've found myself blending the two lifestyles to create my own metro-western look (not to be confused with urban cowboy). Gail once said, "Well, Nancy, you are really girly, but I like you anyway 'cause you've got a strong will and you're capable."

I suppose my "girly qualities" meant applying makeup and wearing something other than Carhartt jackets and jeans. Around here, any sort of fashionable or stylish clothing is looked upon with a certain disdain or suspicion. Back east, almost everybody dressed nicely for work or to shop in town. In Montana I noticed most people seemed never to give fashion a second thought. Tank tops, shorts, or flip flops are common wear—even in winter. And judging by some of the denizens of the local Wal-Mart, pajama bottoms have become the new stretchy pants.

Some folks mistakenly think me a fan of *haute couture,* but thanks to a bit of fiscally responsible Scottish blood, I've found the discount rack and thrift stores suffice quite nicely. Yet even wearing bargain clothes, at times I would feel slightly overdressed and a bit self-conscious when in public. Then I'd be pleasantly surprised by someone complimenting my hat, dress, or jewelry; and I'd find my one-woman crusade to bring mainstream metro-western chic to Montana reenergized. I'm realistic enough to know such ideas will never supplant the day-to-day reality of needing rugged clothes for rugged work—even around my place I wear sweats, jeans, and muck boots to the barn; but I'll never accept the notion that boots coated in bovine scat will ever quite fit into any fashion motif or social event, no matter how egalitarian.

Though Gail often teased me about my appearance, one of the nice, fashionable things I noticed about her was how pretty her hands always looked, and how her nails remained polished and manicured, despite her work regimen.

"How do you keep those nails so nice when working?" I once asked. "Mine just chip off at the barn."

"I wear gloves when I work so they don't get damaged."

"Very nice."

"Oh, it's just a little thing I do for myself 'cause I like it. But my friends give me a hard time about it, teasing me by saying, 'Hey, Gail, are you turning into a girl?'"

"You're female, Gail, embrace your babeness!" I replied, smiling. I suppose I began to rub off on her because as time passed, I saw her wearing mascara, and knew, in some ways, she was becoming less tomboyish and more feminine. Score one for my metro-western makeover!

29

She Thinks My Tractor's Sexy

KEEPING A MILE OF LOGGING ROAD OPEN FOR THE last five winters had been a learning experience. Our first three winters had been relatively mild, but still we managed to get stuck a few times. It had taught us that outside help was not always readily available whenever we needed the road plowed or a vehicle freed from a snow drift. To avoid a repeat of those early mistakes, by the middle of our fourth winter we had purchased from Builder Bob a used four-wheel all terrain vehicle (ATV), commonly referred to as a four-wheeler, which mounted a four-foot plow. Bill, bundled up like an Eskimo, would attempt to remove the heaviest drifts, before returning to the house an hour later looking like a frozen mummy, with icicles dangling from his parka, and his goggles frosted over.

For the remainder of that winter and the one that followed, he used it, and in the process found it adequate for pushing light snow, but it could not clear the heavy drifts. We damaged the ATV and two different plows learning this fact, and still our vehicles occasionally got stuck. After one particularly exasperating escapade, I heard him through his frozen muffler

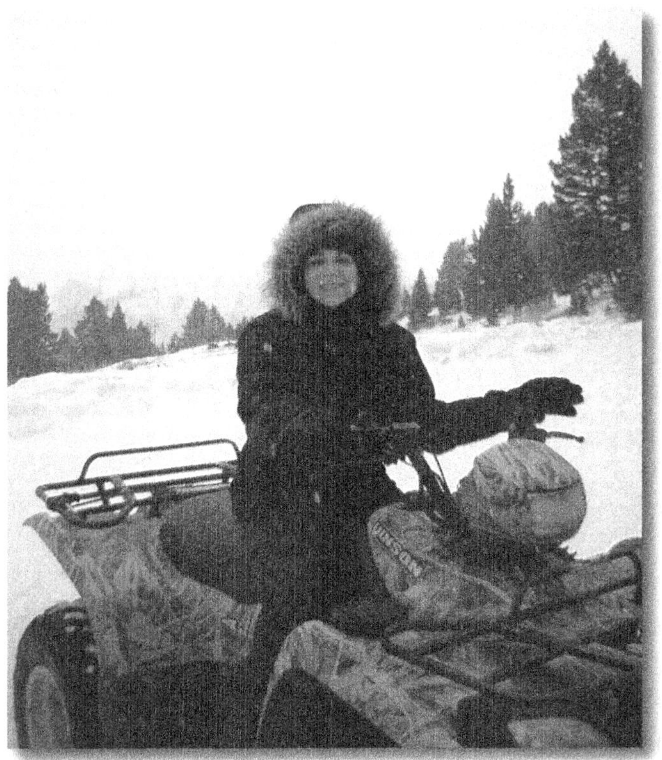

Learning to drive the four wheeler

say, "Honey, if we ever get through this winter, we've got to seriously look at buying a tractor and the biggest honking snow blade we can find."

The time had come to seriously consider purchasing something much larger and more capable. Now that we had a thorough taste of rural life, I completely understood why I saw a tractor in almost every front yard. But a new tractor was as expensive as a new car, and we were largely ignorant of the advantages and disadvantages of the few brands available. About all we were certain of was that it must be capable of plowing in the winter and maintaining roads and ditches in the summer.

When I asked Gail her opinion, she was thrilled. I could tell she enjoyed her heavy equipment; she had enough of it scattered about her ranch. She began rattling off a complete list of features she considered necessary or highly desirable. We talked about engine size, hydrostatic (automatic) vs. manual gear shifts, bucket dimensions, lift capacity, digging depth, whether of not I should put beet juice in my tires (to weigh the machine down and given it stability), enclosed cab features, and winter fuel mixes. Bill and I began a thorough investigation of all tractor brands and tractor attachments. We knew we needed the backhoe feature and a front mounted bucket, so we collected brochures, reviewed manufacturer internet sites, and read blog comments. From this information we built a spreadsheet to compare the dimensions, capabilities, prices, and warranties of each machine.

There was only one local dealer, so we increased our search radius to 150 miles, visiting a dozen dealers, and looking at fifty different makes and models. We narrowed our choices down to three machines: a new Japanese-built Kubota, a used Korean Kioti, and a new Korean TYM. The Kubota had the best performance and reputation, and a friendly, well equipped dealership was an hour and a half away in Missoula, but it was the most expensive unit, and more importantly, it lacked an enclosed cab. A Canadian built aftermarket cab kit was available for it, but this only increased the price well beyond our budget. Even if we could afford the modifications, it would still be lacking some of the creature comforts that came standard on both the Kioti and TYM. Regretfully, we removed it from further consideration.

The Kioti and the TYM were very evenly matched machines in terms of capabilities and features, and could nearly pass for twins. The Kioti dealership was only thirty-five miles from us, which was a strong selling point, but the machine they had in stock was one which had been damaged, and was currently under repair. It was nearly halfway through its warranty life and there was no extension program. We could order a brand new one, but the price would be higher than the TYM. Bill tried to negotiate with them, but being the only tractor dealership in a 100 mile radius, they felt no compunction to parley.

In the end we chose a new TYM 50 HP T503. Like the Kioti, it had everything we needed such as a six-foot wide quick-release front bucket, good digging and lifting capacity, an enclosed cab with heater (no more frozen ears or fingers during the winter), along with some nice added creature comforts such as an automatic transmission, air conditioner, radio, and CD player. It also had the best warranty and lowest price of the three machines, and the dealership was friendly and helpful. Since TYM did not build their own backhoe units, we had the dealer attach a tough Canadian built Wallenstein unit with a twelve-inch bucket, which added enough weight in the rear to make the tractor heavy enough to operate without adding beet juice to the tires. The only serious challenge we faced was the distance to the dealership, which was located 150 miles away. Even with the warranty, if we ever needed any repair, we would have to pay him to pick up and deliver it, for we had no trailer of our own.

"When is your tractor being delivered? I want to come and see it," Gail asked excitedly. She understood that a monetary expense like this was really an investment in the future. It meant we planned to stay, permanently, if possible. Even I began to realized how "permanent" this was all starting to feel.

I began to tease her, "It's a beautiful shade of fire engine red, all bright and shiny!" I could hear moaning over the phone. I suppose tractors really do have a certain sex appeal.

The big day arrived, and I watched the semi and flatbed trailer snake its way up the hill to our home. As it turned around, I saw our fully decked-out tractor come into view. It was a rather intimidating looking machine, with its huge tires and hungry bucket itching to dig up some dirt and gravel. The backhoe looked like a retracted claw ready to spring forth, as if from some prehistoric beast. In a few short minutes it was unloaded and Bill was having his first lesson.

"Don't turn the wheels too fast or too sharp, or you could tip over," I heard Cody, the dealer, yell over the loud rumbling of its diesel engine, as Bill practiced in our driveway. Soon it was my turn to try. I was not in a big hurry to drive it, but I did get inside and familiarize myself with all the controls. I even practiced raising and lowering the bucket, feeling like a real farm girl. Of course, we had to take photos of each of us sitting in it, to send to our friends and relatives back east. We received a lot of excited responses, probably because we were the only people they knew who actually *owned* a tractor.

It was only a few days after the tractor arrived that Gail was standing in my yard, admiring our latest acquisition.

"It's nice," she said with enthusiasm, looking over every detail of the machine. I knew she secretly longed for it. "I love the cab; you won't be cold this year when plowing."

"I think I should learn how to drive it," I said confidently. In truth I was feeling intimated and small inside this great beast, a beast I considered much bigger and more challenging than a horse.

"Of course you should," Gail replied matter-of-factly.

She was encouraging, but my weak smile probably exposed my false bravado.

"You can do it," Gail offered again. "Come on, if Bill is sick or laid up, you may have to clear the road. My kids started driving farm equipment as soon as they could reach the pedals. It's not that hard."

I knew she was right. Bill and I had talked about it many times before. I wanted to be able to take care of all the aspects of our rural life. It did not take physical strength to drive a tractor; it just took a little nerve. But I started off slow. We had acquired it too late in the season to do much winter plowing, which was just as well, because we quickly discovered the front loader made for a very poor plow. We would need a real plow attachment, but that could wait till fall. I became fairly proficient at working the backhoe, but I refrained from actually driving the tractor because I feared one mistake might topple the machine. That entire spring and summer we repaired our road and completed ground projects that normally would have required the services of a contractor. We built a beautiful flagstone patio with a dramatic waterfall and crescent shaped pond just outside our dining room window. It was our first real backhoe project and I was proud of the way the girls pitched in on our "rock hunts" around the property. We purchased colorful round river rock and pea rock to add some extra color, and all of it we laid by hand.

The only major problem we encountered nearly became a minor disaster while Bill was digging out the crescent pond. He had just scraped off the last bit of dirt when he noticed a wide streak of white. Curious, he stepped off the backhoe to investigate, and discovered he had uncovered part of our septic drain pipe. Had he dug down any further, raw sewage would have leached out, and we'd have been facing an expensive repair bill. As it was, he had to refill the hole and start over. Not having a more suitable place to locate our pond and patio, and now aware it lay right over our septic line, we decided to overcome this problem by building the patio and pond several feet higher. Bill spent a day bringing in more dirt to raise the mound three feet, and then dug down again. It was all a learning experience, and a worthwhile one, for we were pleased with the final result.

With the patio and waterfall project completed, the day had come for me to master a new skill when Bill announced, "Let me teach you how to drive the tractor, just a short lesson."

My thoughts immediately shot back to the day when he tried to teach me how to drive a stick shift, a decade before. We were in a small field on a dry sunny day in Florida, and I was in the driver's seat of Bill's old Datsun 280Z sport car. I could still feel the car stalling as I struggled to coordinate the shifting of the gears and clutch. The car would lunge forward awkwardly or stall. Then there was the yelling, cursing, and growling each time I ground the gears. I never did quite master the manual transmission, and Bill never quite overcame his frustration at not being able to teach me, yet we're still happily married.

I took a long deep breath and said, "All right, but no yelling." I looked seriously into his deep blue eyes, and he stared back into my dark green eyes and grinned.

"Just do everything I tell you and I won't have to yell at you."

He explained how to use the console-mounted hand lever that served as the throttle, the left side floor-mounted twin brakes, and the right side floor-mounted, forward and reverse pedals. It was simple enough, but alien and awkward. I turned the key and waited for the glow plug light to come on, then turned the key a bit more, and felt the rumble of the diesel engine as the dragon came to life, belching black smoke from its snout. The noise and rumble created a vibration throughout the vehicle that made it feel raw and alive. There was no soft purring and no insulation from the outside world, save for the thin Plexiglas and sheet metal. I comforted myself, thinking *so far so good.*

Bill was scrunched in beside me on the rear wheel well while I occupied the only seat. It was a dangerous perch, and I worried about him falling out if the door popped open. We began to move forward slowly, and I could feel the tires bouncing up and down on the gravel road.

I called out, "This feels really unstable and I can't see the ground all that well."

"You'll get used to it," Bill replied in a comforting tone. "It bothered me too at first."

Our road was fairly narrow and twisting, and there was no room for two cars to pass, but that was unlikely to happen I told myself. I was much higher off the ground than normal, and this fact only made the tractor feel that much more enormous. I crawled along the road at less than five miles per hour.

"Go a little faster," Bill urged. "You're moving too slow."

"No thanks," I replied smartly, gripping the steering wheel tightly with both hands. "Do you have to be somewhere?"

"No, but this is boring. You can go a little faster; let me show you." Bill reached for the throttle control on the console and moved the lever from the turtle icon at the top toward the rabbit icon at the bottom. The tractor instantly lurched forward and began picking up speed.

"Don't do that; we're going too fast! I want to be a turtle! I like the turtle. I want to stay a turtle!" We were now moving at nearly ten miles per hour, where even the slightest dip in the road caused the seat to spring up and down. I was riding a seesaw, not a tractor.

"You were going too slow and wasting time. I thought you wanted to learn how to drive this?"

"I do, but SLOWLY. Who's driving this anyway?"

"Okay, back it down," Bill replied with disappointment.

I returned the lever to the turtle position and the tractor immediately returned to its crawl. We hummed (well, crawled) along, practicing turns and reverse maneuvers. We bounced and lurched when I practiced maneuvering the bucket. My thoughts bounced right along with my aching back. *I don't know if I will ever feel comfortable doing this.* But I was proud of my first lesson. It went much better than the sports car experience.

ʊ ʊ ʊ

As fall approached, the first signs of early snow appeared, so we had our dealer order a large eight-foot plow from W.R. Long in North Carolina. They drop shipped it to our place. Well, the shipping company actually dropped it a mile from our home. The driver wasn't willing to risk taking his rig up the logging road, so Bill detached the front bucket and drove the tractor down to pick up the plow blade. When he returned, he asked me to guide him while he disconnected the plow and reattached the bucket. I decided to stand off to the side, thinking it was a safer place to observe. He almost had it hooked, but every time he got close enough, the "quick-detach" coupling slipped out, so he backed up and tried again, and again. He was becoming frustrated, and motioned me to stand in front so he wouldn't have to keep swinging his head back and forth between me and the bucket. I stepped forward and motioned with my hand; the units snapped together with a solid clunk. I started to step back when the tractor suddenly lurched forward and caught me in the leg, banging and scraping me below the knee. It was a painful lesson and I was lucky I was not seriously hurt. After that, I maintained a healthy distance when assisting with the dragon.

30

Hoarse Horse

I T WAS THE FIRST WEEK IN MAY, AND I WAS very sick with a flu that seemed to have spread through half the county. I was too weak from the fever to do much of anything, so I sat near the upstairs window wrapped in a cozy blanket, with a box of tissues, trying to enjoy the view. I watched the horse graze and thought all about the things I had to do once I felt better.

Belle rested in the grass and had a short nap. She stood up and walked a few feet and lay down again. *How odd.*

She stood up and walked about twenty feet, then lay down once more. When she did this several more times, I knew something was wrong. Belle was sick too. I asked Bill to go down to the barn and check on her. I explained the situation and told him I believed she had a form of colic.

When he returned to the house, I was anxiously waiting. He told me Belle was definitely sick. He explained how miserable she looked and sounded, and that she seemed to be very cold. It had started to rain and was cold outside. I was unprepared for this. I did not know how to doctor a horse, and I was too sick to go down and see her myself.

"I should go and see her," I said in a *hoarse* voice. Gripping my robe, I stood up, and a wave of dizziness reminded me I was in no shape to do this.

"Sit back down," Bill commanded. "You don't want to get worse off than she is."

"I'll call Linda; she can give us some advice."

After talking to Linda, I felt a little better. Belle was not rolling in pain; she looked sick, but was fairly stable. She offered to call her vet, Hanna, and let me know what she advised. If Belle got worse, then a vet would have to come out. Time passed too slowly, and Bill and the girls tried to keep Belle in her stall where she could stay dry. In the meantime, Linda had called a mutual friend, Connie, and asked her to bring us a horse blanket. When Connie arrived, she showed us how to put the blanket on Belle, and she listened for belly noises with a stethoscope. It was important to hear some gurgling or churning sounds that would indicate some kind of activity in the digestive system. It was hard to hear anything, but Bill thought he heard something. It was getting late, and Connie needed to return home, so we thanked her for the use of the blanket, and promised to return it as soon as possible. Connie wished us luck and hoped Belle would get through the night.

The hours passed without sign of improvement, so Bill decided to call a local vet for advice. He was a surly man we hated dealing with, but he was the closest vet to us. He curtly told Bill under no circumstances would he treat colic, and from our description, it sounded to him like that was what Belle had. If he did come out, it would only be to euthanize her. What did we want him to do?

Bill had to bite his tongue to keep from telling him what he really wanted him to do. He simply replied, "I'll have to talk to my wife."

Bill described his conversation and we both agreed there was no way we would take such drastic measures. We would check on Belle through the night. If she made it, there was a good chance she'd recover. It turned into a very long night. As sick and tired as I was, I could not sleep, and I would quiz my husband after he returned from checking on her each time. I felt guilty that I was not able to be of more help.

By the time the morning light was breaking through our bedroom window, Bill had a surprise for us. I heard a small tapping at the front door and went downstairs. When I opened it, there he stood with Belle by the front entrance, looking well. I know if I had moved aside and invited her in, she would have come through the front door.

"I'll go get the girls. Stay here," I said excitedly.

I told the girls to come down stairs for a surprise, and they quickly scurried down the stairs, two steps at a time. They were so relieved to see Belle up and about, that they bounced around like two kids on a pogo stick.

We monitored her food for the next few days, and although she seemed a little tired, there were no further episodes. Hanna did call to check on Belle, and we discussed her condition and progress. The next day I ordered a horse blanket and stethoscope. If this ever happened again, I was going to be prepared.

31

TKO

I WAS FEELING THE JOY OF A TRUE "MONTANA MOMENT" when I saw my daughter trot and canter across the open meadow of green lush grass, dotted with flowers. Her dishwater blond pony tail bounced in the breeze as she sat tall and poised. Belle's beautiful head and tail remained up high with each step, while her mane and tail flowed in rhythm as she moved gracefully through the field. In the background stood the rolling hills and tall pine trees, and further back the mountains, silhouetted by the bright sun high above in an ocean of clear blue sky. The sweetness of the air only added to the dreamlike quality of that moment in time. It has been a favorite memory of mine, and I often think back to it.

Along with such beautiful dreams, sometimes a nightmare slips in when you least expect it. Bill and I were setting flagstones in our new patio and waterfall area just below the dining room bay window. It was the continuation of our big summer project which we worked on every evening. I was just finishing up and planned to join Sandy down at the barn when I heard her call out to me.

"Mom, I need help with Belle!" I heard the strain in her voice.

"Coming!" I yelled as I hastened along, moving as fast as my poor back would allow.

When I looked down the hill, I saw Belle pulling at the lead rope and half dragging Sandy around the corral. The eleven-year-old girl would get her footing and the horse would suddenly decide to walk in a new direction. When she got control for a moment and tried to back the stubborn mare up, she simply turned away.

"Just drop the rope," I called.

But Sandy held on, determined to gain control of the situation. This concerned me greatly, so when I entered the corral I told Sandy to give me the lead rope. I could see that Belle was very agitated and behaving in a belligerent manner. I stood a little off to her right side so she could not run me over if she decided to bolt forward. I let her stand a moment, thinking she would calm down, but she turned and tried to walk away.

With a firm grip on the lead rope, I stepped along with her and told her to back up. She froze and refused to move. I asked her again, tugging the lead rope as I had been taught to do in the past. She still would not move. I took a step forward towards her and bumped the lead rope. She just stood in place. I could not afford to give in to her. I had to do something, and my mind searched for an answer. I took the end of the lead rope and gave it a small swing in a circle in front of her face. *This should back her up* I thought in earnest. She still did not move. *Unbelievable! But I can't quit now.* My thoughts were racing.

"Sandy please get me the training whip," I ordered.

I asked Belle to back up again, and again she refused. With the whip in hand, I gave Belle a bump in the chest with the rubber end of the handle, along with the verbal command to back up, and she finally moved a step backwards. *Thank goodness that is over* I thought to myself. Suddenly, Belle swung her head in my direction and hit me in the side of the head, knocking me to the ground. I was so angry that I jumped up quickly, the lead rope still in my hand, and backed her up again. She immediately complied. It was then I realized I was hurt. I had broken my own cardinal rule and forgotten to put on my helmet when I entered the stable area. I was so focused on helping Sandy and keeping her from getting hurt, that I had placed myself needlessly in danger. I put both hands to my head as the spinning started, and then a terrible pain began.

"Oh no, Mom!" I heard Sandy's fearful cry. "Are you hurt?" She rushed over to me.

"I'm okay," I lied, breathless, as I leaned against her. "Take the halter off...and come home." I said.

"Oh, it's all my fault! I don't like helmets, but I should have reminded you."

"No...it's mine," I said. "I forgot. I was too focused on helping you."

Sandy wanted to argue, but thought better of it, and instead took the lead rope without another word, and walked her horse back to the hitching post. I started heading to the gate, and somehow made it halfway up the hill when Bill rushed to join me.

"What's wrong?" he asked, his face pale.

He took my arm and helped me the rest of the way into the house and onto the couch. I briefly told him the story as I lay there at what seemed like death's door. Then I added weakly, "I just want to rest awhile. I'll be fine." Inside I kept thinking *How could I have made such a mistake?*

My headache worsened through the night and into the next day. I became sick to my stomach, so that anytime I tried to move, I nearly vomited while choking and gagging. By the afternoon of the following day we decided I should go to the emergency room.

I hate hospitals. I have spent too much time in them in different areas of the country. Some health problems I have managed to overcome, but a few I just manage to live with. *Would this be one of those conditions?*

Horse versus head was probably the note written on my chart. The nurse was nice to me, stating that they get horse related injuries in the ER quite often. This was Montana, after all.

I was lucky. The scan showed no permanent injury to my brain, just my pride, but I did have a head injury, a concussion with brain swelling and bruising. My headache lasted for over three weeks. All I could do was wait for the pain to end.

"I'm a Western girl now; It's official," I joked on the phone with Gail one beautiful summer morning, while I lay on the couch missing the chance to enjoy the day.

"At least you can keep a sense of humor about it. These things do happen, Nancy. Last week my son's mare swung her head and hit him in the face, breaking his brand new glasses." I could just see her shrug as she added, "It's better than breaking his head."

"No kidding. Oh I know I'll be okay in time. You always said I was hard-headed. Now we have proof."

Gail laughed and completely agreed with me. I hung up the phone, my head still sore and pounding, thinking once again *this was not in the brochure.*

With little to do but lay about, I had plenty of time to think. I knew this was an avoidable accident, but the idea that it might happen to one of my daughters was very disturbing. Part of me began to question the wisdom of my relationship with horses. I did not want my girls to stop riding. They loved that, but Belle, I now fully understood, carried quite an attitude.

"What are you thinking about?" Bill quizzed me when he saw the concentration on my face. "How are you feeling?"

"My head hurts, and I'm having second, third, and fourth thoughts about this horse."

Bill studied my face intently, "What are you saying?"

"Maybe I shouldn't do this anymore, or maybe a different horse would be more suitable for our skill level."

Bill slowly sat down on our bed across from my recliner. "You can't quit. This was an accident. It happens. I see how much you love ground training. You'll learn from this and get better at handling her. Any horse is a handful when you're still learning. Belle does have some good qualities, you know. Have you talked this over with Linda?"

"I did; she thinks I can still continue training Belle. She says horses are always a risk. Belle's difficult at times, but she says there are much worse types out there. Time and practice is what I need. She doesn't think we have to sell her...but I wonder."

"I don't want to sell her," Bill interrupted.

"I suppose I don't really want to, either," I replied.

"But now you're scared of her."

"I'm not scared of her. I'm scared of what could happen to me, or the girls, even accidentally."

Bill stared seriously at me, "You still can't quit. I'm no horse lover, but even I can see what this means to Sandy and Sonja. If you give up now, how will the girls interpret it? When things get tough, just quit? Honey, there's risk associated with almost anything we do. You knew that when we bought a horse. So you made a mistake. You're going to make more. Learn from them and press on. You always have before."

It was one of his "colonel speeches," but I saw the wisdom in his advice. And maybe I wasn't being totally honest with myself. Maybe I was scared of Belle. Horses can cause serious injury, or even kill. The thought of getting physically close to her again made my stomach jump. I also understood that horses feel your fear, so how could I hide my feelings from her? How would she react if she sensed that fear? How could I overcome it? I had no answers, but I continued to ponder the questions over and over in my mind.

After almost four weeks I was feeling better again. I was up and about and back to my normal routines. I was also getting ready for my friends, Grace and Russell, to visit from Florida. I had only been down to the barn once since the accident. I sat and watched a riding lesson that Linda gave Sandy and Sonja. I knew I would have to "get back in the saddle" and halter Belle again. *After all, wasn't I the one who knew her and could handle her the best?* In fact several people, including Linda, had told me Belle should be my horse, and perhaps we should look at another one for Sandy.

"She does like you best, Mom," Sandy would tell me. "Besides, they are good for people with back problems."

I found her idea was a little strange. I didn't ride.

"Oh you'll ride," said Gail one day, in her matter-of-fact voice.

"I would rather ride a cow," I teased her. "They can't go as fast as horses." I regretted that statement the moment I said it because I just knew Gail would offer one of her cows, but she didn't. She was on a mission.

"You can't have a horse and not ride one. Sooner or later, if you own one, you're going to get on."

She sounded awfully sure of herself. I decided not to argue the point and just mumbled, "I don't know." Apparently that was good enough for Gail because she let me off the hook for a while.

Grace and Russell arrived soon after, on a lovely warm summer day that only Montana can provide. The meadow flowers were in full splendor, and I was fully up and about again.

"So, how are you feeling?" Grace asked in her brash Bronx accent.

As I escorted my friends down to the stable, I replied, "Fine." I was hiding the fact that I was sick with fear. The closer we got to the corral, the more I felt my stomach tighten. I kept thinking, *Don't do this to yourself. You can't be afraid of your own horse. Be confident and expect a good result. Have faith.*

I stepped into the corral trying to look as confidently as I could. I introduced Belle to my friends and decided to get the halter. At this point I had only seen her once in the last thirty days. I had forgiven her and decided to move past it all. I approached her like I always did and watched for her reaction. She seemed unconcerned as I went about my business. With my helmet on, I haltered her up and began getting acquainted again. I backed her up, moved her hind end, turned her at the shoulder, and moved her into the round pen. As I worked with her, I explained what I had learned about the round pen activities, about building respect and trust between horse and handler. I also predicted how Belle would react, and she responded perfectly.

"Nancy," Grace began, "I can see that you really love what you're doing. Look how well Belle did that."

Russell chimed in and echoed Grace's sentiments. I was pleased because I knew Russell had owned horses and had a great deal of knowledge of them. I felt a great joy of relief. It was true Belle had responded perfectly to my every request without challenging me in any way. She made me look much more skilled than I felt inside. I reached up and stroked her neck, thanking her for her good work, as she stood next to me, a model of grace and dignity. It was as if nothing wrong had ever happened between us. We were back on track. I had a huge smile on my face the rest of the day. How long would it last?

32

Dressed to Kill

THE NEXT MORNING AFTER BREAKFAST, GRACE AND I talked about clothes. Fashion was a subject few of my local acquaintances seemed interested in. But Grace hailed from New York, so a discussion of couture came easily to her. She had recently told me about her favorite store, and I started looking at their online sales page. Grace leaned over my chair and looked down at what I was wearing.

"How come I don't see you in your nice clothes anymore?" she queried.

"Oh, I still wear them; but they've become my go-to-town clothes."

She looked a little puzzled. I knew her everyday clothes were nice enough that she could go just about anywhere in them, so I explained further, "I don't like to wear them around the house because I'm afraid I will ruin them. I never know what I will be doing next."

From the look on Grace's face I knew she did not completely comprehend me. "What do you mean?"

"Well, when we first moved up here I thought living on a mountain meant you just built a house and lived in it the same way you would live in a neighborhood house. I was wrong about that, and I've been learning just how different it is here every day."

Grace soon got a small taste of what I meant when we later sat on the patio. We heard a strange squealing sound as the girls came running up to us, jumping onto the patio.

"Kobi caught something," Sonja said breathlessly.

"What is it?" I asked.

"I don't know," she replied. "Come and see it."

We left the porch and walked around the girls play area to the woodpile. There we saw Kobi with a poor struggling animal between his paws. I walked closer and saw he had caught a gopher.

It was hard to watch because Kobi, like most dogs, was playing with the injured animal. I took another step closer. "What do you have, Kobi?" I asked him gently.

He looked so pleased with himself. I must have distracted him because all of a sudden, the gopher jumped from his grasp and started to run across the yard. Kobi, hot in pursuit, snatched the gopher and carried it back to me. One look at the gopher and I knew it was now dead.

"Sandy, please go ask your father to bury Kobi's prize." As I had done before with other kills that Kobi hunted, I would offer him a trade. Kobi was happy to swap the gopher for a large dog biscuit. But now he was covered in blood from his chest down to his feet. He could not come in the house like that, so I got a rag and a pail of soapy water, and proceeded to clean him up. On the patio stones, down on my knees, I offered my explanation to Grace. "This is only *one* of the many reasons why I don't wear my good clothes around the house."

Grace laughed with a mixture of amusement and distress, and said, "Now I understand. I don't blame you."

"Good clothes and gopher blood just don't mix," I joked. Everyone laughed but the poor gopher.

By now, Bill had effected enough modifications to the dog kennel that he felt certain our "Houdini dog" would be safe inside, unable to escape. This allowed us to use the car instead of the truck for a tour of the local area, and we all piled into the Highlander.

On our way to Helena, Bill acted as tour guide, describing the history of the pass, including the French woman's murder, among other gruesome lore. He concluded his lecture with the comment, "Thank goodness it's no longer a toll road, or we'd go broke."

"How do you know this stuff?" asked Grace, impressed.

I chimed in, "Oh, we pass historical markers for these roads every time we go to town. When we were new here, we used to stop and read each one."

Bill added, "When we first purchased our property, we found out that part of it was used as a stagecoach line from Helena to Clark Fork, Montana."

"So what's it like crossing the pass?" asked Russell.

"Most of the year, the drive across is enjoyable. The roads wind and climb, and offer spectacular views for miles. In the winter the drive can be treacherous. We've been caught in white-out conditions and had our experiences with black ice. It's the main reason we try to be home before dark in the winter."

We often had long days in town because of the numerous errands—medical appointments, food shopping, and other supplies; but with Grace and Russell along, there wasn't room for much, so we curtailed the traditional stops and spent more time sightseeing. We took them on a tour of the Charles Russell paintings at the state museum, and returned home before dinner. As we pulled up the drive, a familiar figure darted toward our car.

"He got out again!" Bill's exasperated voice boomed. "I put two chains on the kennel door and he still got out. How did he do it this time?"

We found the answer to our question when we examined the kennel door. He had managed to pull the door frame inward and bent the metal until the entire frame twisted away from the door.

"This dog has amazing strength," said Bill shaking his head.

"I don't know how we're going to keep him in here," I wondered out loud. I grabbed Kobi's collar and stared him down in frustration. "This is for your protection. Do you understand?"

Kobi stared up at me in bewilderment, lowering his ears while wagging his tail, still proud of his latest feat, as I continued my tirade. "Beside the fact you are becoming destructive, these constant repairs are costing us both time and money."

To Kobi it was all blah, blah, blah. He knew his name and words like "treat." The rest was unimportant. We were completely frustrated, trying to think of a new way to keep him in his kennel when we were away. Kobi, however, was having a grand time bouncing and quivering around my feet.

"When will you ever learn?" I said as I patted his head in defeat.

33

Dead Heads
and Dead Ends

TWO DAYS LATER GRACE AND RUSSELL DEPARTED, and I resumed my search for a horse for Sonja. Linda had been keeping an eye out for a beginner's horse, while I again placed calls regarding horses I thought might have potential, only to find out they were poor choices. But at least I was getting good at asking the right questions. By now our quest had taken over seven months, and although she never complained, I could see Sonja was becoming disappointed. I renewed my promise to her and continued looking.

I had long ago settled into a predictable routine, and was no longer surprised by the unpredictable reactions I received from touchy owners when I asked them detailed questions about their horses. One Internet advertisement had a common post of "A horse anyone can ride" and went on to describe a willing-to-please mare. When I sent an email query asking if the owner thought the horse was suitable for a child who was a new rider, the reply I received was a bit stinging for such an innocent question. It read, "My horse is not a dead head, so she is not right for a child!"

I had to ask Linda what a "dead head horse" was, and she laughed, "It's a term people use to describe a horse with dulled senses or a lack of spirit.

Usually it's describing a horse that's not very intelligent. These are often the kind of traits people look for in a beginner's horse because they aren't a challenge to the rider. I wouldn't take the insult seriously, even if the owner overreacted."

I found it was not just the people who sell horses that have odd reactions and behaviors. Sometimes it applies to the buyer as well. I responded to an ad about a grey gelding that was supposed to be good with children. I called the number posted and spoke to a very nice woman who answered all my questions.

"I'm sorry, but a family has already come to look at the horse. They're undecided, but it looks like they want him. So I told them they could have a few days to think it over. But I could call you back if I don't hear from them Monday."

She began asking me a little more about what I was looking for in a horse, and listened sympathetically to my story. "It sounds like you know more about horses than the people interested in my gelding."

Since I usually didn't receive any compliments from my inquiries, I just *had* to ask, "What do you mean?"

"Well," she paused and took a deep breath, "They were originally interested in my yearlings. The grandmother was trying to talk her daughter into buying the colt for the grandchildren. The strange part was that none of them ride."

"That is weird," I replied.

"I tried to explain to them these young horses need a few years to grow before they're physically able to carry a rider, and they must be trained before anyone can ride them."

"True," I agreed. I was not exactly sure where this conversation was going since this information was common knowledge and just made sense. What she said next made me feel as though I was a pinnacle of equine knowledge.

"My comments didn't deter them; they still wanted to buy one." Her voice began to falter as she laughed, "They wanted to take a yearling home that day in the back of their SUV!"

"What!?" I exclaimed. Even I knew that was impossible.

"I know; it sounds crazy," the woman hastily added. "I told them they couldn't do that, and how unsafe it was for all involved. That's when I decided to show them my gelding for sale. He's much more suitable for children who are learning to ride. They liked him, but it was clear they knew nothing about horses or how to handle them. It was then I suggested they take a couple of days and think this whole situation through."

I thought to myself, *Why would she even consider selling her horse to these people?* I did not want to offend her, but it seemed obvious that selling any horse to them could prove dangerous for all involved. I respectfully asked, "Are you having any concerns about selling horses to people who clearly aren't prepared to care for them?"

"Well, I will just have to wait until Monday and see what happens."

"I understand," I replied. "Good luck, and I hope it turns out well for everyone." I hung up the phone, realizing I was not the most uneducated horse person in the world. It was mid-week when I got a return phone call from the gelding's owner. "I never did hear back from that family," she said. *What a relief. That's one potential tragedy avoided.*

We discussed the horse in greater detail, and I had some concerns that only could be addressed if Linda were present. It was a bit of a drive to her place, and the owner was unwilling to negotiate the price. I pondered the issue before deciding to go with my gut instinct. I appreciated the owner's candor, at least she was honest upfront, but, I decided to pass on this one. It just didn't feel like the right horse. And so it went.

While I searched vainly for the perfect horse, Bill busied himself with the task of making the dog kennel Kobi proof. He wanted to find out just how he was getting out, so he put Kobi inside, set the lock and chains, and went inside to watch him from the upstairs window.

Kobi howled and whined, trying to call us all to him. When we failed to come, he bit into the chain link door, locking his teeth around the metal, and began to pull backwards with all his might.

"He's going to pull out his teeth!" I said to Bill with great concern.

"Look how strong he is," Bill replied with clear admiration.

We both watched intently as Kobi began stepping backwards. With both Shepherd and Malamute traits, Kobi was mentally and physically strong. His color was shepherd, but his stocky legs and sturdy chest was all malamute. With incredible strength, he pulled and pulled, and the door frame began to slowly buckle. He pulled some more, but the chains held the door frame in three different places this time. He seemed to be at a standstill. The frame was bent, but not enough for him to squeeze through. Kobi stopped pulling and began to push and paw at the door. He tried to dig at the floor of his kennel, but we had reinforced the bottom with rebar. Next, he sat down. I could tell by the look on his face that he was thinking. This was not the kind of dog to give up.

He paced the chain linked walls and began to test the sides. He was hoping he could break the wires that connected the floor to the walls. This time it would not work. Bill had secured heavy gauged hog panels to all four sides, and they would not flex enough for Kobi to push them out and crawl under. Still, Kobi tried forcing the sides of the kennel, hoping to bend one of them. When Kobi at last jumped on top of his dog house and took a look around, I felt a flush of success.

"I think he gave up. We have finally secured him, at least for now," I said with relief. "He won't give up you know."

"I know," Bill replied. He smiled and I looked up at him. I thought again just how handsome he was, and how devoted he was to me and our little family. I locked my arm into his, and we walked from the window down the stairs and outside. When Kobi saw us approaching, he at once became a wriggling mass of happiness. He looked at me with pleading brown eyes that seemed to say, "*I could not get out. Where have you been?*"

"So you couldn't get out this time, eh little man?" I reached out to him as Bill opened the door. Kobi pressed against me so hard, I thought he was going to knock me over. I braced my legs and rubbed his sides.

"We'd never leave you for long periods, Kobi; I promise. We just want you safe when we're not at home to protect you." I stopped a moment and thought about what I had actually said. *Funny, we originally bought him to protect us.*

ʊ ʊ ʊ

Flush from victory over our dog, I renewed my horse search with increased vigor, but it wasn't long before my fondest hopes were dashed yet again. Linda and I had just finished looking at an older mare of nineteen. She was showing her age and needed some additional training. But our main concern was her teeth, which were in bad shape. Linda believed within a few months the horse would need equine senior, a type of horse food supplement, similar to that for older dogs.

Linda warned me, "She would most likely not be able to chew grass hay, and would need to eat manufactured food. It's very expensive, exclusive feed."

We decided to keep looking. On the way home, Linda mentioned a palomino gelding she had seen the other day.

"A palomino?" My ears immediately perked up and I turned to her with interest. That was Sonja's dream horse color.

Linda elaborated. "I've evaluated the horse and really like him. His price is right at only $850. You should take a look at him."

I eagerly agreed. Perhaps this was a chance to make Sonja's dream come true. Even so, we decided not to tell the girls we were evaluating this horse for purchase. We did not want to get their hopes up too high, so we told them, as part of our horse lessons, Linda was taking us out to learn about all kinds of horses.

We drove the few miles from Linda's house to the ranchette where the horse lived. We pulled into a long drive that ended at a very large barn and arena. There we met a middle-aged, petite, blond woman and her horse, Clif. He was a very handsome pale palomino quarter horse. I watched Sonja's face instantly light up. Linda saddled him up and examined him as we talked. After a few minutes of groundwork, she led him over to us, smiling.

"I love this horse," Linda began.

"Tell me everything."

"He's gentle and well mannered, very willing to do as you ask, and calm too," Linda said as she popped into the saddle.

We watched intently as she walked and then trotted around the arena. He moved well, but was a little out of breath.

"He seems to be breathing hard," I commented.

"He's a little out of shape and needs some exercise," the owner replied. "He hasn't been ridden on a daily basis for a while. I bought the horse for my older daughter, but lately she's lost interest in riding, so I'm selling him. I hate giving him up, but the he can't stay around with nothing to do."

I turned my attention back to Linda as she rode up to us. She leaned over the saddle and said, "Would anyone like to ride him?"

The girls responded in an eager chorus, "I would."

We let Sandy go first since she had more experience. The horse did well for her, responding gently and quickly to each command. Soon it was Sonja's turn. We set her in the saddle and she smiled broadly as Linda led her around on the lead rope.

"She loves him, I can tell," I said to Bill. "Look at her face."

Sonja's delicate features were all upturned in hope and happiness. Even after her little feet dismounted and hit the ground, she was still floating on air. She removed her helmet and stood patting the gelding's neck.

It was cold outside, so I told the girls to get in the car and warm up. I could see Sonja's concern as her little chin turned to me and said, "Mom, is this horse for sale?"

She rarely asked for anything. She was and still is, sweet and polite, and often selfless. Such a grown-up little six-year-old, she was always grateful for anything she received, and wanted little more than our time and affection.

"Yes, honey girl, I think so," I replied. Her huge blue eyes, a gift from her father, locked into mine as they opened wide. I could see the question she was burning to ask, but I knew she would remain silent. She just stood there frozen in time. I kissed her on the cheek and said, "You're cold and the wind's picked up; please wait for me in the car."

She gave me a weak smile and walked towards the Highlander while Bill and I talked in low tones. Linda tried to negotiate a price, but the owner was firm. We finally agreed on her price, but there was a sticking point. The owner wanted Clif taken today. Linda explained that we did not have a trailer and that she would have to pick him up and take him to our home in Mullan. Linda also requested that the owner hold our check for a week so we could try out this horse.

The owner was really bothered by this request, and wanted the sale to be final that afternoon, but Linda was adamant.

"I can't recommend the sale if we can't give the palomino a try. It's common practice to try a horse for a week or two. We can write a contract between the parties so everyone knows their responsibilities."

Grudgingly, she agreed and we wrote the check. Linda was to pick up the horse in a couple of days.

I could hardly contain myself once I was in the car. Sonja's birthday was only a couple of weeks away and this palomino was her gift!

"Mom, I really like the horse we met today," Sonja said with a tentative voice. "He was really nice."

Sandy chimed in, "He was, Mom; you should buy him. He was great!"

I smiled all the way home, but kept my secret just in case. On the day Clif was to be delivered, the weather turned. We had a snow storm move in and Linda called to postpone the delivery. That was fine with us, since we didn't relish the thought of her pulling a horse trailer over the pass in a blizzard. The problem was she was not sure she could pick up the horse before the end of the week, and we had to be in Great Falls for a medical appointment for Sonja the following Monday. I didn't want to leave a new horse alone with Belle, or to have our trial period interrupted. I also had not heard back from the owner regarding Clif's vaccinations. Linda agreed to handle everything for us. I was so happy that Sonja's new horse would soon arrive at our door. Our little trooper really deserved it.

We returned late Monday evening from Great Falls to find the message light blinking on our answering machine. I recognized the terse voice of Clif's owner, "I'm returning your check. I'm not comfortable selling you my horse."

That was it, nothing more. I just stood there in shock. I could not believe it. I played the message again to make sure I heard it correctly. *Who would do this?* Multiple thoughts cascaded through my mind as I felt the anger well up inside me. *Why on earth would she go back on the sale? She is crushing Sonja's dream and ruining her birthday surprise. She KNEW the horse was for her big day. How the devil can she do this to a seven-year-old child? And after everything she has been through! How would SHE feel if someone did that to HER?*

My thoughts tumbled over one another, and I had to sit down to catch my breath.

There was another message on the machine from Linda, "Call me when you get back. She cancelled the sale."

I called Linda, trying to contain my frustration, "What happened?"

"I don't know. I left a message asking if we could talk it over, but I didn't hear anything back from her."

"You won't," I replied acidly. "I just don't understand. There's something here we don't' know about. I'm sure of it."

"I admit I've never had a check returned and a sale cancelled. This is the first time this has ever happened to me," Linda mused. "We *will* find a horse for Sonja, I promise. We just have to keep looking, and go on with our lives."

"I agree," I said. "I just feel bad about it." I knew Sonja really liked that horse and so did Linda.

All that effort and nothing to show for it. I tried convincing myself that it was probably for the best, and that there must be a better choice out there somewhere for her. Thank goodness I never told the girls our real plan.

"Hey, Mom, we really liked that horse. Will you buy us Creamy Hay Bale?" Sandy blurted out a few days later.

"Who?" I replied, puzzled.

"That palomino we went to see. That was what we named him. He was the color of straw. Besides, 'Clif' doesn't suit him."

Both of the girls' faces turned up to mine. I knew they were still secretly hoping we would buy the palomino. Now I began to question the decision of not telling the girls about the failed purchase. Bill and I thought it was best not to let them know about it because of the huge disappointment factor. However, they had been talking about this horse for nearly two weeks, and I could see they were not able to move on as long as this gelding was still on their minds.

Bill and I talked it over, and called a family meeting after dinner. We explained the whole story of how we had bought the palomino for Sonja and the owner had returned our check. Sonja understood, and stoically accepted it, though I knew she was sad. Sandy was very bitter, and feeling cheated, she snapped, "How come she went back on her word? How could she ruin Sonja's birthday like that? It's not right!"

We talked for a long time about how life wasn't always fair, and how we must do our best to keep a good attitude. We also discussed how it damages your spirit to keep hold of a grudge. We ended our meeting over ice cream (which still didn't make Sandy feel better) and the promise that we would keep looking, and find a good horse for Sonja.

I was so proud of my youngest one when she put her arms around me and said, "Mom, I believe you. I know you will find a horse for me."

Sonja did have a wonderful birthday that year, even without a horse as a surprise gift.

My search ground on. I soon spotted another listing, this time from a family who owned a ranch only five miles from nearby Stratford. They were downsizing their herd and had a horse that sounded suitable. Gail wasn't available, so another neighbor, Connie, who had some knowledge of horses, agreed to go with me. The area was still covered in deep snow, and the ranch a bit off the beaten path, so we followed some written directions their son had provided. He would be the only person at home, and would show us the horse.

His directions weren't entirely clear, and when we came to an unexpected fork in the road, we weren't sure which way to go. I asked Connie to call the young rancher, but she had forgotten her cell phone, and at the time I didn't own one. Since he made no mention of an intersection or turnoff, we continued straight ahead on the recently plowed section. We drove several miles without seeing any houses, and the road was getting narrower. We were about to turn around when Connie spotted a large backhoe a few hundred yards ahead of us, plowing the road.

"That must be the owner," she said. "He's plowing a path for us."

"I wouldn't go any further," I said. "We might get stuck."

She stopped the car, and we began hiking toward the backhoe. Connie, being much taller, easily outdistanced me, and was talking with one of the men for several minutes before I arrived. Her news was disappointing.

"These people aren't the ranchers. They're plowing a road to their mining claim. We're on the wrong road."

"Then let's turn around and go back to the intersection."

We hiked back to the car, but when Connie tried to turn around, the back tires got stuck in an irrigation ditch hidden under the snow. It was obvious we couldn't free ourselves without help, so back to the backhoe we went. The freezing weather was beginning to burn my lungs, and by the time I caught up with Connie, she had borrowed a cell phone from the backhoe operator, and was calling the ranch. The son answered, and Connie explained our situation. He offered to come help us, but Connie said the backhoe operator had already agreed to free us. Connie added, "If we're not at your place in an hour, it means we're still stuck out here." With that, she ended the call and handed the phone back up to the driver. Connie then asked, "Okay, how do we do this?"

The man smiled down at her from the cab and replied, "Well, I'd like to help you, but I can't do it right now. I gotta finish plowin' to the claim. I can help on the way back. Then I need to find the closest hotel with a bar."

Connie's smile faded as he eyed her.

I interrupted, "But it could take hours to finish your plowing, and it's almost dark now."

He frowned at me and shrugged, "It won't be that long."

"Then can I borrow your phone to call my husband?"

"No; I gotta get back to work."

"I don't mind reimbursing you for the minutes I use. Please let me use your phone."

"No, I'm behind schedule," he added gruffly, and then revved up the engine and started plowing again.

I looked at Connie and said, "Let's get back to the car. I've got a bad feeling about this guy." She agreed, and we once more returned to her SUV.

Meanwhile, back at the ranch, the son had tired of waiting for us, and left for a basketball game fifty miles away. By now, it was dark, and Bill had begun to worry. He called Connie's daughter, and asked for her mother's cell number. When he learned she had left her phone at home, he began searching for the number of the rancher. I had scribbled their cell phone number on a notepad, but not labeled it. Bill found it, and since he had no other information, he tried it, and reached the son.

"Is my wife there?"

"No, she never showed up. I'm on my way to a ball game."

"She never made it?"

"No, but she called me an hour ago and said she was stuck on a side road. I offered to help, but she said there was someone there with a backhoe that was gong to take care of them. When she didn't call back, I figured it was because it was dark and they just went on home."

"Well you figured wrong," Bill replied, trying to suppress his anger. "Where exactly are they?"

He gave Bill a description of the turnoff before his cell signal was lost. Bill called Gail and explained the predicament.

Gail said, "I know the family that lives at that intersection, the Andersons. I'll give you their number, and you can call them for help. They're good people, but if they don't answer, call me back, and I'll have one of the boys help you."

Bill managed to reach Mrs. Anderson, and after hearing his story, she replied, "I'll send my son, Jake, on the tractor to find them. If they're still there, he'll pull 'em out."

Meanwhile, back at the SUV, we discussed our options. I expressed my concern that at least one of the men might have ulterior motives, and I really didn't relish the thought of being placed at their mercy. If they'd really wanted to assist us, they would have done so then, and not later at their leisure, in the dark. Connie thought I was overreacting, but even she agreed the one man she'd spoken with was a bit creepy.

We decided it was too dark and cold to hike back to the main road, so we stayed in the car for warmth and protection. We had nothing with which to defend ourselves, if my worst case scenario became true, so we scrounged around and found two fairly stout sticks with pointed tips. It wasn't much, but our choices were extremely limited. I fretted quietly as to how I could have so easily gotten myself into this predicament. In retrospect, it was due to a general lack of planning. I promised myself, if I got out of this situation unscathed, I would never again venture forth without some means of communication and protection.

Several hours passed before we saw the headlights of the backhoe coming back down the mountain. Connie said, "Look, they're finally coming back. Do you feel better now?"

"I'm undecided."

She started the engine and switched on the headlights. When their vehicle reached us, they had to stop because her SUV straddled the narrow road. To my dismay, it was not the backhoe, but a pickup truck that had been accompanying them. I counted four men inside; the backhoe operator was behind the wheel. We got out and approached the truck, and the driver rolled down his window. Without warning, Connie began scolding him for his ungentlemanly behavior earlier. This did nothing to improve the mood, and he glared at her in return.

I tried to calm the situation by pointing out that we were all blocked now, and would need to work together to get out. I then asked politely to use his phone. He did not respond, so I asked again more firmly. He remained silent, therefore I looked past him at the other men and said, "Will one of you loan me your phone?"

The first man had no phone, the second one had no charge on his, and the third man did not respond. I again looked at the driver, and this time said, "I know people are looking for us. The rancher we were going to see, knows where we are. I'm sure my husband has called the sheriff by now, so I know that people are looking for us." I stepped closer to the truck and added firmly, "I want to use your phone—now."

He begrudgingly handed it to me. I walked away from the truck and called Bill. I explained our predicament, and gave him the license plate number on the truck. Bill advised me that help was already on the way. As we talked, two of the men got out of the truck and started milling about. I handed the phone back to the driver, and then Connie and I got back in the SUV and locked the doors.

Thirty minutes later we saw the lights of the Anderson's large tractor approaching. Unbeknown to me, Bill was in regular contact with Mrs. Anderson about the situation. She stood sentry at the end of her driveway when our parade of vehicles finally arrived.

She comforted us by saying, "You're not the first people to fall into the trap of taking that blasted snow road. Folks here prefer to leave it unplowed in the winter." She then threw an icy stare at the men in the truck and added, "We curse anyone who opens it up—because of the confusion it causes strangers."

The truck drove off, none of its passengers offering a word of thanks. Twenty minutes later I was finally home, after 10:00 pm. We'd been gone almost seven hours. Two days later I bought a cell phone, and dropped a grateful thank you note in the mail to the Andersons. We never did see that horse.

Go West, Young Woman!

34

Rory

S HORTLY AFTER SONJA'S SEVENTH BIRTHDAY, I WAS sitting at my dining room table with Gail discussing, once again, the frustration of not yet finding a good horse for my younger daughter. Though sympathetic to my plight, her interest in them really centered around their utility on the ranch. Now cows were another matter. Gail was always interested in discussing them in great detail, since they were her bread and butter. With my dear friend's birthday so close to Sonja's, I liked to invite her up so I could surprise her with my latest cow-themed gifts and share some tea and cake in privacy. This time I had found her several bovine bowls with cows on them, a set of salt and pepper shakers in the shape of very fat Herefords, and a tea set made in the shapes of cows. She was admiring the creamer as milk poured out of the cow's mouth, when we started talking about the price of beef.

Gail was hopeful because beef prices were going up and she was looking forward to increasing her profit this year, once the cows were sold.

"You know what this means, right?" she quizzed me.

"More money for you?" I smiled, lifting an eyebrow.

"Cattle rustling," she said. "We have to watch our cows."

"You've got to be joking. Does that still happen?" I replied, completely taken aback.

My mind wandered back to the old Western movies I had seen on TV. I thought for sure that rustling had died out with the stage coach.

"Of course," she continued. "We've been lucky, but some of our neighbors have lost thirty or fifty head from their herds. They disappear, just like that." Gail snapped her fingers.

"They have brands and I know you tag their ears. Who'd buy them?" I asked, intrigued by the whole idea.

"Cows can be re-branded. If someone really wants to sell them, they'll find a way." She sipped her tea and bit into a biscuit.

I shook my head. *Some things never change.* "Maybe you should raise bulls. I understood they can be sold for hundreds, if not thousands of dollars. Rustlers might not want to mess with them."

"Yeah, and neither do I. Bulls are a lot of trouble, and we don't need the headache. They have to be raised separately from the herd; you know, bulls will be bulls," she laughed. "And if you register them, you're responsible for making sure their offspring are pure-blooded."

Gail then leaned across from me and whispered *sotto voce*, "You know the bull can damage himself if he's too eager." She nodded seriously.

I thought about this for a moment, then grinned sheepishly, "You mean he can break his man-part?" I was trying to choose my words delicately. "Is that possible?"

"Yep," she replied, spacing her hands in the air about two feet apart. "You know it's about this long!"

I burst out laughing. "Won't it heal up on its own?"

"No," Gail said, laughing with me. "Once it's broke, the bull is hamburger. He has no future."

"I'm sorry, Gail," I chuckled while trying to pull myself together. "I shouldn't laugh at such a thing. It really is not funny, the poor bull." I was still trying to quiet myself down, giggling between my words.

Gail just grinned, "It's funny and okay to laugh. That's why I only have a few of them."

"And that's no bull!" I blurted out as we both broke into hysterics.

Later that evening I repeated our conversation to Bill. His only comment was, "If I were that bull, I'd sure wanna die."

The following morning I found myself back searching through internet advertisements again. I decided to widen my search and look at neighboring towns. I had not seen anything in Helena for some time, so I looked in Butte, Bozeman, and Missoula, hoping I would see a horse that would fit our needs. I knew it was a gamble. There were numerous intermediate horses and young green horses to be found everywhere, but horses for beginners or children were very hard to find. They often sold the same day the ad was posted. Many times I called about a horse, only to be told that someone was buying it that afternoon, or it had already been picked up that morning. So while the idea of traveling several hours to look at a horse didn't seem very feasible, I had to at least investigate the possibility.

I found an ad posted in Missoula for a horse that was about twenty years old, a little older than I wanted, but if he had been well cared for, he might be worth meeting. It said he was a child's horse that had been used in the 4H horse program a few years prior. I was familiar with the program because Sandy was currently enrolled in it with our horse, Belle. This horse, Rory, was supposed to be good with children and was priced at $750. I called and spoke to a woman who turned out to be the broker. She was stabling the horse, and helping the owners by taking calls and showing the gelding to prospective buyers. "Their son has grown out of the horse and the family can't keep him due to a personal crisis, but they want him to go to a good home."

"Does he have any problems?" I asked.

"He does have a problem in one leg, but it doesn't affect his soundness any. He'll never be a barrel racer, but he's fine for a beginner child," she replied.

"When was the photo taken?" I asked.

"I'm not really sure; it was given to me to post, but I don't think it's too old."

"I'll let my trainer know and call you back if we want to set an appointment."

Linda agreed it was worth investigating, so we set an appointment on the condition that we were to be informed in advance if the horse sold before we got there. Linda's schedule prevented her from going to Missoula until the end of the week. The broker offered to hold the horse for a couple of days until we could come by.

"My main concern is finding a happy home for this horse and I really have a good feeling about you. I've had several inquires, but felt you could give him the best life."

I was so pleased to hear this news, that it seemed almost too good to be true. If it was true, we had found Sonja's horse. When we arrived in Missoula, my feelings were immediately dashed. I saw a horse in the round pen, but wondered whether or not it was the one that we had come to see.

The short-haired brunette who greeted us was the same woman I'd talked with on the phone. Next to her stood a middle-aged man whom she introduced as the owner. "Here he is," she beamed with a warm smile. "This is Rory."

This is not the horse in the picture. A hundred miles of driving and a day wasted for us and Linda's work. This is not good. We all looked at each other. I wanted to get back in the car and drive away. Bill looked really angry. I felt sad for the horse. The poor animal was really showing his age, and looked *nothing* like his photo. He was definitely older than twenty, maybe somewhere between twenty-five to twenty-eight. His back was swayed and his coat was worn. He had a warm gentle look in his eyes, so I knew he was a nice fellow, but he didn't look well. I wondered, *Just how old was that photo?*

"Let's look him over," I said quietly to Linda. "After all, we've come this far."

Linda began to assess the horse as the rest of us moved to the pen to saddle him up. Linda got on and rode him a short lap around one side of the pen before putting him into a trot. He began to throw his head up with each step, but was clearly trying his best. Linda got off and examined his front leg, then questioned the owner about it. They were in the middle of the round pen, speaking quietly, but I could see the owner was becoming angry; his lips now appearing terse on his weathered face. With persistence, Linda asked him more questions. I heard her mention the cannon bone, and then a few more brief words passed between them. I could not make them out, but the man clearly was becoming more agitated and vocal. As their conversation grew more intense, I asked the girls to go wait in the car, but they begged to get a ride on Rory. Linda walked over and said the girls could ride him. Sonja and Sandy both took turns for a few minutes, and this nice horse did what was asked without hesitation or complaint.

As we watched them ride, Linda noted quietly, "Do you see how his head shoots up every time his front foot hits the ground?"

"Yes I do," I responded in an equally low voice.

"That horse is in pain," she went on. "I found out he has been on anti-inflammatory medications and painkillers for almost a year."

"I wondered what you two were talking about. I could see it was getting rather heated." I took a deep breath and continued, "That's so sad. Even in pain, see how hard he's trying to do what he's asked? This guy has a great heart."

I wanted to take him home and help this poor fellow, but the cold reality was this was not the horse for Sonja. Not wanting to hurt this horse any further, I called in Sonja and we all began talking about the horse.

As we discussed our options, the owner became increasingly impatient. He wanted us to take the horse immediately, which wasn't possible because we had not brought a trailer. He also was annoyed that the broker had agreed to hold him for couple of days for us. I saw no point in telling him his horse was not what had been advertised. The broker looked mortified, and I thought she must not know all the details about this animal. She was just focused on trying to find him a loving home. The owner became more frustrated when Linda offered the idea of a trial period.

"I have an excellent vet in Helena; maybe she can help him. If I could arrange to meet you halfway, I could transfer him to my trailer…"

The owner cut her off and briskly snorted, "I'm not doing that. My horse is fine and worth every penny and more. There will be no negotiating."

It was finished. I knew we could not buy this horse and I understood why. We were not skilled enough to help him, assuming he could be helped at all. However, I did not want to step on Linda's toes in front of everyone. She was really trying to make this work.

The broker chimed in, her voice desperate, "He really is a nice horse."

I looked her in the eye and felt her dismay. "I know he is a kind horse with a good heart. I'm sorry it didn't work out..." I paused, looking at Rory, "...for all of us."

We got back in the car, and I glanced at everyone. The girls were once more dejected and disappointed; Bill was fuming; Linda appeared almost despondent at yet another failure; and I was embarrassed that I had wasted everyone's afternoon because I was the one who asked that we see this horse.

"Oh, Mom," said Sandy, "I swear, if I'd known Rory was in pain, I *never* would have gotten on him."

"Me too," added Sonja.

"Every time I see a horse, I learn something. I guess it's all just one big learning experience," I said philosophically. I was upset on our long trip home, and felt sad for poor old Rory. I just prayed that he would find a caring owner and spend the remainder of his time in a loving environment.

35

Meet Mr. Wilson

A MONTH PASSED, AND I WAS STILL FEELING THE BRUISES from our last horse encounter, when the phone jarred me from my thoughts. It was Linda.

"I want to tell you about a horse," she said excitedly. "He is more than you want to spend, but he would be perfect for Sonja. He used to be one of my lesson horses."

"What is more than I want to spend?"

"He's $2,500."

Ouch. "Tell me about him," I said.

Linda was so excited, she repeated herself, "He used to be one of mine; I used him for lessons. His name is Wilson, and he's a flea bitten grey gelding, about fifteen hands high, and eight years old. He has a great temperament and is very calm and sweet. I sold him to a friend of mine in another part of the state. They've had him for a while, but are expecting their first child now, and can't put the time into Wilson. They contacted me and asked me to help sell him."

"Do you think he's worth the money?" I asked her sincerely.

"Yes I do. He is a reliable guy for beginners. He's the lowest ranking member of most any herd, so he won't challenge you much at all, and he's nice and agreeable, which makes him a good horse for a child."

I took in all she said and agreed he sounded promising. "I'll talk it over with Bill and call you back."

I hung up the phone and did some thinking. If he was all Linda said he was, then he was worth the money. I had been looking for nearly seven months, and my first concern was always Sonja's safety. I knew riding a horse was always a risk, but choosing the right horse did bring that factor down.

I slowly walked behind the house to Bill's shop and pondered his reaction to the price. I found him working inside, focused hard on one of his projects. I explained the phone call from Linda, all the while fearing my interruption of his routine, coupled with the asking price of the horse, would cause him to balk. But to my surprise and relief, he said Wilson seemed worth meeting.

"If he's that young and reliable, I don't mind spending the money. We should get plenty of years out of him."

I was relieved and elated, "I was hoping you would say that. I'll call Linda back and tell her we want to meet Wilson."

"Great!" was Linda's reply. "Wilson will be arriving at my barn in a few days. Right now he's living about six hours away."

The arrangements were made, and we were present to see Wilson get off the horse trailer. He was brought into the barn and put in a stall. My girls' eager faces looked through the gate. There he stood, with his white coat dotted with light brown specks, a light grey nose, a white mane, and a matching white tail that brushed the ground. He had pleasant looking eyes and seemed quite at ease after his long journey.

"He has two spots in the shape of hearts on his shoulder," Linda offered as she pointed to them.

"Hearts!" Sonja exclaimed. She loved hearts and was often found drawing them on the cards and letters that she made for me to use as bookmarks.

Linda explained that she wanted Wilson to settle in for a couple of days. "I just want to be sure he's the same horse he was when I sold him. After I've had a chance to ride him, I'll know for sure if I can recommend him to you."

I thanked her for being so conscientious and agreed to wait to hear back from her. Those days anxiously dragged by, and I kept myself busy, in part, by trying some new baking recipes. I was just taking a loaf of fragrant strawberry bread out of the oven when the phone rang.

"He is the same Wilson!" Linda announced gleefully.

"Great," I paused, "so you think we should try him out?"

"I do. When can you come over?"

"I'll check our schedule, but let's try for tomorrow."

The next day we found ourselves inside Linda's new indoor arena. It was a huge facility, with stalls and a tack room on one side, and a riding area over 50 feet wide by 150 feet long. The rocky ground had been covered with several inches of soft clean dirt to serve as padding, in the event someone fell. Wilson stood inside, tied and haltered, calmly waiting for us. The girls began by brushing him, and a beaming Sonja called me over after she located his heart birthmarks. I looked at Wilson, admiring the two cute brown hearts Sonja pointed to. She then set to work cleaning his feet with a hoof pick. As she worked on his feet, Wilson lowered his head and sniffed her hair, gently resting his nose on the top of her head. It was a beautiful sight.

When Sonja had finished all four feet, Linda mounted him and began to give a demonstration of his abilities by riding him around the arena, first at a walk, then a trot, and finally a lope. She backed him up and side-stepped him. She finished by halting him in the middle of the arena, and then standing up on top of his saddle. "You see how gentle he is. I can't do this with just any horse." She stood there with both arms extended like a trick rider. Then after a few moments, she settled back down in the saddle and rode over to us.

The girls took turns riding him about the arena. Sonja was in Heaven, the expression of joy never leaving her face. After both girls had finished riding, Linda turned to me and asked, "Do you want to try him?"

"Oh, no, that's okay," I began to stammer.

"She does, put her on," Bill commanded, as though he were addressing one of his airmen. I turned to look at him, and there he stood, holding my back brace and riding helmet, which he had quietly retrieved from the car.

"Give it a try," he said, as he looked at me encouragingly. I stood there not knowing what to do. "You need to do this for the kids, and for yourself."

"Okay," I smiled weakly.

I slipped into my brace and helmet as Wilson was led over to the mounting block. I climbed aboard, and found it was a strange feeling. I was sitting higher than I had the few times I had been on Belle. And like her, I knew Wilson was very much alive, and able to toss me like a rag onto the dirt floor, if he chose to. Yet he seemed rather unconcerned I was there. He was very solid and heavy, and as I looked down to plant my feet in the leather stirrups, I sensed his muscular sides hidden behind his brown-speckled, soft white hair.

"How does it feel?" both Bill and Linda inquired.

In between the squeals from Sandy and Sonja, I answered, "It feels alright."

Linda told me she was going to take one step, and holding the lead rope, she moved the horse forward. I felt myself sway gently to one side and stop.

"How about another step?" Linda asked.

"Go ahead," I replied, in a voice that sounded more confident than it really was. In only a few minutes Linda had led me around the indoor arena and out the barn doors into the fresh air. I was gently rocking to the horse's rhythm and listening to the delighted voices of my family.

"Mom is on Wilson!" Sonja chortled.

They followed us outside and were enjoying the show. I could see Bill was pleased too, and I had to admit it was a fun, new experience. When my ride was over, I carefully dismounted and unleashed my back brace. The relief was instant, like removing a tight corset. I really liked this horse, and could find nothing wrong, save possibly the price. After thinking it over, we made an offer of two thousand dollars for Wilson. Linda promised to call her friends and let us know their reply later that night.

After dinner that evening, we were sitting in our living room when the phone rang and Bill answered it.

"Your offer has been rejected," Linda explained, "The owners want full price for Wilson, and they won't negotiate."

Bill looked at me, his hand over the phone. "What do you want to do?"

I searched his face for an answer, but I knew it was now my decision to make. I hesitated for a moment. Thinking about the facts of this situation, I mentally listed them, both the pros and the cons. With a deep breath I said, "I believe he is worth the price."

Bill immediately replied to Linda, "It's done; we'll take him."

He handed the phone to me, and Linda and I worked out the details of the sale. Before hanging up she said, "I'm glad you bought him. I didn't want to sell him to anyone but you guys."

After I hung up the phone, I immediately called the girls from upstairs. I could barely contain my excitement before I announced, "Girls, Wilson is ours!"

Two little mouths fell open wide, then turned into huge smiles and squeals of laughter as they hugged me and competed to speak at the same time.

"I can't believe it! I really wanted him for Sonja," Sandy shouted.

"We can really have Wilson?" Sonja asked cautiously. "He really is ours to keep?"

"Just as soon as his papers arrive from the owner, we can bring him home," I answered, with my heart beating a little faster. I was so happy that we could give Sonja her dream. It meant a great deal to me to do this for her.

"I knew you would keep your promise to me, Mom," Sonja said, hugging me tightly and nearly cutting off my breath.

With a small tear in my eye, I told her, "Love Lamb, I do my best."

Several weeks passed as we waited for the paperwork, which still had not arrived. In the meantime we went to visit and ride Wilson at Linda's barn. One afternoon I was alarmed when Linda told me Wilson had had an accident.

"What is it?" I asked feeling a small wave of nausea pass through my stomach.

"I put him in the paddock with some other horses and he got kicked in the front leg."

I knew how serious this could be and wondered if yet another dream had ended before it had begun.

"How bad is he injured?" I asked.

"Not bad enough to cause any permanent damage, but he does have a cut on his leg. It looks worse than it is, and I believe it will heal up."

I questioned her further, and Linda said she had recently moved him to a new paddock with a different group of horses. One of them must have kicked him. She promised me he would be alright, and agreed we should come out and evaluate him for ourselves. When I saw his leg, I was reminded how brutal horses can be to one another. It was scraped open and bleeding just below the knee area. The girls became immediately concerned when they watched Linda clean the wound. But I noticed that even though he was in pain, Wilson remained calm, standing perfectly still while Linda scrubbed the area with an antibiotic soap and rinsed it with the garden hose. This impressed me because I had watched other horses jump away in fear just from seeing a garden hose.

Linda said confidently, "I promise I'll treat his wound until it's healed, along with the rain rot that has showed up on his side."

"What's that?" I asked.

"It's a fungal infection caused by an area of the skin staying wet too long and not getting good air circulation." As she spoke, she applied a Betadine solution on his skin, which she claimed would clear it up after several repeat applications. By now I was becoming anxious, so many problems in such a short time, and we hadn't even gotten him home yet. What might happen next? Would he recover, or develop an infection that would require a more drastic treatment? Might his skin infection leave scarring that would ruin his beauty or make saddling uncomfortable? These were absurd notions, but I couldn't block them from my mind until he was better.

Thankfully, Wilson did heal up quickly. His leg was looking better and his skin condition disappeared. It reminded me of those acne commercials on television where they show the teenagers with "before and after" skin. Now he was like the smiling teen whose skin treatment was successful, and he was looking forward to the future, able to face the world again.

His papers finally arrived, and we set a delivery date. We opted to surprise the girls so we could see their expression when Linda's horse trailer came up our drive. I also was curious to see the expression on Belle's face when Wilson arrived. I hadn't long to wait; the following morning I heard the sound of a Linda's truck and trailer coming up the road. She circled and parked near our front door. As Linda exited the truck, the girls raced up to greet her with a barrage of questions.

"You brought your trailer," Sandy observed. "Do you have a horse in there?" she asked anxiously.

"Don't I always have a horse if I bring a trailer?" Linda mused.

"Is it Wilson?" quizzed Sonja. Her blue eyes were huge with anticipation, as her words hung in the air. Her little body stood still, almost petrified the answer might be "no."

"It's Wilson," Linda answered with a smile, as she unlatched the back of the trailer door and lowered the ramp.

Wilson calmly stepped out to see his new home, while the girls cheered and jumped about. One would have thought a movie star had just descended into a group of his adoring fans. Hearts were fluttering and excitement ruled the air. But down below, a hundred yards away, someone else was not so admiring or welcoming. Belle, upon hearing the commotion at the house, looked up from the barn area and walked to the edge of the corral, starring over the gate. She let out a loud whinny that caught our attention. *"Who is this intruder?"*

"Somebody's anxious to meet the latest member of the family," I commented.

"Then let's not keep her waiting," Linda replied.

We walked Wilson down to the corral, and as he strolled he looked about the pasture, pausing occasionally to sample the green grass. *Wow, all this for me?* As he approached, Belle eyed him intently. Bill went into the corral first and walked Belle over to the side of the round pen.

Linda brought Wilson inside the gate, "Don't worry, Belle and Wilson know each other. They were both at my place. They just need to get reacquainted."

She walked him into the round pen and shut the gate. We placed troughs of food and water in with him. Linda's goal was to keep the two horses near each other, but separated for a couple of days until they renewed their bonds. Once Belle was more accepting of Wilson's presence in her territory, Wilson could be freed from the round pen.

Bill released Belle from her halter and the show began. We all stood back as Belle approached the round pen. Wilson immediately began eating hay, which for the first time, he did not have to share or wait his turn for. It was all his, and he was taking full advantage of the privilege.

My mind wandered back to images of Wilson at Linda's paddock. He was always in a corner, his hind end backed up into the fence line for cover, while his head and chest faced forward, completely unprotected. I would watch as the other horses tried to bite him and force him from his spot, moving him around just because they could. I thought what a terrible way to live, but in horse society, as well as in human society, someone is always at the bottom. *Those days are over, Wilson; there is only one horse to lead you around now.* Even though Belle was bossy, I did not believe she would actually bite Wilson or bloody him.

Belle stood at the edge of the round pen, inspecting this new interloper. She thrust her head over the metal pipe panel. As Wilson lifted his head to look at Belle, she suddenly reared up with her front legs in the air and let out a high pitched noise that I thought only movie dinosaurs could make. It was a mix of a loud shriek and a grunt, complete with waving feet and shaking head, just for the dramatic effect. Belle really wanted to get her point across, which was, *"I'm in charge around here and you must understand this now and at all times!"*

Wilson stood by, quietly looking at her, rather unimpressed, as he munched his hay. This upset our drama queen diva, and so she made another attempt at driving home her point, this time adding foot stomping to her flailing, and making even louder dinosaur noises (or was she imitating Godzilla?). Wilson remained passive, and was focused on enjoying his hay, seemingly aware he was protected by the round pen. He just accepted her theatrics as part of the welcoming ritual. What could be better than dinner and a show?

Belle paced alongside the pen, then decided to get a bite of the hay, irritated that this newcomer was eating *her* hay while all she could do was watch. She pushed her nose through the panel and laid back her ears at Wilson, grabbing a mouthful of the hay. Wilson stepped back without interfering.

Emboldened by her success, she went for another mouthful, but this time

Wilson leaned in and quickly snatched a bit of it right out of Belle's mouth! I thought for sure she would rear up into another tantrum, but instead she relented and acted as if nothing had happened. She continued eating, and so did Wilson. The first thread of a friendship was forming.

"They'll be okay," Linda confidently announced, as she turned to head back to her truck. "Just give 'em some time to settle in."

After a couple of days, we decided to put Belle and Wilson together in the front meadow. We had cordoned off a few acres with temporary electric fence. In case Belle decided to assert herself with Wilson, I wanted him to have enough space in which to run and get away from her.

Bill took Wilson to one end of the pasture and I took Belle to the other. We removed the halters and let them begin grazing. They were so interested in the fresh green grass that they totally ignored each other. Soon they both began to wander toward each other and ended up in the center of the meadow, eating alongside like best friends. Wilson was happy with his new life and Belle was accepting him, so all was well—for now.

"I'm glad that's over," I said with relief. "They were so busy eating, nothing else mattered."

Of course Belle did not always have a gracious and sharing nature with Wilson. We fed them dry hay in two different areas of the corral to avoid any confrontation over food. It was comical to watch Belle race from one end to the other, trying to keep two troughs of hay for herself. Her confidence grew until one day when she walked up to Wilson and pushed him off his trough of hay. He stepped back, but must have been "feeling his oats," because he decided to try getting around her. I watched this exchange with interest. Belle walked over and let him know with ears pinned, *"Wilson move, this is my hay."*

"Okay, sure," his face implied. Then he stood back for a moment before leaning in and slowly opening his mouth to take one more little strand of hay with his lips.

"How about now?" his eyes questioned.

"No!" she clearly said with a nip in his direction. He pulled back.

"But now is okay, right?" he leaned in again.

"NO!"

"Now is good, eh?" He moved his head an inch closer.

"No Wilson." Belle quickly thrust her head at him again.

"It's okay this time, right?"

"I said no."

"This is a good time, huh?"

"No, get away!"

"But now is good."

"Fine!"

Belle finally let poor Wilson get that tiny bite of hay. It was comical to watch, but instructive as well in the psychology of how horses think. She continued to ignore him as he ate on his side of the trough. Belle had confirmed her dominance, but I had to give Wilson credit for being so persistent. I never understood why he didn't walk over to the other trough and eat in peace alone. Maybe that evening he wanted some company with dinner.

After eating, Wilson always went for a drink of water. He would take a sip, raise his head, and hang out his tongue. He flapped and wiggled it up and down while smacking his lips. We always were amused by this cute sight, and I think he enjoyed it when the girls laughed and made comments. It never failed to get him plenty of attention. Sometimes I think that's why he put on such a show.

Now that Wilson had time to settle in his new home, we agreed Sonja could ride him outside her normal lessons, but only under our supervision. She brought him to his hitching post and began brushing and grooming "her Wilson," as she had come to regard him. She really enjoyed herself and was looking forward to a ride, but when Sandy casually announced her eagerness to try him, Sonja suddenly twirled around and emphatically said, "NO! He's my horse and I'll ride him. I don't want you ruining him with the wrong signals."

"Well, Sonja," Sandy coyly added, "if only *you* ride him, how will Linda be able to train him?"

"Fine," Sonja sharply replied. "No one else except Linda and me will ride him."

"But Sonja…," Sandy cooed, as the tension rose, "he's my horse too."

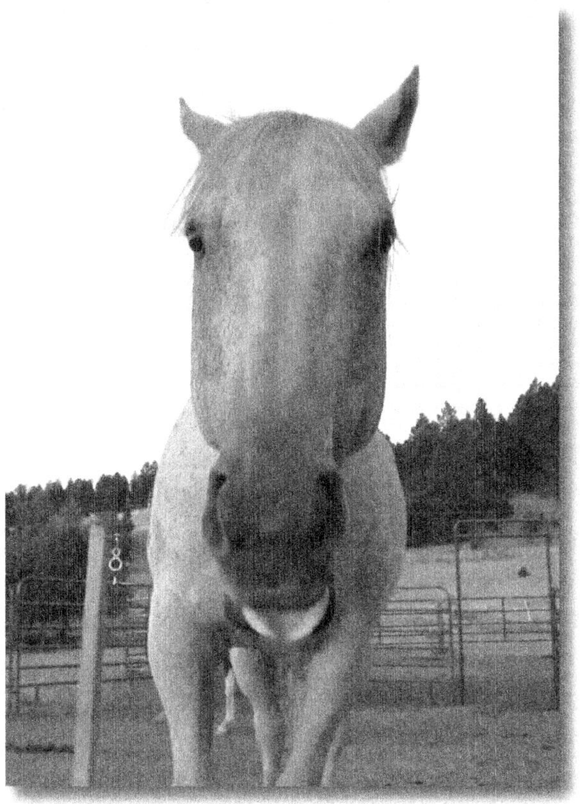

The ever-handsome Wilson

"MOM!" Sonja yelled in anger, while Wilson stood silently, unflappable.

"What is it?" I asked, somewhat startled.

"Sandy says Wilson is her horse, too, and she gets to ride him."

Before responding, I looked at Sonja's red face and watched her little chest quickly rise and fall with each breath. I recognized the signs of stress. Sandy was tormenting her, so I had to choose my response carefully.

"Honey Bear," I said as sweetly as I could, "of course Wilson is your horse. And you are the primary rider. But don't you think it's alright for your sister to ride him on occasion, just as you ride Belle?"

"No, she'll ruin him," Sonja responded in defiance. As if to emphasize her point, she folded her arms tightly and stood rigidly with both feet firmly planted on the ground.

I wasn't going to get anywhere as long as she was upset, so I switched tactics and replied sternly, "Sonja, we can discuss this later. Right now let's focus on grooming and saddling Wilson."

She looked up and eyed me suspiciously, "Okay, but I'm not letting her ride my horse. She might break him."

I laughed at the thought of a ninety pound girl breaking a 1,200 pound horse, but I knew what she meant. "That's enough grooming for now. Are his hooves clean?"

She nodded affirmatively, so I sent her to get his tack. Linda had shown me how Wilson liked to have the bit put in his mouth. All horses are different, and he particularly liked it accomplished a certain way. I had put bits in Belle's mouth many times and was confident I could do Wilson, even if he was a bigger horse. When I approached him, he started to back up and turn his head. I was calm and moved him a few steps forward with reassuring words. I looped the reins over his head and started to bring the bridle toward his face when he suddenly jerked his head up high.

"Now Wilson," I chided him, "stop this and put your head down." I tried again with the same result. I thought about what had happened and mentally checked my procedure. I was doing everything I had been taught.

Sonja stood watching us intently. I glanced back at her and said encouragingly, "I think Wilson just has to get used to me. We'll get it."

But we didn't. Wilson kept flinging his head in the air and even tried to walk away. Bill came over and offered to help. After a couple of tries, he too was frustrated.

"Roy always put the bridle on over the halter when the horse was still tied to the post. Perhaps that's worth a try," I offered.

Bill haltered Wilson and tied the lead rope to the hitching post.

"I'm going to cinch it down so he can't raise his head, then maybe we can get the bridle on him."

But when he approached him with the bridle, Wilson panicked, threw his head in the air, and jumped back. The lead rope held under the strain, but the hitching post didn't. I heard a loud crack and pop. The hitching post had snapped in two pieces and Wilson darted away with the top of the post dragging behind him, still attached to the lead rope.

Now free from restraint, Wilson quickly calmed down and stood beside the tack room. I looked at the two jagged edges of the post and then at Wilson in disbelief.

"What happened?" I said with great alarm.

A very upset Sonja was almost in tears. Bill looked frustrated and angry. He picked up the pieces of the broken post and took the halter off of the now calm Wilson, who stood alongside all of us as if nothing had happened. I offered comfort to my daughter and her horse. I was at a loss as to what to do next. Everyone was shaken, so I thought it was best to end this attempt at riding now before someone got hurt.

Sandy turned to her little sister and cautiously said, "You know Sonja, I think you're right. Only you should ride Wilson. I'll stick with Belle."

"I'll call Linda," I said limply. I felt emotionally drained, unhappy, and defeated at that moment. Had I made a huge mistake in judgment? As I slowly made my way up to the house to get Linda's number, my thoughts turned to reviewing the whole puzzling affair. *Did I buy a $2,500 problem? Why would Wilson react that way? I've put a bridle in his mouth before. Why was he so afraid? Is he so particular that only Linda can saddle him?*

I dreaded making the call to Linda, but I had to find out what to do right now; it couldn't wait. Normally I'd always ask her if it is a convenient time to talk, since I knew she might be in the middle of a lesson or working with a new horse. But this time I just blurted out my problem as soon as she answered the phone.

I heard the irritation in her voice when she snapped, "Oh great, now I have to fix him."

I did not speak for a moment. If she was frustrated, then there really must be a problem. I was doing my best I assured her, but she clearly thought this was my fault. I told her I felt like Wilson was definitely refusing the bit and then he got scared, but I couldn't fathom why. We talked it over and decided it was best not to bridle him until our next lesson with Linda.

"Wilson is used to having the bit put in his mouth a certain way. I'll show you again next time."

By the time Linda arrived two days later, we had replaced the broken hitching post. I showed her the old post which we'd stored in the tack room.

"Broke it like a toothpick," Bill commented.

"Well I'm not surprised," Linda responded. "You never, ever want to tie a horses head down. If they can't move their head around, they panic. It's a perfectly normal reaction."

"Yeah, I know that now," Bill smiled sheepishly.

Once back outside, Linda instructed me again how to place the bit in Wilson's mouth. Her technique appeared no differently from what I had done, and I told her as much.

"That is what I do; let me try again," I said, taking the bit gently out of Wilson's mouth.

I held the bit in my left hand and guided it up to his mouth. With my right hand I held the headstall over his nose and slipped it up his head. I placed one thumb in the corner of his mouth where there are no teeth and urged him to open up.

"Push your thumb back in there more and get him to open up," Linda instructed.

"My thumb is in as far as it will go," I said earnestly.

"Oh that can't be true. I have small hands and no one has hands smaller than mine."

"There is no more," I insisted, looking over Wilson's nose at Linda. I gently wiggled my thumb up and down, and finally Wilson opened his mouth. I quickly slipped in the snaffle bit and lifted the rest of the bridle over his head, secured it over his ears, and fastened the throat latch.

"Let me see your hands," Linda demanded. "Hold them up to mine."

I offered her my hand and we held them up to each other, palms touching.

"Wow, your hands really are small. I've never met someone with hands smaller then mine. Now I know why this was a challenge for you and Wilson."

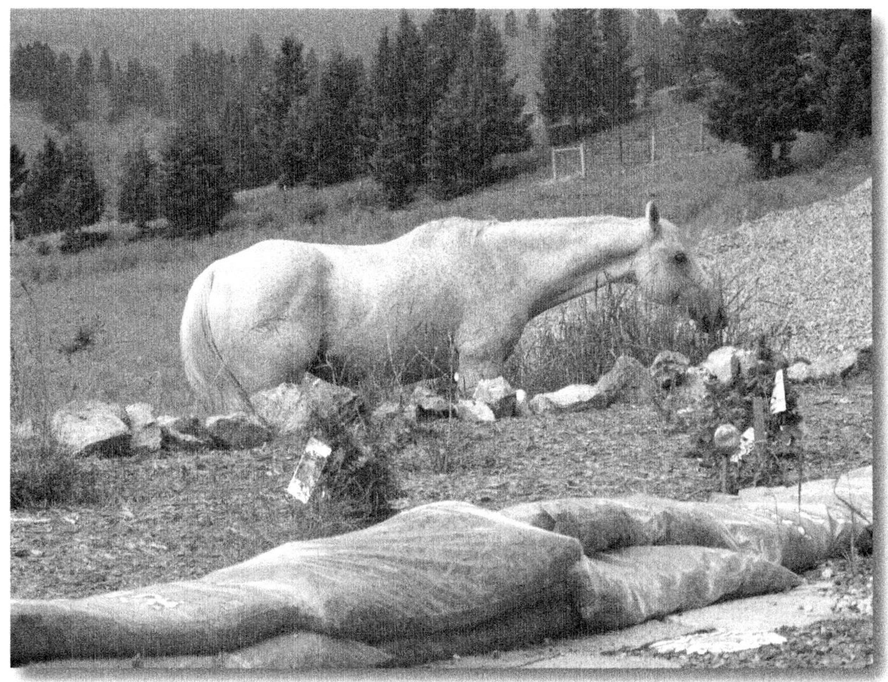

Wilson, our landscape architect

We practiced the procedure repeatedly until I fully grasped it. I still couldn't see where I'd done anything wrong before. Maybe Wilson had sensed my hesitation, or perhaps I wasn't standing exactly as he expected me to. Or maybe he just wasn't used to me bridling him. Whatever the reason, he behaved well now. The rest of the lesson progressed smoothly and I began to regain some of my confidence that we had purchased the right horse. This notion was further bolstered when Sandy once again asked if she could ride Wilson.

The latest crisis had passed, and one more lesson in Montana rural life had been learned the hard way, but it had been learned.

Go West, Young Woman!

36

Trouble's a Foot

I WAS CLEANING UP THE TACK ROOM AS I HEARD laughter coming up the hill from the creek. The girls had been on a short trail ride with Linda. I saw her on the ground leading Wilson by the reins.

"Wilson's feet hurt. I had to get off and walk him," Linda called to me.

She brought him through the gate and came towards me. She was right, he was limping and slightly shuffling his feet.

"You have rocky soil here. I think he has to get used to it. His feet should toughen up in time. He'll get over it."

I watched Wilson carefully for weeks, but he did not improve. He worsened as time passed. In a matter of weeks he was completely lame. He could barely shuffle his feet to walk, and he was losing weight. I felt as sick as he did. Sonja was beside herself with worry. She could not ride him, and Wilson was clearly suffering. I had some friends take a look at him, and they all offered different opinions, or just did not know. I heard everything from founder, to laminitis, to cannon bone. I decided it had gone on long enough.

"We must get Wilson into the vet," I told Linda one morning, my voice desperate with concern. "I would like to use the one you recommend in town; Hanna, wasn't it? Wilson can't go on like this, and frankly, neither can I. We don't have a trailer. Will you come pick him up and take him to

223

the vet's office? I tried to make an appointment, but the vet can't come out to our place for at least two weeks. He really needs to be seen now."

Linda agreed, and assured me she would get him to Hanna right away. It was something of a relief when she arrived the next morning with her trailer. She dropped him off at the clinic in Helena, and we arranged to meet with Hanna later that afternoon. When we arrived at her office, Hanna came out to meet us. She was a tall, sturdy woman, about my age, with light brown hair. She had a kindly smile, and a soft-spoken, easy-going manner. She apologized to us that an emergency had come up, and asked if we could return in a couple of hours. We agreed, and later that afternoon we were all standing in an open air stall. Hanna looked at Wilson's feet and his overall appearance. We waited anxiously for her diagnosis and prognosis.

Hanna instructed me to walk Wilson around. He was such a gentle soul, that even in pain, he was calm and obedient. I held his lead rope and whispered encouragingly in his ear.

"I see the problem. The wall of his front hooves are separating. I'd like to keep him for a few days," Hanna said. "I want to fit his front feet with corrective shoes today, and watch him for a while. I don't want him moving around too much right now. I also want to float his teeth. That may be part of the reason he's losing weight. Horses often lose weight when they're in pain."

Talking with Hanna proved eye opening. She had plenty of experience with horse feet; she'd been a farrier for many years before attending veterinary college. I felt Wilson was in good hands. I looked at Sonja and the tears were streaming down her face.

"I don't want to leave my Wilson," she said. I put my arms around his little lifeguard and explained why this was for the best. Hanna overheard our conversation, and came over. She knelt down and began speaking to Sonja in her soft voice, offering her comfort, and explaining again why she wanted to keep Wilson with her for only a few days. I watched Sonja's face, and soon the tears began to subside. I was glad our equine vet took those few extra moments to help her. I was pleased that she cared enough about our situation to offer such help. Not every vet I've known would have done so.

Sonja hugged Wilson goodbye, and we walked out of the office holding hands.

"It's only for a few days. He'll be home soon," I whispered in Sonja's ear.

The next day I was pleased to pick up the phone and hear Hanna's voice. "Wilson is doing better than expected. I think he needs to come home and get back to work."

Sonja was ecstatic over the news. The doctor was prescribing therapeutic riding, and after all, Wilson's job was to let Sonja ride him around the field, and be groomed by her, and glittered with horse paint. In other words, his purpose in life was to make Sonja happy. Hanna also recommended we start Wilson on a hoof supplement to help him grow a better hoof. I agreed and told her I would make all the arrangements for Wilson's immediate return home. The girls got to spend the afternoon riding their horses. Wilson's feet slowly improved with his new corrective shoes, and he was happier. He also began to put back on some weight. For once, the stars seemed to align.

Go West, Young Woman!

37

Season of the Grizzly

FEW ANIMALS THREATEN MAJOR LIVESTOCK OR HORSES. Wolves operating in a pack may prey on the young or the sick if they are separated from the herd. A cougar, if truly desperate from hunger or pain, might attempt it, but doing so risks injury, and injuries can prove fatal if the ability to hunt is impaired. Of all the predators that roam this state, only bears possess the size and strength required to singly confront a full grown, healthy horse. And among bears, only one subtype is generally regarded as having the predisposition to do so, *Ursus arctos horribilis*— more commonly know as the "grizzly." First recorded in writing by the Lewis & Clark expedition, where it was initially called a "white bear," they had long been the subject of ancient Indian lore. The myths, the legends, and the reality of the grizzly are so intermingled that it is difficult even now to separate fact from fiction.

I had always known that bears roamed our place. Gail and her family had seen them as close as a hundred yards from our back door when checking their herds or looking for lost cows. These were mostly black bears (*Ursus americanus*), a smaller and less aggressive cousin of the brown bear, to which species the grizzly belongs. But even a black bear can be dangerous when properly aroused. One female "blackie" had a den in a cave on the back of our property. Chase, Gail's son, once came upon the

227

mother black bear and her two cubs. She was so upset upon seeing Chase that she charged the truck he and his father were driving, without injury to either party or the truck. I admitted the idea of bears living nearby made me uncomfortable, but what really concerned me was the grizzly bear.

Earlier in our friendship I had commented to Gail, "I'm worried about bears."

"I would be too with your girls so young," Gail seriously replied. "Most of the time bears are afraid of you and will run away, but sometimes…" her voice trailed off and I knew what she was referring to. She had called me earlier that same morning to tell me about a grizzly bear attack on a hunter near Sealy Lake, a rugged wooded area about eighty miles away from us. But any bear attack was worth paying attention to.

She explained the likely reason for the attack. "The hunter had killed an elk and was skinning it out when the grizzly bear came upon him. He was alone and startled the bear when it came on the fresh carcass. He didn't survive the sudden attack."

It was a chilling story for such a beautiful sunny morning, but Gail's point was not lost on me.

"I'll keep an eye out," I promised. I could always count on Gail to apprise me of any current local area news I should be aware of. She was better than the emergency broadcast system.

"You should get the girls bear spray," Gail cautioned.

"And you should carry a gun," I countered. "Bill can pick one out for you. He got me a .44 Magnum to carry when we hike the trail."

"A pint-size like you carrying a big gun? The recoil must knock you off your feet."

"No, it's not that big, and I can handle it, especially if my girls are being threatened. But you're always so far from home when you irrigate your fields, Gail. You need to protect yourself if you run up on a bear."

Gail disagreed. It was just one more thing to lug around and possibly misplace while riding the range on a four-wheeler. Outside of hunting, she had never carried a gun in the thirty years she had been working her cows. Many local residents, who hunted and fished regularly, had expressed similar notions and felt no need to be armed while afield. As children and adults they had roamed the mountains without a thought about their own safety, rarely ever seeing cougars, wolves, or bears.

But still, being new to the region, I wasn't at ease in my surroundings. Maybe I was overreacting and seeing danger lurking behind every rock, shadow, or unfamiliar sound, but I also believed times were changing. For whatever reason, be it lack of game, successful wildlife management, or human encroachment, predators were becoming far more common sights now than they had been ten or twenty years prior. I didn't even have to leave my own backyard to see them.

We talked a few minutes longer about it, when Gail announced, "I have to bolt," and ended the conversation without further explanation. I was no longer offended by such curt behavior, for I now understood the reasons behind it. But I could remember the first few time she had used that phrase, and I had read the queue incorrectly, assuming she meant it was time to start wrapping up the conversation. As a result I committed the social *faux pas* of continuing my train of thought, and ended our conversation with the usual niceties.

Later I began to wonder if I was offending her in some way because it seemed our talks nearly always ended suddenly. I tried not to take it personally, but I had yet to realize that many rural Montanans are not known for their subtleties, and when someone says they have to bolt, they mean they have to hang up right now! I didn't figure that out until during one conversation she elaborated further by adding, "Someone's coming up the drive; I have to bolt." I now understood such phrases are more correctly interpreted as meaning, "I'm sorry, but I have to hang up right now and don't have time to explain why." I chalked it up to yet another Montanan mannerism I would have to adjust to.

With our chat abruptly ended, I returned to my other task at hand and kept busy in the kitchen baking oatmeal cookies. I put chocolate chips in mine, but always made two separate batches, one with golden raisins and one without, because Bill hates cooked raisins. Even though the kitchen was now filled with the aroma of cinnamon sugar, my thoughts kept returning to that poor hunter and the grizzly bear. *Bears are a part of the west like any other predator. You just have to be aware of your surroundings and take precautions.* As always, it was for my girls I felt the most concern.

℧ ℧ ℧

The next two seasons passed, each with its share of maulings, but no deaths. I had grown somewhat complacent, and half convinced myself that since none of the attacks had taken place anywhere near us, we had little to fear. That reasoning was shattered when I read about a fifty-seven-year-old man who was killed by a grizzly bear in Yellowstone National Park while walking with his wife on the Wapiti Lake Trail. They had seen a female grizzly about a hundred yards in front of them, and as a precaution had turned and walked away in the opposite direction. But the grizzly had spotted them and charged, despite their hasty retreat. She caught up with them and the husband did not survive the subsequent attack. The Park Service decided not to pursue the grizzly because they believed she was acting in a "purely defensive nature" by protecting her cubs. They further stated the animal had not been tagged since it had no previous history of aggression. I was horrified. It seemed logical to me that if a bear attacked a human once and killed him, then it would be more willing to do so again. I viewed this bear as a threat and questioned the motives and reasoning of the park officials. I also worried about the safety of any other hikers who walked the trails of Yellowstone.

"That makes two fatal attacks here in Montana so far this summer," Bill remarked as he read me the story from the computer. "I wonder when the next attack will be."

"What makes you think there will be another one?"

"Trouble always comes in threes," he replied seriously. His look softened and he smiled as he added, "At least that's the saying with regard to airplane crashes and celebrity deaths."

I felt uneasy; whether true or not, such things were unpredictable. And we were among the last to hear about them since we had scant access to news of events as they unfolded. Aside from what Gail provided me, we had no running commentary on local matters. We lacked satellite or cable television service, and could not receive any local television signal because the mountains blocked them. Our most immediate news sources were the Internet and the radio, but they concentrated mostly on national and international events. Any other local news was heralded weekly by our county paper, *The Gold Standard*, or by our local postmaster, Leo.

Mullan, being such a small town, with services limited to a grade school, saloon, gas station, and post office, was not exactly a hub of activity. But everyone living there eventually dropped by the post office at least once or twice a week to receive their mail. That made Leo the unofficial eyes and ears of all the local news fit to print, or not print, as the case may be.

It was the only government presence in our tiny hamlet, a small oasis of semi-officialdom. Aside from our builder, Leo was the only other local person with whom we established contact before moving west. I remembered the first conversation I had with him while still living in the metro D.C. area. I had called to find out what was needed to forward our mail after we closed our mail service in Maryland. It was complicated; the Postal Service had created a new rule, presumably as part of their war on terror, requiring anyone wishing to establish a post box, to appear in person at their gaining post office so the postmaster could satisfy himself that he wasn't dealing with an enemy saboteur.

Being such a small, spread-out community, it was not economically feasible to provide home mail or rural free delivery service, so everyone was assigned a box number instead. Therein lay the conundrum: We could only open a new post office address in Mullan in person, but we were living 2,000 miles away.

At the time, my local post office in Maryland had loaded me down with paperwork to forward our mail, yet I had no place to forward it to. I was classified as having "no forwarding address." No one seemed able to offer any useful suggestions regarding how I could have my mail forwarded during the week long transition from one state to the next. I was told my new postmaster in Montana might require that I fax him some proof of identity, or else he might not hold any of our mail. So I called the Mullan Post Office with some trepidation, not really knowing what to expect. When Leo answered I told him who I was and explained my predicament.

"Tell me your name again," he interrupted in his deep gruff voice. "Okay, I'll just hold anything with your name on it. You can collect it when you arrive and I'll set you up with a P.O. Box."

I was stunned. Based on my previous experience, I was expecting an indifferent or unhelpful response. Too much time living around D.C. had jaded me.

"Don't you need me to fax you the change of address papers, or my driver's license, or something?" I was recalling the nightmare I had gone through to get my driver's license changed from Florida to Maryland.

"No, we don't do all that here," he answered. "We'll work it out when you arrive in person. In the meantime I'll just put your mail on the shelf. It'll be here when you get here. You don't have to worry about it."

I let out a sigh of relief, "Thank you, Leo. I look forward to meeting you."

I hung up the phone, thinking that small town living had its advantages. And so it did. Once we settled in, I looked forward to dropping by the post office at least once a week to pick up or drop off my mail. As part of this ritual, Leo would apprise me of the local gossip in colorful descriptions that often rivaled Gail's knowledge. It was only natural that on my next visit we would discuss the topic of bears.

"Did you hear 'bout the grizzly bear that was hit by the semi truck up in Lincoln?" Leo belched out in his deep baritone voice.

"Another grizzly?" I asked. "They are really moving around this year."

"That's not all," Leo said, as he leaned over the counter that separated us, his ruddy face pressed forward toward me. "Here in Mullan a black bear has been causing trouble. He came right into town and killed some sheep in a nearby field."

That was disturbing news. Bears seemed to be everywhere and they were getting closer and bolder.

He leaned back and pulled on the red suspenders he liked to wear over his Hawaiian shirts. I couldn't help but think how his appearance always reminded me of how I pictured Santa Claus on summer vacation: Bermuda shorts, sandals—all that was missing was the beard.

Leo continued, "Your builder, Bobby, told me he and his wife was out walking just up the road behind us." He pointed his thumb back toward the hill above the town, "And what do you suppose they saw? A blackie just sitting in a tree right there among all them homes."

Leo was referring to the houses scattered along the road leading up the mountainside. I knew that Bob and his wife, Jan, liked to take walks every evening, but this one must have been unnerving, or so I assumed. Bob was an avid outdoorsman, so perhaps he was used to such sights. Jan, on the other hand, was the local beautician, and I doubt her reaction would have been the same as his. I guess I would have to ask her at my next hair appointment.

I thanked Leo for the news update, disturbing as it was, and departed with my mail. I found myself peering about as I returned to the car, thinking some bruin might suddenly appear and threaten me. It was absurd, of course, but one cannot always keep absurd thoughts at bay; and in Montana, the absurd has a way of becoming the accepted.

It did not help matters that, as I ascended our logging road, I remembered the dead bloated cow in the field below us that had been left unburied for the past two weeks. The land was leased to someone out-of-town who rarely checked on his stock. It was a sore point with Gail because carrion always attracts predators, including bears. Luckily, my emergency broadcast system was in place. Today was no exception. When I went into the house I found the light blinking on the kitchen phone. It was a call from "game warden" Gail.

"There's a black bear down in the field below you, Nancy. I saw it this morning when we were checking cows. You need to be aware of it. It could wander up your way."

I returned the favor by calling her back and telling her about the grizzly bear that got hit by the truck in Lincoln. Of course, she had already heard about it. She then informed me she had lost another calf to bear attacks.

"We notified FWP. They agreed to set a trap for the grizzly. Nancy, I've never seen a summer like this one."

As we moved deeper into that summer, the bear activity increased, and then I received some very upsetting news from Gail.

"Two horses were attacked by a grizzly bear and killed when they got caught up in a fence. It happened only seven miles from my house," she exclaimed desperately.

It was a horrible incident, and naturally the owners were devastated. They, too, thought of their horses as friends and companions. I could not imagine the reaction one would have finding such a gruesome scene. I thought about our own two horses, Belle and Wilson, and about my family;

a feeling of uneasiness quickly enveloped me. I knew the bears and other predators lived here when I moved to Montana, and I understood there was a risk associated with living so close to them. But I had not anticipated a season so full of potential danger.

Despite what had just happened, I had no desire to see them punished or killed. I reasoned they had a right to exist, just not at the expense of my family or my home. My line was firmly drawn in the sand; I simply refused to live in fear of them. Bill discreetly placed a shotgun loaded with slugs near the front door and made sure I was trained to use it. I took the logical precaution of arming myself with a handgun whenever I walked outside, even if I was just going to the barn. I had considered buying some pepper spray, but given its limited reach and our frequently strong westerly winds, it was more likely I'd be out of range or have the wind in my face if I really needed to use it. If my family or animals were in danger, I did not have to be close by to discharge a firearm, and the sound alone was known to frighten bears away. It was an imperfect solution, but not our only course of action.

We cautioned the girls again that they were never to go to the barn without Kobi and one parent with them. In the meantime, I was hopeful the local grizzly would be caught as I anxiously waited to hear from Gail. She had told me the game department had set one trap, but only for ten days. Neither of us knew the reason why, and the trapper seemed unwilling to elaborate. Before the week was out, I received a frustrating call from Gail. It was not what I was hoping to hear.

"The grizzly sprung the trap, but got away!"

"Are they going to try again?" I inquired hopefully.

"Yes, we have a few more days. They'll only do it for ten days, you know. Chase has been going to check the trap everyday. We'll call them if we see anything."

In the interim more bad bear news arrived from the West Glacier Park area. Another man, a fifty-year-old hiker, had been attacked by a grizzly bear. He was mauled, but survived the attack and was currently recovering at the hospital in Browning.

With this latest news, Bill and I agreed it was time to brush up on our shooting skills, so we practiced all afternoon with the shotguns. My old Remington 1100 was a 20 gauge, but all I'd every used it for was bird hunting back in Florida, and the lighter bird loads did not compare with the heavy slug loads I now tried. The recoil proved brutal on my tiny frame, even with padding added to my shirt. The gun was too unwieldy to carry about with me on my daily chores, especially since I needed both hands free to work with the horses. That left me with the handgun, which I considered a last ditch effort. Even a revolver as powerful as my .44 Magnum is only effective on a grizzly at close range (unless one gets in a lucky shot on one of his few vital soft spots).

Whenever the horses became nervous, or I heard an unfamiliar sound in the bush, I'd wish I'd brought something bigger like a rifle or shotgun, or better yet, a bazooka. Such was the kind of fear the unknown and the unseen could engender in me. I thought this must have been what it was like for those early pioneers before bears learned to fear them. It certainly wasn't what I had expected, doing my poor impersonation of Annie Oakley. Well, we were about the same size, at least.

The next day Gail called, her voice tense, "Our time is up. We didn't catch the grizzly. Parks and Wildlife think it moved on but I don't think so. They removed the trap."

"That's ridiculous," I responded flatly, "you're still losing livestock, and horses have been killed, all within a few miles. What's next, a person? It's only a matter of time before someone meets up with it. We know it lives around here. This just isn't right, Gail." My frustration was working itself into a lather. "I'm tired of the animals having more rights than people. This bear is a real threat, not an imagined one. And I think he's lost his fear of humans.

"When I worked in Florida at the Fish and Game Commission, we killed alligators that were a threat. We valued life and property and protected both. We often removed dangerous animals before a serious loss occurred. I just don't understand this stupid ten-day attitude."

Gail answered calmly in her usual deadpan way, "Eh, what are you gonna do?"

Well, I'd done about all I could do, remaining alert during the day and maintaining a vigil at night (thanks in part to my light sleep habits and Bill's chronic snoring). I was becoming fatigued, but my intuition kept telling me there was more trouble ahead, and my intuition was rarely wrong. Three days later the phone rang and I heard Gail's voice, but this time it wasn't calm or even tense, it was nervous.

"Nancy, you won't believe what happened to me."

"Gail, what's wrong?"

"I was on my four-wheeler in one of our meadows about a half a mile from your place, checking the irrigation. I saw what I thought was an elk further down the field. I wasn't wearing my glasses, so I couldn't really tell. Still, I didn't think too much about it. I had my dog, Shep, with me, riding on the back." I recalled Gail once showing me the little box she had mounted on the back of her machine so one of her dogs could always accompany her in the field.

"I got back on my four-wheeler and drove nearer to it because I needed to check another spot. When I got closer I thought it was a moose because I saw a hump at the shoulder. I went on with my work and continued to move closer to it. I figured it'd move away because of the four-wheeler making noise."

I was getting an awful feeling about this; I knew Gail would not be frightened by a moose. I listened intently without interruption, my hand gripping the phone tightly. Gail continued.

"I was still heading its way about a hundred yards off, when it stands up on its hind legs! Nancy, it was the grizzly!"

"Oh, Gail!" was all I could manage before my voice choked.

"He started chasin' me! It was coming at me faster than I could run. I have never been so scared in my life. I turned 'round as quickly as I could and drove that four-wheeler at top speed. I was too afraid to look back. I didn't stop until I got home by my own door. I'd even forgotten about Shep. I spun around, and thankfully, he was still in his box. I was afraid he might have bounced out on one of the bumps."

"Thank goodness you weren't on foot and couldn't get away," I said. I tried to lighten the mood a little, "At least Shep didn't bounce out. I'm glad you're both safe." I quickly added, "I wish you would carry a gun from now on."

Her voice shook a little as she replied, "Better than that. I just told Herman I am *NOT* going out there again. He can check his own damn fields from now on! I mean it!" Gail added a few other, more colorful choice words. I had come to understand her and knew it was born of her frustration.

"Thirty years I've been doin' this without one incident, and now all of a sudden I'm dealin' with bears everywhere. And not just any bears. It had to be grizzlies. I blame that stupid federal judge who banned wolf hunting this year."

"What do you mean?"

"Oh, you know, the one who said we couldn't shoot wolves in Montana 'cause there were too few of 'em back east. Well, we've got too many of 'em here, and they compete with the bears for game. When game's short, they turn to easy pickins like sheep and calves.

"Now listen to me, Nancy. It's a good thing you pack a gun 'cause this happened just over the rise next to your barn, less than a mile from you. You have to really watch out; that grizzly could wander over the hill to your place in a few minutes. He could come right through your front yard. Oh, I see someone drivin' up. Gotta bolt, bye."

The line clicked dead before I could respond. That's the way things seemed to happen around here; *sudden like*, I thought. Now I wasn't just acting like a Montanan, I was starting to think like one, too.

ʊ ʊ ʊ

Several weeks passed without further incident and I was settling down into my new routine when my world was disrupted by the sound of the phone ringing. It was Gail.

"We lost a calf yesterday," her voice was heavy with concern. "And that's not all; my neighbors had five sheep killed."

"Do you think it was wolves?" I asked.

"No, there were marks in the dirt where it looks like there was a scuffle. It looks like the mother cow tried to protect her calf. Nancy, from the looks of it, it had to be something big to drag off a large calf. I think it was a bear."

Once again those words left me feeling cold inside. I had overheard some conversations between other local ranchers, whose collective opinion was that we had become overpopulated with wolves and cougars. There was more talk of opening a hunting season on wolves despite the temporary federal ban. They firmly believed that wolves and cougars were competing with the bears for food and territory, and were driving the bears down from the upper elevations to the lower valley areas where they saw cow and sheep herds abound. The young calves were plentiful and easy prey, and for the bears it was as though the buffet line was open.

"Gail, please be careful when you are out in your fields," I pleaded, but she quickly changed the subject.

"I heard sugar prices are going up. You should buy yours now before it becomes too expensive. With your love of baking, you'll soon run out."

"Well you have never *steered* me wrong—get it?" I had to think of something to lighten the mood.

"Oh yea, very funny," Gail replied, though I could sense her eyes were rolling at my lame humor.

We had to be in town that afternoon to pick up some supplements for the horses, so I added sugar to our shopping list. On the drive in I told Bill about what had happened to Gail's calves and the neighbor's sheep. He nodded in agreement, but seemed to be preoccupied with other thoughts.

"Anything wrong?" I inquired.

"No, I'm just thinking about what you said about a sugar shortage. Where did Gail get her information?"

"I don't know, but she's been right about everything else, so maybe we should stock up."

"Alright, let's stop at Costco and buy it in bulk," he responded.

I didn't give it anymore thought and went about my normal shopping with the girls while Bill looked for sugar. When he met us at the checkout line, I was surprised to see over a half dozen huge bags of sugar piled on a rolling cart.

"I got you 75 pounds of white sugar and 15 pounds each of brown and confectioners sugar. This should last us through any shortage," he announced triumphantly.

"Wow, you really took Gail's warning to heart," I said, trying to suppress my laughter.

"It'll keep and I don't want to pay more for it later, or not be able to find it at all. Remember that time we had so much difficulty finding flour? This sugar will last us for years."

"I'm sure you're right." I was not about to dispute that fact. I was just thinking about where we were going to store it.

We left the store as the weather began to change. The wind had picked up, making it difficult to cross the parking lot to our Highlander. As we neared the car, the air billowed though my light jacket, inflating it like a parachute. I felt as though I might be blown into the air at any moment. It had nearly happened to me once before on a visit to New York City when I was in college. I was climbing the steps of the Metropolitan Museum of Art, but found myself reeling backward until I was caught by the strong arm of an attentive museum custodian. He pulled me up to the entrance and commented, "Lord, child, you need rocks in your pocket to keep you on the ground."

Right now I felt I should have heeded his advice. Bill was ahead of me pushing his sugar cart. Sandy and Sonja followed with the grocery basket. I trailed them with one hand on my jacket and the other clutching my purse. I leaned forward, bucking the rapidly increasing wind, trying to balance myself and reduce my exposure. I was too far back to grab the grocery cart and too embarrassed to call for help. I could just see the headlines on the evening news: "Tiny local woman disappears in wind storm...." Just then, a huge tumbleweed rolled swiftly across the parking lot and briefly hit our grocery cart before rolling away. This caught everyone's attention, and momentarily forgetting my plight, I laughed out loud, "Tumbleweeds? I thought that only happened in the movies. We really are in the West."

Bill looked at me and replied, "You having a little trouble there, Quinn? Girls, grab your Mom before she gets blown away." He smiled and slyly added, "Better put some rocks in your pocket, Nancy, or you'll wind up like that tumbleweed."

We returned home without further incident, the wind bucking our car the entire way. It was always quite a thrill to cross the pass under such conditions, a thrill I could do without. It wasn't just the thought of plunging off the highway into the canyons below—that was an extremely rare occurrence, usually reserved for anyone driving too fast. It was the realization that strong winds usually meant a change in the weather was coming. Summer was ending and fall would soon begin.

ʊ ʊ ʊ

With the weather growing cooler and the days growing shorter, the girls hurried to get in as much riding as possible. I was in the tack room cleaning up after their last ride of the day, when Bill's voice crackled over the intercom.

"It's Gail on the phone. Pick up."

As an additional precaution, we had placed a cordless phone extension in the tack room, but it was barely within range and I had to step outside to receive a clear signal. With one finger in my ear, I answered the phone while crossing the corral to a spot where I knew reception would be stronger.

"It's the grizzly again," my friend said tersely.

"What happened this time?" I asked.

"We had a bow hunter come to my place today. He said he hit an elk and it walked onto our property and died. He wanted permission to come on our land and retrieve it. We said that would be fine. The elk had gone into our back meadow behind the house. He walked back to the meadow and saw that the grizzly bear had already found the elk and was eating it. The bear stood up and growled at him. The guy was so scared that he just ran away. He said he didn't want the elk that bad; the grizzly could have it."

"Have you called the trapper again? Maybe he could set another trap."

"Please, you've gotta be kidding. He already told me he'd set the trap for ten days and it's their policy not to go back and try for the same bear in the same place. A fat lot of help he was."

"Gail, it's getting to the point where you're afraid to leave your home." Then I realized I was standing in a corral with my back to the woods, a hundred yards uphill from my own house. A shiver went down my backside.

"I know. I'm always looking over my shoulder, and I don't want to go irrigating," she replied.

"Are we just supposed to wait until it's cold enough for the bears to hibernate?"

"What else can we do? The boys want to track him down and kill him, but they're a protected species. It's illegal to hunt them, but *they* can hunt *you*! See how dangerous this is?" Gail answered, exasperated.

"Well, just be careful," I cautioned her again.

"You too, kid. It lives around both of us, you know. And watch those girls and your horses. Now I have to bolt."

I knew my that was my cue, and said good bye. Without hesitation I told the girls to finish up quickly; it was time to go back home. I promised them they could ride again tomorrow, but I felt uncomfortable with the notion. The good riding weather was fading fast, and I didn't want to disappoint them, but the uneasiness continued to gnaw at me. Was it such a wise choice?

We were at the barn the next afternoon, grooming the horses at their hitching posts. It was surprisingly warm, and felt more like mid-summer than early fall. I was lulled by the sweetness of the air, and made drowsy by the sun beating down upon my face. Mingled with a light cool breeze, it was a perfect afternoon. But the tranquility was soon interrupted by Belle, who began to pound her feet and snort. Her head flew high into the air and she suddenly stood very still. I saw her nostrils flair open wide as she sniffed the air with great puffs and snorts. She started to back up, the whites of her eyes were showing, and a wild look appeared on her face. She was staring straight ahead at a clump of trees.

Wilson too was becoming distressed, and he stared at the same place as Belle. Once again she began stomping and snorting, tugging hard on the lead rope that held her fast to the post. She began snapping her head wildly, and I feared she would break the post and injure herself, so I quickly untied her. This calmed her somewhat as we stood together. I tried to comfort her but I sensed a fear in her I had never witnessed before.

"Release Wilson," I said hurriedly to the girls.

"What is it, Mom? Why are Belle and Wilson so scared?" Sandy asked me nervously as she untied Wilson.

I could see nothing that might upset them, but my mind turned to thoughts of the grizzly bear. I strained my eyes from tree to tree and still could see nothing wrong or out of order. By now even Kobi was sniffing the air and alerting, but he did not seem quite as upset as the horses. I expected them to dash to the other side of the corral, but they did not move. Freed from their restraints, they now stood motionless, intently staring, smelling, and listening for the slightest change in the bush. I didn't like it. They'd never been so agitated or afraid.

"Girls," I commanded, "go into the tack room and call Dad on the intercom. Ask him to come down to the barn and tell him the horses are very upset." I wanted to stay with the horses, fearing they might panic if I left them alone. I had Kobi by my side, and he seemed to sense my apprehension, for he would not leave me. Together we retrieved the shotgun and stood watch. By the time Bill arrived, Belle and Wilson had calmed down. Bill took Kobi and his shotgun, and walked in a wide circle around the meadow near the tree line, searching for signs.

When he returned, he said with relief, "Whatever scared them is gone now."

"Do you think it was the bear? We couldn't see it, but I know horses can smell something from a distance, before anyone can see it."

"Could have been, but I didn't see any tracks or disturbances," Bill replied.

We looked at each other and sighed. Gail's recent experiences were running through our minds. Maybe the grizzly had crossed that last half mile and was on our land. Just to be safe, Bill decided to stay around for awhile, and propped himself in a lawn chair by the tack room door, the shotgun cradled across his lap. We watched Belle, Wilson, and Kobi. They all seemed calm now, so I told the girls they could ride. We decided to keep them in the corral area and away from the tree line, and despite these restrictions, they had an enjoyable ride without further incident.

Later that night I told Gail about what happened at the barn.

"It was that grizzly," she said confidently, "I just know it. The horses smelled it and that scared them. It may have been further away than you could see. The wind can carry a scent pretty far."

I decided to change the subject and interrupted, "I may be stopping by in a day or so."

"Okay," Gail replied, "you can drop in anytime."

Before she could say anything more, I added, "Well, I gotta bolt, bye!" and hung up the phone with a laugh. I was becoming more Montanan everyday. In truth, I wanted to surprise her and went into the pantry to take inventory of my supplies.

"I need to get that cake made," I told Bill as I stood by the bakers rack, searching through the massive bags of sugar piled on top of one another.

"Sugar prices never did go up, did they?" he replied wryly.

"No, I guess I'll be putting a little extra sugar in the frosting this year."

I had unknowingly started a tradition the first year of my friendship with Gail. I knew how hard her family worked at haying in the fields, and so one year I surprised them with a *haying cake*. I had shaped a simple vanilla cake into a haystack and put apricot filling inside. Then I colored the cream cheese frosting a buttery yellow, and used a fork to texture it to look like straw in a haystack. I fashioned several soda straws next to the stack to resemble a "beaver slide"—a large contraption that hay is piled onto and turned over so it slides into large stacks. Most ranchers these days use a bailer to make either large round bales of hay or small squares, but Gail's family preferred the old loose hay stack method ("The hay'll keep for years that way," she once told me).

I knew the whole clan would be in the field, so I left the cake as a surprise on their dining room table with a handmade card stating, "Happy Haying." The family was so delighted to find the cake, they took pictures of it and I received an immediate phone call from Gail. So now that the tradition had begun, each year I faced a new challenge trying to come up with a superior cake design.

Haying normally lasted four to six weeks, weather depending, so I had time to think up something clever. This particular year I was running late. I had experienced some more serious health problems over the summer and did not get one made in time. But I could not disappoint her family, so as soon as I recovered sufficient strength, I got to work on it.

With this summer having been so stressful, I wanted to think of something funny for my theme. I knew chocolate was Gail's favorite flavor, so I settled on making a chocolate sheet cake filled with chocolate chips and chocolate syrup. I placed a toy metal tractor and driver on top, and added a small plastic bear in front so it appeared the tractor was chasing the bear. The accompanying card read, "Heard haying was a bear this year!"

After she stopped laughing, Gail proudly proclaimed, "I told a friend of mine, 'She won't let me down. Nancy will bring a cake this year.'" She appreciated it so much that she decided to keep the toy tractor and bear, and hang them on her Christmas tree that year.

ʊ ʊ ʊ

For the remainder of the fall it seemed bears were the main topic of conversation with everyone. We were all worried about the possibility of another attack and where it would occur. As much as I loved the summer, once the weather cooled enough to drive the bears into their dens, the more relieved I would be. Perhaps then I could relax my constant vigil. By the end of that summer and fall there had been three fatal grizzly bear attacks, and several more people had been mauled in the state of Montana. With winter now approaching and hibernation coming, the season of the grizzly was finally over.

38

A New World Odor

T HE COLDER NIGHTS DEMANDED WARMER COVERS and heavier clothes. We also needed to turn on the heat in the house. We had a propane gas-fired forced air system that produced dry warmth, but since it had sat idle all summer, lint and other fine particles had collected in it. The first time we turned it on, the acrid smell of burning dust filled the air, but it soon cleared itself of such debris and produced a more acceptable odorless heat.

The same was true of our wood burning fireplace in the family room. Soot and dust had to be burned away the first time it was used, and my eyes and nose stung for an hour afterwards. Those rituals now completed, we began settling in to the predictable and repeatable routines of winter life: boots and coats on to go feed the horses, boots and coats off once back inside, boots and coats on to walk the dog, boots and coats off upon return. If it was too cold or snowing, the dog walking was suspended and Kobi was simply allowed to go out and return on his own, while one of us stood a freezing vigil by the door. If the day was pleasant, Kobi was free to roam the place until evening.

Darkness now came early, and we were settling in for the night, so I asked Bill to bring Kobi inside. We usually didn't leave him out late at night, but we were running a little behind our normal schedule. After Kobi was settled on his pillow, I came down from our upstairs bedroom. Bill sat in the family room waiting for me to select some program to watch from the vast horde of movies and TV shows he was constantly purchasing online.

"Do you smell something?" I said, wrinkling my nose.

"No, it's just your super sensitive canary nose. The miners should take you down into the tunnels with them to detect gas," he replied while thumbing through a stack of DVDs.

I had always been blessed with a very sensitive sense of smell, and could detect the faintest odors long before anyone else, even when those odors were outside and I was traveling in a car. But my blessing was also a curse because what might be a faint and harmless smell to others could easily make me feel sick.

"Bill, it's awful; it smells like something is burning, like rubber or an electrical fire. Can't you smell it?"

He lifted his head from his work and sniffed the air, and his face grimaced, "I do now."

We walked around the downstairs, sniffing like two bloodhounds in search of the foul source.

"It's strongest in the mechanical room," I said. "Do you think it has something to do with the heat and air unit?"

It was now beginning to permeate the entire house. I began to get a queasy feeling in my stomach and now my eyes and throat were burning.

"It's almost like a chemical odor. I'll close the bedroom doors before it gets in there," I said as I rushed up the stairs, taking two steps at a time.

When I returned to the mechanical room, the stench had become unbearable. Fearing an electrical fire someplace in the wiring, we considered calling our volunteer fire department. I looked at poor Kobi sitting on his bed in the epicenter of this stench, rubbing his face vigorously, as if trying to wipe away the smell.

"I think it's affecting Kobi the most," I said, as I sat down to comfort him. "Poor fellow, his nose is even more sensitive than mine."

As I reached over to touch him, the stench hit me like ton of bricks, stinging my eyes and clogging my nostrils.

"It's Kobi!" I cried, choking and quickly backing away. "Get him out of here!"

Bill coaxed him into the garage and closed the door. The odor lingered in the air as he passed by, and I simultaneously tried not to pass out. We pondered futilely, trying to figure out what he had been exposed to.

"It smells like chemical fertilizer. Do you think he left home for a while and got into something one of the nearby ranchers use?" I asked.

"I don't see how. I doubt they'd be putting any out this time of year."

We had no answers, but one thing we were certain of, he needed a bath immediately. The last thing we wanted to do was bathe Kobi at night in the cold, especially after we'd just gotten clean ourselves and had prepared to settle in, but we had no choice. Bill agreed to perform the foul deed, so that I would be spared anymore physical suffering from the olfactory invasion.

I went about the house opening doors and windows, hoping to air out that horrible and debilitating odor. The furnace would kick into high gear as a result, but it wasn't a very cold evening, and I reasoned we had little choice. It was either choke to death or shiver. But the putridity would not depart. It hung like a cloud all over the house, and was creeping up the stairs.

Now that I knew there was no immediate danger, I told the girls to go to bed and keep their doors closed and blocked with towels so they would not be affected by the smell. I then stood in the garage doorway watching Bill scrub a miserable looking Kobi. They were both covered in white suds, which Bill would rinse away, then repeat with more soap and water. Kobi stood there, silent and indignant. He seemed to understand our goal, and so endured it as best he could.

"Do you think he met a skunk?" Bill said as he scrubbed Kobi's thick black and tan fur.

"I doubt it; I've smelled dead skunks before; it's different."

"I guess you're right. Whatever it is, I hope it's nothing dangerous or poisonous."

"If we watch him, we'll know soon. If he starts vomiting or drooling, or acts sick in any way, we should take him straight to the vet."

Since Bill had the bathing under control, I decided to investigate possible causes of the still unidentified odor on the Internet. I started reading about anything I thought might help—chemicals, poisons, odor sources, and so on. Some of it fit our situation and some of it didn't; but I just wasn't finding a good match until I came to a site about removing bad smells from your dog. It described how to remove skunk odor from your dog. What really caught my attention were the number of reports of people who had called the fire department or their furnace repairman because they thought the awful burning smell was coming from the house itself, when it later turned out to be their dog. This intrigued me, so I read on. Apparently, freshly applied skunk musk did not produce the same effect as it would after a few days have passed. People described the smell variously as overheated electrical wiring, chemical poison odor, and burning rubber. So there was my answer; Kobi had tangled with a skunk and lost that battle. It was the one thing he could not catch and kill, and we were all paying the price for it.

The information from the website proved to be accurate. After a few days, the whole house smelled like a dead skunk on the side of the road. Kobi was no better, and slept in the garage when he was not outside. We tried all the home remedies such as tomato soup, shampoo, and dishwashing detergent, but they all failed. We bathed him numerous times, cleaned everything in the house, even burned scented candles, but nothing worked. We would have to wait for the smell to fade away.

After a month I thought it was finally over, then one morning Kobi came into the laundry room after being caught in a gentle rain shower. The smell was there again. Back out into the garage he went, to sit and ponder on his newly cleaned bed. *Would this ever end?* It did end, but only after two months had passed. It was that long before I could not smell "skunk" in the house. Luckily, the rest of the family did not have my sensitivities. I was the one who had to endure our new home potpourri, or as Bill called it, "poo-poorri."

39

Swap Meat

NOT LONG AFTER THE SKUNK INCIDENT FINALLY ENDED, I was preparing one of my family's favorite meals, spaghetti. Kobi sat loyally at my side, watching as I stirred the pot, ready to offer any assistance I might require, such as royal food taster or floor mop. His vigil was a bit too constant and too close, so I gave him a small taste and sent him outside to look after the girls.

After a short time I heard them all come inside, the girls pausing to remove their boots at the door, while Kobi headed straight into the kitchen and the bubbling pot of meaty spaghetti sauce. He paused by my side, tail wagging gleefully, and dropped something right at my feet. Then he happily stepped back and sat down, offering me up his paw with a smile of satisfaction. I glanced down, then shrank back and shrieked in horror at the sight of a rodent in my clean kitchen! Kobi could not understand my instant mortification at this wonderful prize. His ears flattened out sideways and his poor head went down to the floor.

I demanded rather harshly that he pick it up, and his puzzled eyes seemed to say *but I got it for you.* Before I could speak another word I heard Sandy say, "Mom, I see it moving."

Alive? This creature was still alive and in my house! My eyes widened as I thought of the consequences: A rodent scampering about the place with

Kobi in hot pursuit, knocking over furniture and lamps, making a home for itself in my linen closet, leaving little droppings everywhere, or even raising a family of its own that would think of our house as their home. I had to act fast—get it out of the house *NOW!* Then I glanced down again and saw that, although it was moving, it wasn't moving much. It was too injured to get up and crawl away. Suddenly I felt sorry for the poor, dying little creature.

"Sonja," I called, "go get your dad and tell him to come get this mouse out of my house."

By now both girls were giggling and pointing, while Kobi continued to sit in confusion, wondering why I was not completely thrilled with the gift he had worked so hard to give me. I patted him on the head and soothingly reassured him he was a good boy. This cheered him up, and once again he wagged his tail. Bill came in, and I ordered him to get rid of it. To distract Kobi and prevent him from making a game of "catch the mouse," I offered him a small bowl of spaghetti sauce. While he munched happily on it, Bill removed the still squirming mouse and disposed of it outside. Handling it didn't bother him in the least, but I was too busy to care as I quickly began scrubbing the affected area with bleach. It was only when he returned from burying the now deceased rodent that I reconsidered the wisdom of my hasty trade, as Bill smugly said, "Don't be surprised if Kobi brings you a dozen more, now that he knows there's spaghetti in it for him."

40

Kickin' Cousins

Y COUSINS, FAITH AND RICK, HAD COME FROM Michigan to visit us
for a week, and see what was the great appeal of Montana. After
only a few days enjoying the summer weather, they both agreed that
Montana would be a great place to retire. We were sitting on the front
porch, enjoying the last rays of light as the sun set behind the mountains.
It was growing dark, so I switched on the porch lights as the darkness
grew.

"But what about all the snow and cold?" Faith asked.

I looked at her a bit puzzled and replied, "And you're from Michigan?"

"Oh, right," she laughed. "I'll bet Glen [Faith's husband] would love it
here, especially the hunting. What do you think, Rick?" She was staring at
her brother.

"Oh, it's great, but I'd never be able to convince my wife to move here."
He reflected for a moment, and added, "Maybe this would be a good place
to retire after all."

We laughed, and enjoyed the evening chatting about family and friends
back in Michigan. I'd left the greater Detroit area as a child, and moved to
Florida when my mother remarried after my father's tragic death from a
car accident. For years I had very limited contact with my grandparents
and many cousins "up north." It was only when I was an adult that I

reestablished and strengthened those family bonds. In the last few years, my friendship with Faith had grown close, and we felt more like sisters than cousins. The idea of them possibly moving here held great appeal for me, but I knew it would be a tough sell on their families, who were deeply rooted in their home state. Still, it was something to consider.

As we chatted on, I noticed Kobi suddenly alert to something behind the planter by the front door.

"Oh look, Faith; Kobi must have a chipmunk cornered by the planter," I said.

"I want to see it," she said excitedly. "You're always telling me about them and your 'chipmunk wars.'"

We got up and went over by the door where Kobi had just flushed the small creature out. It ran towards us, and I heard Faith emit an ear-piercing scream, "MOUSE!!! It's a MOUSE!!!"

Faith grabbed my arm, and half pulling and half pushing from behind, she frantically dragged me from the patio, and nearly into the front fountain. At that exact moment, Sandy opened the front door, as Kobi chased the mouse, close on its tail.

The rodent made a beeline for the open door and Bill screamed, "Shut the door!"

Rick, confused by the rapidly unfolding events, blindly, but quickly kicked my heavy resin black bear sculpture with his right foot. It slammed into the mouse's head, stunning it and pinning it between the wall and the resin bear.

"I think I got it!" Rick shouted, gleefully.

"Is it dead?" Bill inquired.

All four of us slowly made our way onto the front porch and leaned over to peak. Faith, still tightly gripping my arm and laughing nervously, apologized for nearly forcing me into a nighttime swim. There, behind the resin bear, lay the deceased rodent. Death by garden ornament seemed a most unusual epitaph. My arm was turning numb, so I told Faith she could let go now.

Until that moment, I had never met someone more afraid of mice than I. Perhaps it is a family trait.

41

Ride Like the Wind

AUTUMN WAS IN FULL SWING, WITH CHILLY MORNINGS that succumbed to sunny afternoons, and cool evenings. The wildlife busied themselves each day eating and storing food for the winter. The deer boldly presented themselves everywhere, and even large elk herds moved into our open fields to graze. I wondered if they knew something about the coming winter of which I was yet unaware, for they no longer seemed concerned about our presence.

I had little time to ponder the matter further; Linda was giving the girls their riding lessons at our stable, and I had promised to assist.

"You should think seriously about riding," Linda commented. "It's something you could do with your girls."

"I've been telling her that for some time," Bill chimed in. "But she'll need her own horse."

Linda's eyes lit up at the prospect. "I know I can find just the right horse for you. I've got so many to choose from. But we can start you today on Belle or Wilson."

Here we go again, I thought. She'd already tried to talk Bill into getting a palomino, but although he had ridden some in the past, he took no great pleasure in it, and firmly rejected the idea of owning an animal he would

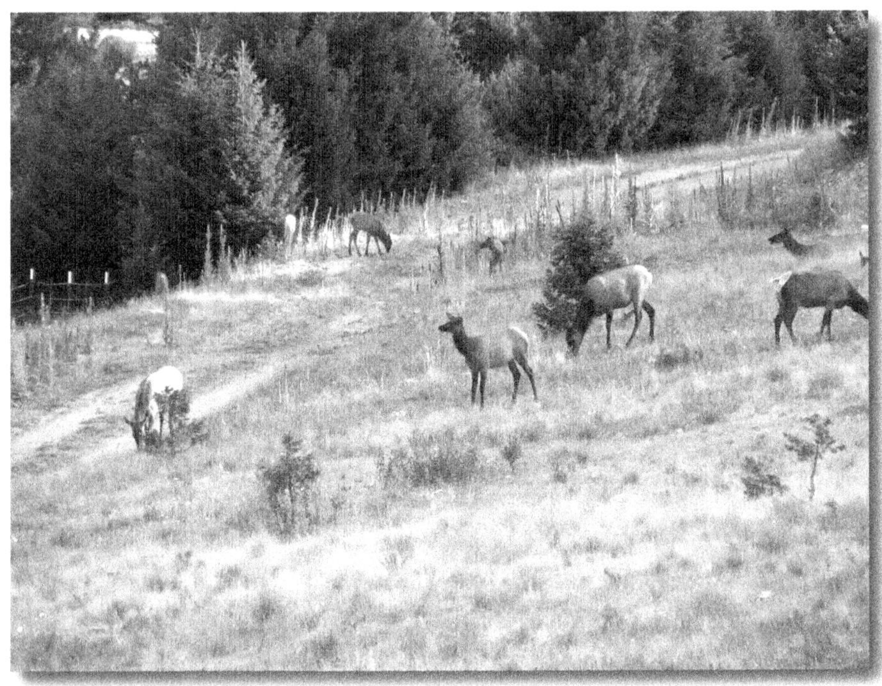

A herd of elk grazing in the front yard

not ride. The girls teased him and joked about what an "illegal" Montanan he was since he didn't have a horse. Perhaps his eagerness to get me one was just a way of deflecting their attention toward me, but he also was aware of how much I enjoyed learning how to train horses. Riding seemed the next logical step. I too had been thinking about it, and I wanted to try, but I suppose part of me thought I was too old.

"You are not too old," Gail's irritated voice echoed in my mind. "I'm older than you and I ride."

"Yes," I remembered replying, "and you've been riding since you were a child. You know what to do. I've never spent any real time on a horse."

That conversation now rolled through my mind as it had numerous times before, like waves on the beach that never cease.

"So, who do you want to try?" Linda's voice snapped me back from my momentary repose.

"Wilson," I replied. "He's a little slower than Belle."

Before I could protest my sudden decision, I found myself climbing up onto his broad back and settling into the saddle. It was Sandy's saddle and fit me just fine, so I had no excuse to immediately climb down. We were in the round pen, and there was no danger of him tearing off at a gallop, not that he ever would, so I practiced moving him slowly around. The girls were cheering, Bill was smiling, and you would have thought I had won some kind of contest. I suppose in some way I had; I felt good about giving this a try, and Wilson was very obliging.

The world seemed different from up there. For once I was looking down at everything instead of up. And I could feel the power and control I exerted over another living creature, one that would obey my slightest command— well, usually. A whole new experience was opening up for me, and I excitedly anticipated our next meeting as I later gave Linda a check for my first five riding lessons.

42

A Horse of a Different Color

"A THIRD HORSE, BILL— REALLY?" I looked at him, unsure.

"Nancy, I always knew we'd get more than just one horse. I always assumed it would be more than two."

I digested this for a moment. I was concerned about the added work and expense. On the other hand, I did admit to myself that having a horse of my own would make me happy, but it had to be someone special, a friend and companion who was just for me. I enjoyed Belle and Wilson, but the girls had already developed special relationships with them, and they found it hard to share them with me. The ground work, the grooming, and their general company were things we could all share. Riding was more personal, and the bond between rider and horse was not something we could share equally, at least it was not for me. Sandy was happy to ride any horse, anytime, anywhere. I was different. I needed to be invested. I wanted to really know and care about the horse I rode. I needed to have a trusting partner.

It was September, and Bill had been asked to speak at a local September 11th memorial dinner. We had dropped the girls off for a few hours at

257

Linda's and continued on into Helena. We were a little late getting back because people stopped to chat after his talk, so when we returned to Linda's place it was almost dark. Sandy and Sonja greeted us excitedly, telling us all about the latest "boarders" to join Linda's ever growing stable.

"Do you want to see them?" Linda remarked.

"I'd love to." It was on such tours that I initially learned about the different breeds and their personalities. I enjoyed seeing all the various colors and markings, and in her menagerie one would always find horses of every shape and size. It was like an equine candy shop.

"Would any of these horses be a good candidate for Nancy?" Bill asked.

"Yes," she replied, "and I have a couple in mind. I'd have to work with them a little more, but I have a dappled mare out back with a very gentle personality. She's small and dainty, very refined. We named her Dolly because she looks like a Barbie doll."

The description of Dolly appealed to me, a small dainty horse for a small dainty woman.

"And over here, I have a gelding called Pancho and another mare named Trina."

We walked across the paddock and she introduced me to Pancho and Trina. Pancho was a small horse of reddish-brown color, only two years old. Trina was an older broodmare of about fourteen. Although larger at about fifteen hands, she was the same color as Pancho. Darkness was closing in fast, so we could not get a good look at them or handle them. I just listened to Linda's description of them and looked on through the fence with a small flashlight.

"What about Dolly?" I quizzed.

"Dolly's isolated in the back round pen. She has a virus right now, so please don't touch her; you don't want to transmit anything to your horses. But you can at least see her. "

I approached the round pen with caution. Linda turned the lights on so I could get a good look at Dolly. I stood outside and peered into the round pen. Dolly was a dainty, delicate looking mare, and very exquisite. Her beautifully shaped face would have made a lovely painting. She almost reminded me of a little deer. She approached me, walking from the other side of the pen. She came right to me, with only the pipe panel between us. She moved her head closer and gave my hand a delicate sniff. She moved two steps away and then in a few moments, returned to me, watching me thoughtfully.

"I really think she would be perfect for you," Linda said. The night shadows danced across the pen, and a gentle breeze had begun to move the trees. I buttoned my coat against the invading cold and put my hands in my pockets.

"What exactly is wrong with her?" I asked.

"She has a fever and a runny nose."

"So, you don't think it is anything serious?"

"No, she'll get over it in a week or so, then you can try her out if you feel comfortable. You can see how calm she is. Even sick, she's gentle and sweet."

All this time Dolly had not left my side. Even with all of us standing there, she did not approach anyone else.

"I think she likes you, Mom," said Sandy. "She keeps standing with you."

I just smiled and did not reply. She was a pretty little horse, and I felt good standing next to her, so quiet and calm.

"It was nice to meet you, Dolly. I hope you feel better soon," I whispered under my breath.

"It's getting late and we need to get the girls home," I said.

I thanked Linda for everything, and we talked about our next lesson later in the week. The girls were tired, and the ride across the mountain was quiet. As I looked out the window at the towering trees rushing by, my thoughts returned to Dolly.

43

Ride On

M Y FAVORITE THING ABOUT THE AUTUMN IS the changing colors of the leaves of the quaking aspen. Heart shaped, they turn a bright golden yellow, with streaks of red. The trees grow in large clusters, so I enjoy watching them shiver and shake in even the slightest breeze. When they do move, you can hear them rustling, almost ringing, like a thousand soft cymbals. The sounds drift and swirl through the air. There is nothing like the wind through the leaves, the soothing timbre that breaks the silence of the life on the mountain.

I have learned the mountain has its own rhythm. In the morning are the songbirds that praise the light of day. Come noon, the silent butterflies dance among the poppies that open their petals to welcome the sunlight. The tall pines spread their needles toward the sky, and the wind sways their branches as they stoically stand together. By evening, the sky is painted with both subtle and dramatic hues, as the creek, always the creek, rushes headlong in its endless journey to the river below. We move through this natural cycle with gratitude and appreciation, or we ignore it, and are the lesser for it. The choice is one we must make each and every day.

It was on such a beautiful morning that I almost hated to leave and go to town, but we were due at Linda's for our riding lessons. I was now a veteran of five lessons. As we crossed the mountains over to Helena, I wondered who I would ride this time. I had tried Pancho and a couple of other horses at her barn, but none really quite suited me. As we pulled up and readied our gear, Linda appeared.

"I think Dolly is well enough to ride, if you want to try her out," Linda commented as I began to strap into my back brace and put on my helmet.

"I do want to try her," I smiled. I had found her a very interesting equine. I also liked the fact that she seemed to like me too.

"May I try to bridle her?"

"Sure, give it a go," Linda replied, handing over the setup.

I remembered some of my other experiences trying to put the bit in Wilson's mouth, so I was expecting some resistance. When I approached Dolly, she immediately lowered her head and waited. I was so impressed that I simply reached over and slipped the bit into her mouth, and had the headstall in place in about twelve seconds—a record for me.

"That went well; she did not fight me at all!" I said with some surprise and admiration. I did not have to reach up over my head and struggle with the bridle or the horse.

"She wants to please you," Linda said. "She is that kind of horse."

"She did," I replied.

Saddling Dolly was also a good experience. She stood still and did not offer up any trouble.

My first ride on Dolly went well. She was smooth and easy, and made me feel like I was a better rider than I was. She was a confidence builder, and did everything I asked of her without any negative attitude. She had a rhythm that I could easily match, and her legs felt like they were my own. Her dainty steps moved me across the indoor arena with the grace of a ballerina. Riding Dolly felt more like dancing a waltz, and I experienced a kind of joy I did not know was possible on a horse. I had never had an experience like this one.

"So, how do you like her?" I heard Linda's voice, pulling me back from my own thoughts.

"I like her very much," I said. "I didn't feel the slightest bit nervous, like I have on other horses. Maybe it's because I'm gaining more experience in the saddle, but I think it has more to do with *who* I'm riding."

I glanced down at Linda, and for a moment I thought I detected a shadow pass across her face. She was still smiling, but it was there in her eyes. I wondered what it possibly could mean, but I turned my attention back to Dolly. My first lesson with her was nearly over, and I wanted to enjoy every moment of it.

In a few minutes it was time for the girls to have their lessons. We always booked the three of us back-to-back, so we had to take turns. I watched the girls ride, then helped them groom the horses before visiting all the other horses at the barn. When we finished, we piled in the car to go shopping, before heading home. Tomorrow was a school day.

ʊ ʊ ʊ

It was an interesting school day. Belle had managed to get out of the hot wire fence, and Wilson followed her across the field until both were nearly out of sight. This happened occasionally, thanks to the elk and deer that pranced across the meadow, unaware of the temporary electric fence until after they broke a section of it down. For this reason, I periodically glanced out the window to check on them. This time it was Sonja, who looked from her study of verbs to notice their latest escape.

"Mom, please let me get Wilson," Sonja asked with pleading eyes.

I hesitated for a moment, but knew she would not concentrate on her school work if she was worrying about her horse.

"You may go get him, but halter him and bring him straight back to the corral. Belle will follow; she doesn't like being left alone. Take Kobi with you."

Sonja was out the door by the time I'd finished speaking. I was not fond of having our school lessons interrupted by a horse, but this took priority. Bill naturally groaned when I told him about the fence. It had become an almost daily repair routine, and he uttered a few colorful words about the fence manufacturer before heading down to make repairs. Fixing temporary fence was taking such a tremendous amount of our time that we promised ourselves to budget for a more traditional smooth wire fence next year, so we could cordon off the property into smaller grazing sections. But this year we had to make do with the fragile hot wires and temporary posts.

After the horses were safely corralled, Sonja returned to me at the dining room table.

I told her, "Dad's securing the picket line. Belle and Wilson will be back out in the meadow eating in a few minutes." When the fence was down, our temporary alternative was to place Belle on her picket line. Wilson would eat near her, and not wander far from her side.

"I'm glad," Sonja replied with a smile. She plopped down in her chair, swept her bangs out of her eyes, and again picked up her book. "You know I worry about Wilson when he's loose."

"I know, Love Lamb. That's why I let you go get him. Now let's get back to work."

The rest of the morning was uneventful, and we moved through her studies rather quickly that day. Home schooling is a commitment, and honestly, there were days when I just didn't want to do it. But most of the time I enjoyed it. I loved seeing my girls learn and accomplish things with my help. I loved the flexibility of setting my own schedule and choosing the curriculum. Most of all, I liked having them around during the day, and all of us sharing lunch together. We would have the most interesting conversations during those meals. To ensure they weren't denied social companionship, we often invited over several nice friends of theirs for pizza parties and sleepovers. We also entertained with barbeques and long afternoon lunches. All in all, it was worth the effort, as this day would exemplify.

Sonja looked at the clock. "It's time to take the horses back, Mom."

Sonja was happy for any opportunity to see her Wilson. She did not even mind cleaning corrals, because it meant she could be near him. We only had one reading lesson left, so I decided we could take a break. That was all she needed to hear, and she was running down to the picket line as fast as her legs would carry her. I needed some fresh air too, and went outside to meet them. I liked to take advantage of every moment outside in good weather, and we were having a warm, sunny afternoon. Sonja approached me with Wilson on the halter. As always, she was smiling broadly as she led the big horse without trouble. Wilson was happy to follow Sonja. It was a sight, this big freckled horse following the tiny delicate girl.

"How is he doing today?" I asked.

"Oh, he's fine," she beamed. "Do we have to go back now?"

"We still have reading lessons," I quietly reminded her.

"Oh."

I saw the disappointment in her face as she looked down to the ground. I had to admit, it would be hard to put Wilson away and leave this beautiful day to go back in the house. Then I thought about it some more. We'd had lessons outside at the patio table many times. So I made a suggestion.

"Give me Wilson's lead rope and you go get your book."

We were currently reading *Little House in the Big Woods* by Laura Ingalls Wilder, my favorite series.

Sonja looked quizzically at me, "Are we going to read outside with Wilson?"

"Yes," I replied. "We can sit here outside the dining room window and Wilson can graze on the grass here by the waterfall."

"That's great!" she exclaimed. She read out loud to me until she came to a page with an illustration. She paused and I saw a twinkle in her eye.

"Wilson wants to see the picture," Sonja announced, and she moved the book over to Wilson's grazing nose. He looked up, taking a small snuffle and sniff at the page. Sonja broke into a giggle as her blond hair tossed in the breeze.

"He likes me to show this book to him," she stated.

"I'm glad he's enjoying it."

I kept my head down, but grinned under the brim of my hat. How many parents got to teach school with a horse grazing by their feet? Yet, here I sat, listening to Sonja read aloud while Wilson contentedly munched the long grass. I knew Bill would be pleased, since this was one less patch of grass he'd have to cut. It was a win-win for all.

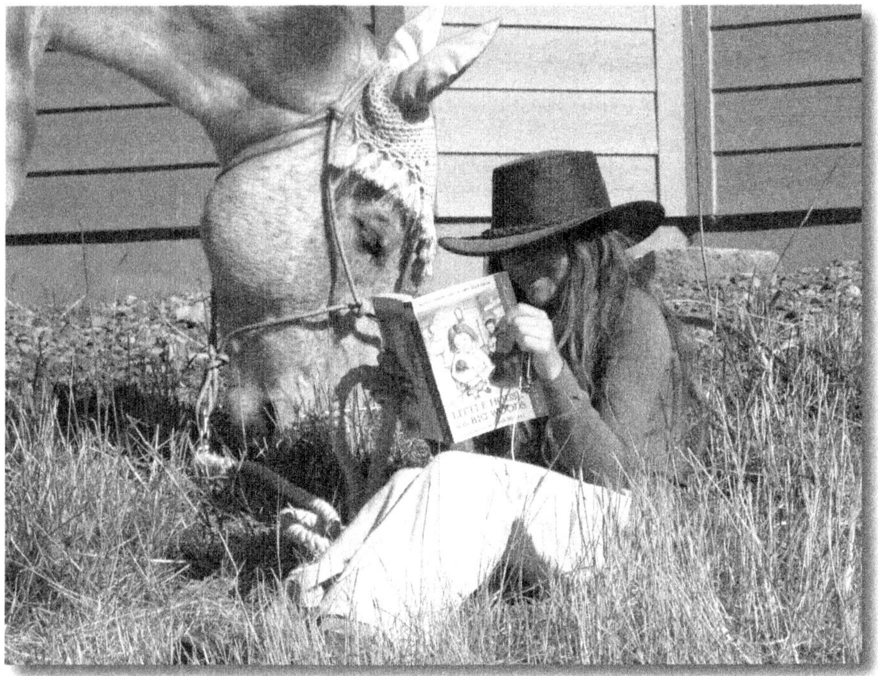

Wilson's reading lesson

44

Hello Dolly

LINDA'S TRUCK AND TRAILER PULLED UP INTO THE TURNAROUND area in front of our house. The rumble of the diesel engine stopped, and out she hopped.

"I brought three horses for you to try out at home," she informed me. "I like to train them here because you've got trails to roam and creeks we can cross. It gives them a different environment other than my indoor arena."

We were always glad to meet new horses, and the girls enjoyed riding them. I looked on eagerly as Linda opened the large metal doors of the trailer. Dolly was the first to emerge, and she gracefully stepped off the trailer onto the rocky ground. She stood and looked around, her gentle face assessing her new surroundings. She was unconcerned and remained calm. Sandy offered to hold Dolly, and took her by the lead rope. She began a conversation with her, telling her how delighted she was that she had come to visit.

Next off the trailer was Ziggy, a sorrel quarter horse who stood about fifteen hands, just a little larger than Wilson. She was young and was not yet finished growing. In time she would be a big girl. She was also calm, but more interested in all the pasture around her than our presence.

"Hold Ziggy for me, Nancy," Linda called.

"Of course," I replied, taking the lead rope from her hand. We stood together as the last horse, Trina, stepped out of the trailer. She was slightly larger than Ziggy, and also a sorrel, but in a lighter shade of red. Trina was the oldest at around sixteen years of age. She was such a patient horse, and very easy to handle on the ground. It was one of the reasons I liked her, but this day would be my first time riding her.

We all walked down our winding drive toward the barn area. Once inside the corral, we tied two of the horses to the hitching posts. Because we were short a couple of posts, we tied Dolly and Ziggy to the red pipe panels that enclosed our corral. Sandy and Sonja chatted excitedly about who would ride which horse first.

Linda piped in, "I suggest Sonja have her lesson on Trina."

Sonja was excited by the idea, and we saddled Trina with the youth saddle. She looked so small on such a big horse, but Trina seemed to understand this, and took slow, deliberate steps with Sonja on her back.

"I'm impressed even more with Trina, look how careful she is with Sonja," Linda commented.

"I can see that," I said, watching them with interest. I had faith in the horses Linda recommended for us, but I admit I was always a little tense when the girls tried a new one. Sonja had a fun ride, but her heart belonged to Wilson, and she quickly lost interest in Trina. Sonja also wanted to ride Dolly, so we brought her into the round pen and Sonja continued her lesson.

"She's easy to ride, Mom, and kind of fun," Sonja informed me as Dolly glided past me, moving in a continuous circle in the round pen. I watched them through the red steel panels as they moved about with ease.

Next it was Sandy's turn, and she enjoyed riding all three horses, each responding to her commands without complaint. Ziggy was last, and Sandy easily rode her in the round pen before taking her into the corral where she maneuvered gracefully around the huge fir tree. She then proceeded to back her up, turn her, and walk her in the opposite direction. I wondered if Ziggy would be a good match for Sandy. She and Belle were continuing to have their difficult times, mercurial as they both were.

Sandy dismounted Ziggy and remarked, "I think you'll like her Mom; give her a try."

"I guess that means I'm next, then." I stepped onto the mounting block and placed my pink boot into the stirrup. I hoisted myself into the saddle and gently settled into the seat. Ziggy felt tall and big after my experiences with Dolly. I enjoyed riding her as I gently swayed with her movement. Next, came Trina, who was as gentle with me as she had been with Sonja. I could detect the unique feel of each horse, in turn, as their gaits differed slightly from one another. It made sense; they were unique individuals, just as people are.

Now it was time to ride Dolly. A stiff wind hit me in the back, and I noticed the trees started to sway and shake.

"It looks like rain is blowing in," I said with a frown. I did not want anything to spoil my lesson. I looked at the horses, wondering if the change in weather would facilitate a change in behavior, since they're often frightened by wind and inclement weather. Ziggy, now tied to a corral panel, looked a little nervous, and she danced a bit on the lead rope. Trina and Dolly seemed completely unconcerned by the wind as it now whipped the trees.

"Let's try to finish our lesson before it starts raining," Linda offered.

I mounted Dolly and began to ride her in the round pen. The weather was becoming increasingly unpleasant by the minute, but Dolly took no notice, and we finished our lesson without incident. I was pleased that the weather did not upset her; I had seen many horses become frightened and difficult to manage under similar conditions. I mentally added this information to my increasing list of "reasons I like Dolly." A rain cloud passed over and peppered us with massive droplets.

"I'm finished," I announced, as I moved Dolly back to the block and dismounted. "Let's get everyone unsaddled and put this gear back in the tack room." I did not like my tack getting wet; it dries out the leather and will ruin it if it is not cared for properly. True to the nature of Montana, the clouds blew over, and by the time we were finished unsaddling, the sun was starting to break through the clouds.

"The weather here is not boring," I commented. We walked the horses back up to the trailer, and Linda began loading them, one by one. Trina was the last, and was showing some resistance.

"That's strange," Linda remarked. "Trina usually doesn't have any trouble loading into a trailer."

"She wants to live with us, Mom," Sandy chirped. "She doesn't want to go home."

"She does seem to like it here, Linda." I turned to the red colored mare and said, "You are welcome anytime. Come back again, Trina." I patted her shoulder, and with that she consented to get onboard.

I looked at Linda, and with a deadpan expression said, "You just have to know what to say to them." With that, she swung the heavy doors shut and latched them in place.

45

Saddle Up

You know you are in Montana when you see a leather saddle perched on a dining room chair by the table where you usually eat your meals. It was something I had never considered, yet there I was cleaning another used saddle I had just purchased for Sonja. It was, in truth, an English saddle. This was something you didn't see as often as a Western saddle, but Sandy had one, and now Sonja wanted to try riding English style.

After several lessons, she decided she liked it enough to try it at home, and perhaps in local competition. I agreed to support her and went back to my favorite leather shop in the Helena Valley. We found a saddle that fit her, even though there weren't many to choose from among the racks of Western rigs.

So there I sat, cleaning up her third saddle in the comfort and good light of my dining room. I always enjoyed the challenge of taking something worn and making it beautiful and useful again. Whether it is a piece of furniture, clothing, or in this case, leather, it felt good when I could take a step back and look with admiration at what some hard work can accomplish. By now the leather had become supple and shiny again. Score one more victory for home economics.

"Isn't it time you bought a saddle of your own, instead of working on everyone else's?"

I looked up to see Bill watching me.

He grinned, "We are looking at a horse for you; perhaps you need a saddle too."

A saddle of my own? I hadn't really thought about it. "When do you want to go look for one?"

"The next time we go to town we can stop at the saddle shop."

"Great, let's go tomorrow. We can get all of our errands done. It'll be fun."

The next day we walked into the leather shop. We had become regular customers and by now, the owner, Ben, knew us well.

"What can I help you with?" he asked.

"I want a saddle for myself. It has to be a used one," I replied. Despite my excitement, I felt awkward and self-conscious. As usual, I had come straight to the point without any banter, forgetting that Ben was also a custom saddle maker. "I mean I need something affordable, and it has to be pretty." I had no sooner said that when visions of Gail rolling her eyes entered my mind.

"Well, let me think, I know one you might like." He walked around to the back of the shop and came out holding a black leather saddle. The leather was hand-tooled with scrolls and flowers, and it had diamond shaped brass edging all along the Cheyenne roll that topped the cantle, or upper back of the seat. Brass accents also flowed down the wide leather fenders to the stirrups. Mentally, I was already cleaning it up and could see its shiny future. It reminded me of something the Lone Ranger would have owned.

"What kind of horse are you buying it for?" Ben inquired.

"Honestly, I don't have the horse yet, but probably a small or medium sized quarter horse mare. I'm still deciding."

"Well, if it doesn't fit, you can always bring it back," he replied.

Ben placed it on a saddle rack and told me to sit on it so I could tell how it felt. It felt just fine, except for the fact that the seat jockey (the part just below the seat) was dry leather that had curled up and dug into my thigh. I mentioned the problem to Ben, feeling disappointed because it was so pretty.

"I can fix that," Ben assured me. "I'll put sandbags on the leather and condition it to make it more pliable, and then I can reshape it. I can also bend the stirrup leather so it sits more forward and takes some of the pressure off your legs. Then it should be more comfortable."

I was pleased, but still decided to try two more saddles, just to make sure I had looked at all my options and was making an informed decision. It was in my nature, as Gail had put it, "to research everything to death."

The black saddle was the one I wanted, even if it required the extra effort Ben had described. I apologized for being so choosey, but he simply smiled and said, "I just want the Lady to be happy."

I then inquired as to his opinion about the cinch. It was made of a fuzzy pale blue polyester material. Not only did it look completely out of place, I was worried it would become hot and cause unnecessary sweat and skin irritation on my horse.

"It came with the saddle, but if you want a different one, I can replace it with a new cotton cinch."

"Do you have a recommendation? Am I worried over nothing?"

"I prefer the cotton ones; they're more comfortable."

Bill asked, "Is there an extra charge for it?"

"No," Ben said. "Once again, I just want the Lady to be happy."

"I am," I chirped.

Bill said, "Sold."

We paid for the saddle and Ben agreed to have it ready for us in about a week. When we left the saddle shop I was feeling very "cowgirl." Even though she was not mine yet, and there was no official choice made, I had secretly bought the saddle with Dolly in mind.

It was lesson day again, and we were at Linda's barn trying out horses. I rode all three candidates, but again decided Dolly was my favorite. It was Sandy's turn to ride her, so I handed over the reins and stepped outside for a few moments while Linda began her lesson. When I returned to the barn, Linda and Sandy were at the far side of the arena. Within moments, Sandy trotted up to me on Dolly.

"Sandy, you should finish your lesson and not come over to talk to me," I said.

"I didn't come to you. Dolly did. I tried to turn her around, but as soon as you came in the door, she wanted to see you. She really likes you, Mom."

Linda walked over and tried to return Dolly to her lesson. Dolly was resistant and seemed content to stand next to me.

"Come on, Dolly," Linda said, trying to push Dolly away from me and back to her lesson. "I know you really like this lady, but you have a lesson to finish."

Once again I saw a shadow briefly cross Linda's face, and wondered what it meant. After the lessons ended, we stood around chatting. Linda was holding Dolly's lead rope loosely, while talking with another one of her clients. At the first opportunity, Dolly left Linda's side and took several steps in my direction and stood next to me. I knew this was a major no-no. I was always told your horse cannot move its feet without permission when you are holding the lead rope. I waited for Linda to finish her conversation and then I said, "Linda, look at Dolly."

"Dolly chose you!" she exclaimed. "Twice in one day! I will have to tell the owner Dolly chose Nancy!"

Instead of admonishing her, Linda expressed her elation. I felt like I had found a friend in Dolly. It was such a good feeling to know that Dolly wanted my company and felt safe with me. I really wanted her to be mine, since it's hard to resist someone who so obviously likes you and gives you such special attention. I have always loved animals, which is why I became a wildlife artist. I had enjoyed training dogs because of the bond I formed with them. I just never thought I could have a similar relationship with a horse. But I had to be sure, so I asked Linda if she could bring Dolly out for a solo lesson at our place. Linda agreed, and within a few days she was unloading Dolly off the trailer once again, and leading her toward our corral. It was a beautiful day and the soft green grass quietly whispered under our feet with each passing step.

"I bought a saddle," I commented to Linda as we were walking.

"And who did you buy this saddle for?" I heard the amusement in her voice.

"I was thinking maybe for Dolly."

The shadow reappeared in her expression. I could tell now it was apprehension, so I asked, "Is something wrong?"

"Well, maybe. The problem is that Dolly was offered to me as a gift by one of my best clients. When I told him I'd found a good match for Dolly and wanted to sell her, he balked. He still has the papers on her, and he's not prepared to give her up."

I was hurt by this revelation, but couldn't blame Linda. She had assumed the owner wouldn't mind. After all, he'd given the horse to her, presumably with no strings attached.

"I'm going to try to convince him to sell her to you, so let's just wait and see what happens."

I agreed and decided to remain hopeful. Linda was on another mission.

"I just sent him this text." She handed me her phone as we sat under the big fir tree in my corral. Her message was short and to the point: "$3,000 for Dolly?"

"I'm just trying to establish something to work with; I'm really trying to get him to agree to sell her at all," she assured me. Within a few moments a long winded reply came in. The owner lamented his love for Dolly and his desire to keep her. We were both disappointed, but decided not to give up.

"This is silly. The man trades and buys horses every month at the Billings sale," Linda said. "This isn't the first time I've dealt with him like this," Linda confessed. "He often pays me to train and sell his horses, then cancels at the last minute. It's so frustrating. If he weren't one of my biggest clients, I'd say…"

The phone buzzed; the answer was still no. The emails and phone calls flew back and forth between us and the owner for weeks. I knew it was more than a bargaining tactic; it was a control issue. I'd seen it before, and the idea disgusted me how some people lived to manipulate others to their advantage or simple whim. The longer it lasted, the more disenchanted I became. He must have sensed how much Dolly meant to me. I wouldn't have held on this long, except for her.

When Linda finally reached an agreement with the owner, she told me he would sell her for $5,000. My heart sank, and I felt a blend of anxiety and relief when I told Linda that I could not justify the price. Linda agreed; it was far more than she was worth. I was depressed about it for several weeks. The only consolation was that I still got to ride her at Linda's place. There were no other offers made on the little mare, and at one lesson Linda came to me and said the owner had dropped Dolly's price to $4,000.

"It's still too much." I said.

Linda's voice was etched with concern. "What do you want to do about riding her today? I don't want you to keep getting attached to her. Maybe it's better if you don't ride her anymore."

I thought it over, and what she said made sense. I went out to the car and told Bill. He could see how much this was hurting me, and he listened intently, being careful to gather his thoughts before replying.

"Why don't you ride her one last time? Maybe this time will tell you how sure you are about her?"

I brightened up some at the thought and agreed. I looked forward to my time with Dolly, even if it could not last. Linda went out to Dolly's corral, and brought her into the barn. When she tied her to the hitching post, I immediately noticed something was different. She was nervous and shuffled her little feet. She was very unsettled. This was not like her at all. Did she sense this was our last ride together?

Bill and I went about our business. I began brushing her and getting her ready for the saddle pad, but she continued to shy at my touch and kept moving her feet from side to side. I called Linda over.

"Something is wrong with Dolly. She won't stand still for the saddle. She's never been this way with me before."

Linda's face soured, and her brow furrowed up. She was plainly upset. She blurted out, "I hope he didn't ruin her!"

"What do you mean?"

"He was here yesterday afternoon, riding her. He treated her roughly; you know, jumping on her back and acting all cowboy. I don't know everything that had occurred. I wasn't in the arena the whole time, but I saw enough. He'd brought his girlfriend with him, and when I came back in, they were riding double on Dolly."

"What? That horse is too small for two people."

"That horse is too small for him," Linda added. "That's why he gave her to me."

"Look, I'll get on her first. I want to make sure she's still okay. Go ahead and finish saddling her up."

Linda got on Dolly and began to put her through the paces. She backed her up, moved her from side to side, and then rode her around the arena a few times.

"She seems to be responding well. I think she's alright for you to ride." Linda dismounted and handed the reins over to me.

I eased myself into the saddle the way I had been taught. If I were a horse, I wouldn't want anyone to slam themselves onto my back. So I was respectful when I mounted. With a gentle squeeze of my knees, Dolly moved off as smoothly as she had always done for me. We walked to the other side of the arena and I felt the familiar gliding motion as I began to slowly sway to her rhythm. *I guess she's alright, she feels the same, what a relief.*

I continued to ride her through the cones, and to and from different barrels and other landmarks I'd pick out from across the open spaces. I was completely enjoying the challenge of moving and steering Dolly around the obstacles, but overall it was relaxing and fun. I saw Bill standing by the door and I walked Dolly over to him.

"What do you think of her?" he asked. He was watching us intently, as always.

"She is wonderful," I replied. "I really enjoy her."

"You *would* pick her—at $4,000," he groaned. He was joking of course, but his voice trailed off.

I looked at him and wondered what he was thinking. Was he considering actually buying Dolly? My birthday was coming up soon. What a gift she'd make! Then I experienced a mixture of joy and guilt. It was too much to spend. My chest tightened a little.

"Move her a little faster and tell me how it feels," he said.

I was still a novice rider, with less than a dozen lessons under my belt, but I felt safe on Dolly. I wanted Linda's permission to trot Dolly, but I knew I could safely move her into a faster walk. I urged her on a little faster, and she responded. Our pace quickened.

"Wow, Nancy, you're almost trotting!" I heard Linda's voice shout from across the barn.

"I asked her to move a little faster. I wanted to see what it felt like. But I don't want to trot her without your help."

"I'm almost finished over here with my other customer. I'm multi-tasking today. I'll be right over."

I slowed Dolly to a walk and took her back over to where Bill was standing.

"What do you think?" I asked him.

"That was really good. I'm going to go talk to Linda." He turned and walked away.

I slowly took Dolly toward the open barn doors. The sunlight was streaming in and I could see the sunbeams strike the sandy floor, casting shadows all around them. *What a beautiful day!*

We stopped for a moment to admire the view and feel the cool breeze on our faces, and then started walking back inside. Suddenly, she began to violently pull at the reins and shake her head from side to side. In an instant, before I could think *Dolly, what is wrong?*...I found myself wondering why I was looking at the ceiling and feeling so disoriented. In shock and disbelief I realized I was falling backwards, still holding onto the reins.

Let go of the reins! my brain shouted at me and I opened my hands. I have a vague recollection of them snapping back at Dolly. *This is going to hurt* I thought as I landed flat on my back. I let out a small cry of some sort and skidded, as the back of my helmet smacked the ground with a whack.

I couldn't breathe; the wind had been knocked out of me. I turned over to my side, gasping for breath like an incredibly embarrassed fish lying on the beach. *What happened? Pain! Oh how my head and back hurt. Could I move my legs? Ouch! Ouch! Ouch!* That was all I could think about at that moment. There was a flurry of activity as Bill, Linda, and my girls all rushed over to me.

"What happened?" Bill exclaimed.

"I was thrown," I gasped.

Bill tried to help me up.

"Don't!" I cried. "It hurts too much."

"Don't move her," Linda warned. "Let her rest a moment."

In a minute my breathing returned to normal, and I relayed my story as best as I could remember. Linda got a chair, and I took off my helmet and eased myself down in it. We tried to reconstruct what happened. No one knew for sure because nobody saw it. They were all doing something else. In and among it all, Dolly never left my side. She waited patiently next to me when I was on the ground and while sitting in the chair. We all looked at her; she seemed completely composed and unaffected by events.

"Do you want to get back on her?" Bill asked quietly. His face showed concern, but he still gave me a compassionate smile.

"No," I barely whispered and shook my head.

Linda decided to ride Dolly. She wanted to see if she could recreate the problem, and discover what was bothering her. Other than a little head shaking, she acted like her old self. None of us could figure out what happened. Everyone had a theory. Maybe a fly had gone up her nose; maybe she lost her footing; or perhaps she had a pinched nerve or some bruising from yesterday's treatment. Or maybe we had simply misjudged Dolly, and she was not the horse we thought she was. There was no answer to this question. In truth we would never know.

Linda motioned to her assistant. He had been watching the drama from the other side of the indoor barn. "Take Dolly away," she ordered.

I watched as he approached and took Dolly's reins, leading her slowly out the big barn doors to the fresh air and sunshine. As she walked away I could not help but watch my dream go up in smoke. It burned my face and stung my eyes. I fought back the tears. I stood up and immediately felt the pain in my lower back. I was grateful I had my soft back brace on under my clothes. *It probably saved me from a more serious injury.* I began slowly making my way to the car. I vaguely recall hearing Bill's voice instructing Linda to call the horse's owner. He was fuming.

"Tell him we won't be buying Dolly for any amount. I wouldn't take her now if he gave her to us."

I settled into the front seat and decided I was well enough to go on with the rest of our day. When we reached the Costco parking lot, I told

Bill to take the girls inside, and I would join them in a moment. I just wanted a few minutes to myself.

They were barely through the entrance of the store when the tears began to fall. I could hold them back no longer; the pain and anguish were just too much to bear. I cried not a few remorseful tears, but a gut wrenching flood that made my whole body shake as I hid my face in my hands. I cried because every muscle in my forty-eight-year-old body was screaming in pain. I cried because I was embarrassed and I felt betrayed by the horse I had been building a friendship with over all these months. I knew that relationship with her was completely over. I even cried because I had ruined my new jacket, a jacket I stupidly thought I could not get dirty riding Dolly.

When I ran out of tears, I took a deep breath and let it out. I checked myself in the mirror on the car's sun visor. If you ever want to make yourself stop crying, take a look at how awful you look with red swollen eyes. Vanity will take hold and the tears will cease. *Pull yourself together, Nancy* I ordered sternly.

I cleaned myself up with a tissue from the glove box, and ran my hands through my hair, smoothing and combing with my long fingers and my pastel painted nails. My head throbbed, and I knew I probably had a mild concussion because it was one whopping big headache. With a sigh of resignation, I stiffly got out and shut the door with a thud, and hit the lock button on the remote, listening for the customary beep. I stood a little straighter, put a smile on my face, and slowly limped into the Costco. After all, I had my pride and they had food samples. Life goes on.

Later, back home on Cimarron, I stood looking at my beautiful saddle sitting on the tack room rack, and I wondered if I would ever use it. I found myself tying on the beautiful leather saddle crosses my friends and relatives had sent me. The one that Gail's son, Chase, had handmade, was embossed with brass brads outlined in the shape of a Celtic cross. If I ever left the saddle again against my will, I would certainly be well protected!

℧ ℧ ℧

I was sore for about two weeks when a card arrived in the mail from Gail. It pictured a bright and colorful cartoon cowboy flying through the air. His hat was going one way and he was going the other, with a bucking horse on the ground. The inside read "What does not kill us might not make us stronger, but it does give us pretty good bragging rights! Hope you are all fixed up soon." Where else but in Montana would one find a card like this? I had to laugh. In her own handwriting Gail had added, "I just had to get this. Hope you are better real soon and BACK ON THAT HORSE. Love Gail. P.S. Happy Birthday."

Anytime I talked with Gail, the conversation usually included cows, horses, our children, our feelings, or rural life reality checks—such as how to keep a house clean that everyone else is messing up. This particular conversation was about my feelings. I was still struggling with my horsemanship skills and my place in a rural life in general. I remember her advice.

"You're being too hard on yourself, Nancy. You haven't grown up in this country. You can't learn everything at once. It takes time."

"I know, Gail, but I'm used to accomplishing what I set my mind to, and I try to do it well. I know it sounds egoistical, but I always expect my hard work and efforts to pay off. I'm disappointed I haven't mastered the basics of riding."

I knew Gail would understand my frustration. We were both very practical minded, logical thinkers. That was one reason why we got along so well. We had similar childhood difficulties that shaped us into who we were now.

"I have to do something to increase my confidence. I know I can't ride Dolly anymore, but I'm going to ask Linda if I can work her on the ground. I have to get over this and not feel like a complete failure."

Gail agreed and encouraged me to try. "Let me know how it goes, I have to bolt."

Go West, Young Woman!

46

Goodbye Dolly

I REALLY ENJOYED WORKING WITH HORSES. Riding and ground work skills were imperative, now that I had two of them living at our home. I had to be able to manage them safely and effectively, and I wanted to set a good example for my daughters. How could I quit now? Linda was receptive to my idea when I suggested I try doing groundwork with Dolly instead of riding her.

My heart pounded the first time I saw her approach me, being led by Linda on the lead rope. *Does she remember what happened? Will I be able to handle her? Did she sense my lack of confidence? Would she take advantage of it?* These questions I asked myself over and over as she softly stepped up to me. She stood silently in front of me, refusing to make eye contact. She appeared almost as nervous as I did.

"Here, you take her." Linda handed me the lead rope. I took the thick twisted cotton in my right hand and draped the excess rope in my left hand, just as I had been taught to do.

"She's ignoring you; don't let her look away," Linda ordered.

I turned Dolly's head toward me and said, "Dolly, if you were going to throw someone, it should have been your owner, not me."

"Yeah!" said the girls in unison.

Linda snickered, "Start out by walking her."

I made a small clucking sound and began walking. My horses know I like them to walk in a particular place. It is about three to four feet away

283

from me, just a little behind by right shoulder. If their nose is parallel to my shoulder, they are too far ahead and I back them up. Dolly started in her usual place and we began to walk together. *Maybe she does remember what I expect.* But I no sooner thought it, when she began to push forward, trying to pass me. I immediately, but gently, tugged at the lead rope, and quietly told her to back up. I started gently; if she resisted, then I would use more pressure. Dolly responded immediately and stepped back into place.

"She's licking and chewing her lips," Linda called to me. "That's a really good sign."

I felt a little better. Dust kicked up in little clouds around our feet as we continued our walk, moving in a big circle around the arena. We came to a stop where we began, in front of Linda.

"That went well," she said. "What do you want to do next?"

"I want to try crossing her feet." Foot crossing is a challenging exercise that involves moving a horses shoulder and hind quarter so that their front feet cross. It is not a natural movement for them, hence the difficulty. I stepped into her shoulder with my feet firmly planted on the ground. I placed the extended fingers of my left hand along the side of her head, while my right hand was against her neck. I began to walk into her space until she crossed her front legs, one over the other, then I stopped and praised her. After accomplishing the same on her opposite side, I gave her a rest. She was a little resistant on her left side, but I persisted until she moved.

Next, I decided to move her hind end. This can be a dicey move because horses have so much power in their back legs. Instinctively, they resist giving up this control to anyone else. My location at her rear put me in a potentially precarious situation. Should she decide to kick, I would not have time to maneuver out of the way.

I pointedly looked at Dolly's left hind quarter and took a step towards it, flicking my wrist and commanding, "Move, Dolly." She ignored me.

"Move!" I said, this time more forcefully, and I lifted my arm a little higher and faster. Dolly suddenly jumped sideways and threw her head up in a panic. Her eye was wild, and she acted as though afraid I was about to beat her.

"Goodness sake, Dolly, calm down," I chided. "I'm not going to hurt you." I stood still and shook my head. Dolly relaxed, and I approached her, gently reaching out to rub her withers. "You really are okay," I said. "Let's try again."

At first I had been tense, but now found myself relaxing as I again moved Dolly's legs forward and backward. From side to side she moved with ease. She seemed calmer, as was I, but my triumph at ground work did not fill the void I felt in my heart.

"I have another lesson to teach." Linda's voice broke through my thoughts.

"Of course," I mumbled, suddenly feeling self-conscious. "I guess I should say goodbye to Dolly." I tried to sound cheery, but my tone rang hollow. Dolly looked at me and leaned her head close to mine. I started to move her away. I don't let horses get this close to my face, but something inside of me said, *Just wait.* She put her delicate nostrils to mine and started taking long deliberate breaths. I was slightly frightened and almost pulled away, but again my inner voice said, *Just wait.* Dolly continued her strange breathing for another minute or two, and then she pulled her head away and just looked me. We stood staring at each other, and I felt what she had just done had some meaning to it, something important, but I could not fathom what.

"What was Dolly doing, Mom?" Sandy asked.

"I don't know," I replied softly. "I didn't understand it either."

I walked Dolly a few steps over to Linda, who had been talking to another customer, and handed her the lead rope. She turned and walked away with Dolly. I watched their silhouettes grow smaller and smaller as they walked across the expanse of the arena and disappeared out the barn door. I turned to my daughters and said, "Let's go home girls." Little Sonja's hand slipped into mine and the three of us walked out those same barn doors into the cool fall air.

I rested my chin on my hand, with my elbow propped against the passenger side window sill, deep in reflection, all the way home. I said nothing, but watched aimlessly as the scenery darted by. As promised, I called Gail later to report my experience. I explained everything to her, lightly glossing over the odd breathing incident.

"You know something, Gail," I said quixotically, "I thought facing Dolly was going to make me feel so much better. It didn't, and I don't understand why. Maybe I should give up trying to understand horses, and let the girls focus on their riding. Perhaps I should just draw and paint horses, instead of riding and working with them. I may not be meant for this."

"You can't quit now!" was Gail's staunch reply. "It takes a long time to learn all this. You've come a long way in a short time. Besides, Chase made you that cross to wear on your saddle. One day I'll bring my horse, Gentry, up to your place and we'll ride together. You just can't let one horse and a single bad experience sour you on the whole idea. I know you really connected with that animal. Someday there will be another Dolly, a horse you really care for that won't hurt you, one that wants to take care of you. I really believe if she had not been treated roughly the day before, Dolly would not have thrown you off. I think she was in pain or simply afraid. I don't think it was directed at you. That's what I believe."

I knew there was forty years of experience behind that opinion, so I tucked it away, and every now and then would think about it.

A week later, I saw Linda pull up and park her truck in the driveway. She made her way down to the corral for the girl's lessons. After our usual greetings, she told me her latest news.

"I'm going to the Billings sale and taking some of my horses. I can look in the 'loose pen' and see if there are any horses that might be good for Sandy. I'm pretty good at picking them out. You know Wilson was a loose pen horse."

"Who are you taking to the sale?" I asked, but I already knew at least one of her answers.

"Some of my customer's horses, and Dolly," Linda responded, looking at me.

I did not reply; I just stood there. The tension proved awkward.

"You can bid on Dolly if you still want her. We can work it out so you can bid over the phone. You don't even have to travel to Billings," she offered, hopefully.

"Part of me really wants to buy her, Linda. But I haven't been able to ride any horse since she threw me. I'm still unsure how it would work between us."

"Well, you think about it. If you change your mind, let me know."

I nodded silently, and she turned to the girls. "Let's start our lessons. Who wants to go first?"

Later, I called Gail and told her about the conversation with Linda.

"What did you decide about Dolly? Are you going to bid for her?"

My voice was resigned. "I've been thinking about it, and decided not to put in a bid. I have to let her go, Gail. Whoever buys her, I'm sure will want to take good care of her. She's up for auction in the catalog, not in the loose pen where horses sometimes end up at the slaughter house. I think it's for the best. At some point tomorrow she'll have a new home."

Painful as it was, I knew I was making the right decision, but I still felt bad about it. The next day Dolly sold for $1,500, a far cry from her original asking price of $5,000.

ᴗ ᴗ ᴗ

The weeks passed, and fall entered its full splendor. The days were cooler, but still beautiful. As always, I looked to the mountains for comfort. Feeling the breeze on my face, and seeing the immense blue sky and rolling green hills, with the far mountain peaks as backdrops almost fifty miles away, never failed to rejuvenate my spirit. But this time I only half smiled.

"Where is my joy?" I asked when I spoke with Gail that evening. I was tired, fatigued from a day spent "winterizing" our place. I had followed the advice of my dear friend and sprayed vinegar all around the house and the girl's playhouse to keep away mice that were looking for a winter burrow. We had brought in most of the outdoor furniture and all the potted plants, drained the waterfall and fountains, stored the pumps and water hoses to prevent line freezing, and closed the air vents to the subfloor. We were starting to settle in for the winter, but what I was feeling was more than just tired. I was just…sad.

"You're not riding anymore," Gail said, in that direct tone I had come to appreciate.

I was silent for a moment. "No, I'm not." Just like the card Gail had sent me, I got "back on," but not on Dolly. I had ridden Belle and Wilson, but not for very long. I was uncomfortable and did not seem to enjoy it very much anymore.

"I'm not like you, Gail. You ride for a living. You were on a horse before you could walk. It's in your blood."

I knew what she was driving at, that throw had hurt more than my body and my pride. It had somehow affected me inside. It had affected my mood and my confidence. I guess I did not see myself as one of those riders who could get thrown twenty times, shake it off, and mount up again. I did not like the feeling that a situation had gotten the best of me. I did not want one bad experience to ruin something I had enjoyed so much, so I had tried again, but I had to admit the experience *had* changed me. In my mind I had decided if I couldn't trust a horse as gentle as Dolly, I couldn't trust any horse.

"Well, look at the girls. They've just started riding, and they excel at it. Besides, you loved that horse. Dolly gave you the love of riding."

"And took it away," I added. "I feel like I'm in mourning, but I will get over it. I can do anything once I set my mind to it."

"Have you set your mind to it?"

"I will. I can put on my 'man pants,' as you like to say. It just takes me longer than you."

After a few more minutes of conversation I heard the familiar, "I have to bolt," and knew our conversation had come to an end. I was tired, and it was time for my shower. I had no energy left to argue anyway.

It would be some time before I ran across an article, quite by accident, about horses "sharing breath." Apparently this is a behavior they do with each other to show affection. It is an intimate behavior. They place their noses close to each other and breathe deep long breaths. It is not the same as sniffing to investigate something or someone. Horses share breath with each other, but rarely with humans. I was stunned by the revelation. I knew at last what Dolly was doing when she shared breath with me. It was the only plausible explanation for her behavior that day. Upon reflection, I was glad I had not pulled away and rejected her affection.

So now, after months had passed, I finally understood it was a rare intimacy, her way of acknowledging that she cared about me. I now felt privileged by the experience, but was saddened to think I would never know what had become of her. From then on, every time we went by Linda's place, I'd find myself looking for Dolly. I knew she was gone, but she would never be forgotten.

And I didn't give up. I continued to work with my daughters and our horses. After a year of training, and two local horse events under their belts, the girls were preparing for the Governor's Cup. It would be their largest and most advanced professional show. This time they would be competing with adults as well as kids. Their skills were improving and they were very excited. Sandy would be competing in both English and Western disciplines. Sonja would try her hand at a Western lead line demonstration. After the girls finished their practice for the event, it was my turn to have a lesson. Although I looked forward to it, I still wasn't enjoying riding as before.

Linda brought out a Morgan gelding named Image. He was a nice gentle horse who knew his job. Linda saddled him up for me and I mounted with ease. He was about fifteen hands, maybe a little larger, and I slowly moved him off. He was a fairly smooth ride, and I began to relax my mind and body as I walked him around the arena. I turned and moved him into series of figure eight patterns. I was at ease, thinking *This is how it is supposed to feel.* Image felt powerful and strong; and I could hear the gentle thud of his hooves as they moved across the sandy ground. Everything felt comfortable and familiar, the slight creaking sounds of the leather, the smell of dust and horse sweat, the slightly labored breathing of the animal, and the rhythm of the movement. Under Linda's direction I continued through the rest of my lesson. It was over too soon and I moved Image back to the mounting block.

"I thought you'd like him; he's such a nice boy," Linda said as I patted the horse and thanked him for the pleasant ride.

"You know, I really did like him. I enjoyed my ride today. He is a nice fellow." My thoughts turned inward as I brushed Image and talked to him quietly. *This is the first bit of joy I have felt with a horse since Dolly threw me. Maybe my riding days are not over. Perhaps there is hope for me yet.*

I finished brushing out Image, and then cleaned all the dark horse hair from the brushes. I brushed myself off next, and I went to talk to Linda. I told her we were interested in finding another horse for Sandy. She had become so interested in competing in shows, that we thought it was time for her to have a horse that she could participate with in the ring. Her horse, Belle, was a Tennessee Walker, and because she was gaited, she could not show or compete with non-gaited horses. In the West, gaited shows are

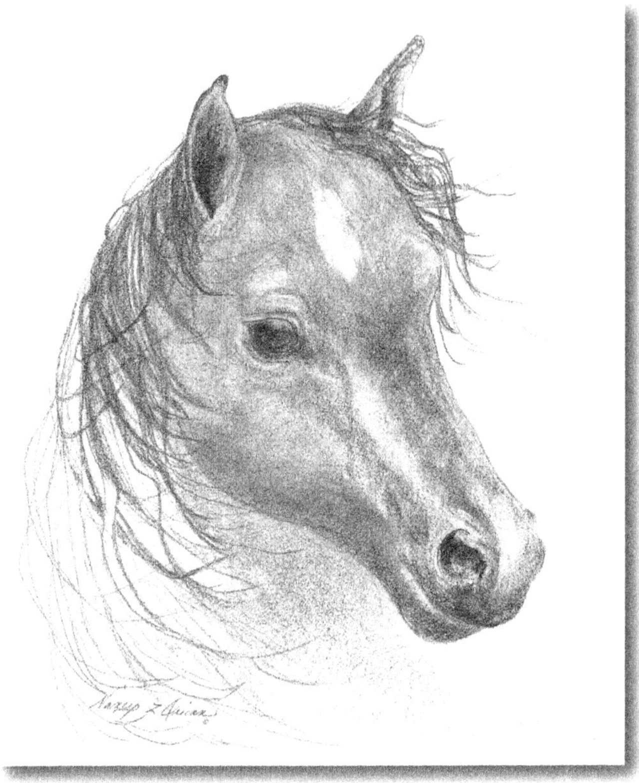

Author's graphite drawing inspired by Dolly

hard to find. We had been borrowing Linda's horses for the shows, and we knew we could not do that indefinitely. Linda did not have any candidates for Sandy, but promised to keep her eye out for one.

The day of the horse show arrived and we were all up bright and early. It was a long day, with the competitions starting at eight in the morning. Sandy's last event didn't end until seven that evening, so it was about seven-thirty before we headed home. Our girls did not mind because they had several showplace wins and went home with a handful of ribbons. It was a fun day for everyone. The ribbons were great confidence builders for the girls, and we proudly hung them on their achievement boards.

47

Bless this Mess?

During the six months of pleasant weather, the animals spend much more time roaming the fields, risking a greater chance of encountering the local fauna. One morning during breakfast I looked through my glass patio doors to see a gorgeous red fox glancing back at me, while on his way to the tree line. For a moment I thought it was a dog. I had seen her before, but never on my patio. I was convinced she had a den close by because I often saw her crossing the yard to the trees. She was no bother to us, so I left her be, and was rewarded with the occasional sighting of this reclusive animal.

The good weather also meant plenty of green grass, and Belle and Wilson very much yearned to leave the confines of the corral to sample it. In early spring we let them roam for an hour or two each day, being careful not to allow them too much green grass at once, for fear of foundering. Because we still did not have proper sections fenced off, they often ended up peeking into the dining room or patio windows. They were friendly horses and liked to see what we were doing. Belle enjoyed being touched and brushed, and Wilson desired to be petted and talked to. They requested such attention often, and so we would stop what we were doing to come outside and visit. Usually I thought it was a hoot, and felt flattered by their need for our company.

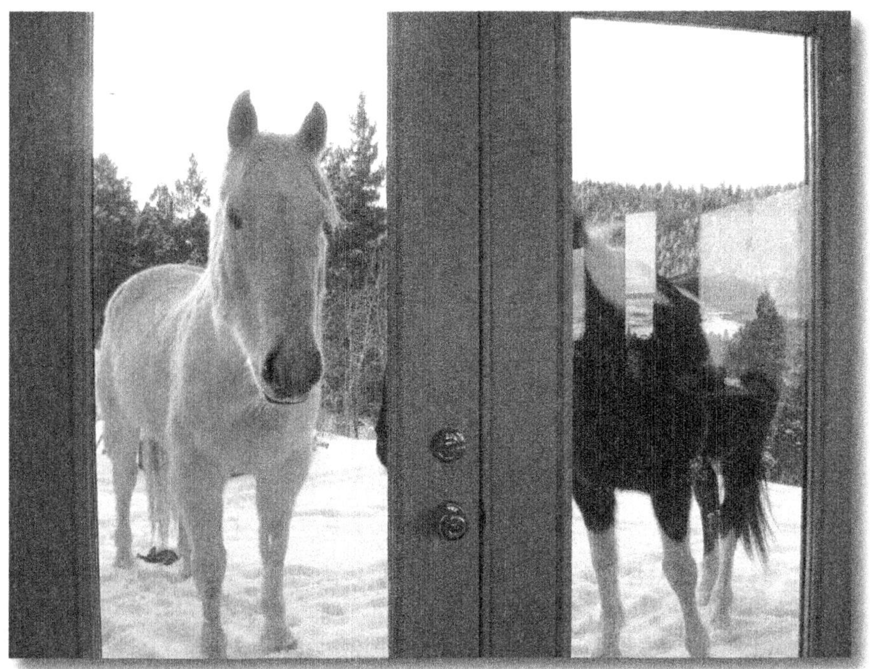

Wilson (*left*) and Belle "window shopping"

One day, however, I realized there was a down side to letting them so close to the house. Not only had I noticed they'd eaten some of my flowers, I nearly stepped in something one of them left behind.

"Who did this in my driveway?" I chastised them, while pointing to the fresh pile of excrement. They looked innocuously at each other, then back at me, but remained mute, admitting nothing. Their poker faces betrayed nothing.

"I know one of you did this," I went on, but they stood there, looking innocent, as if trying to say, *I'm glad you came out and found it; someone made a mess here, probably the dog.*

The horses were not the only ones making a mess. During hunting season, Kobi had disappeared for several hours, and when he returned that night, he became very ill. He vomited up some horrible smelling, foul, black goop, with chunks of what looked like raw liver, all over my maple hardwood floor—twice. The smell was enough to make me gag, and cleaning it up was a nasty chore. I watched him closely after that, worrying at first that he may have internal bleeding, but I knew his happy feet had taken him far afield, probably where some dead animal lay. He could not resist his canine instincts, and gorged on it, but judging by the look on his face now, was sorely regretting that decision. The next day I ran into my nearest neighbor, who said Kobi had come down the mountain for a visit the previous evening, while he was cleaning an elk he'd shot. Kobi had run off with the esophagus!

"I've seen it. Kobi offered it to me after he no longer wanted it." I knew it was not to be the last such incident with him, as long as he behaved like a canine garbage disposal.

Go West, Young Woman!

48

Right-of-Way

ONE GROUP OF ANIMALS I WAS FINDING FRUSTRATING to communicate with was cows. For example, why do cows always prefer to rest and recline in the middle of the road? Acres and acres of grass around them, and they'd rather squat in the road and block me.

"Beep the horn again, and inch forward," I recommended to Bill as we came to a standstill on the road. I really did not want to frighten one of the heifers and cause her to crash into my nice car. I had yet to emotionally recover from all the damage Kobi had done to the paint on my Highlander when it was new, after the first mouse incident. But I couldn't sit all day, trapped by a herd of dumb cows. After much grunting and groaning, the disgruntled Angus moved off the road, and we continued our descent down the mountain and turned onto the highway. What I did not know was that on this particular day I was not done with cows.

"Moving Montana Beef" the large hand-painted wood sign announced. It was driven into the ground on the right side of the highway as we started up the pass.

"It must be a cattle drive," I said. I began earnestly looking for road scat. I did not see anything at first, but rounding the corner we were met with at least a hundred cows spanning both lanes of the highway. An old truck was parked in the emergency lane. A bored looking woman inside the cab held out a yellow flag from the window, which she flicked whenever a vehicle approached. I remembered Gail explaining to me that a flag car was always placed at the beginning and end of the herd to warn drivers to slow down.

We came to a complete stop. The cows were supposed to stay on the side of the road, but at this time they were all over it. Two weather-beaten old cowboys flanked the herd on horseback. The one man closest to me was lean and leathered looking. The bandanna around his neck could not protect his darkened, wrinkled skin from years of working outdoors. What impressed me most was the way he sat in his saddle with confidence. *He has spent his life doing this*, I thought. He knew his job well, and when I saw one of the cows break away from the herd and run up the bank, his horse immediately took off after it. The stray could not get away. The cowboy's horse was urged into a fast gallop as he raced ahead of the cow, and began to push it back to where it had come from. I started thinking the horse knew what to do, as much as the man. They seemed unafraid to run straight at a cow and make it move over, or push it a little, to get it back in the group.

I opened my window to listen to the sounds. I heard the men calling and whistling as the horses cut in and out of the herd, forcing the cows off the pavement. To me it looked like a mass of confusion, but to them it was as well choreographed as any ballet. I thought most of the cows looked frightened or confused. But it was clear some were just plain angry. They caused the most trouble. I was a little worried someone might get hurt, but it was apparent the men and their horses weren't worried. They just looked perturbed and determined, as they continued to move the cows, trying to clear a path for the backed up traffic to drive through.

When one lane opened up, I was surprised to see a car from well behind us break line, and pass everyone at a high rate of speed. It was stupid and dangerous for everyone involved; they could have spooked a horse, or a cow, or even killed someone.

"What's wrong with that guy?" Sandy asked in disgust.
"He's frustrated from sitting so long," I told her. "But he made a dangerous choice." Bill offered a more colorful opinion.

The cows were finally moved off the road, and we slowly started up the mountain pass again.

"We're twenty minutes behind schedule," Bill said, irritated.

"I know," I replied. Secretly, I was thankful for the experience. I had never seen anything like it. It was like being at a Western movie.

"I'm renaming this bend in the road," I said.

"What do you mean?" I heard someone ask.

"From now on I'm calling it Cross Cows Crossing!" I thought it was funny, but nobody laughed at my joke. I guess cows were starting to rub off on me. I'm glad Gail didn't know.

Go West, Young Woman!

49

Snow Days

T HE WEATHER WAS DEFINITELY COLD ENOUGH, but the day after Thanksgiving there was still no snow on the ground. From my limited experience, this was unusual, but welcomed, and we decided to take advantage of it.

It had become our family custom to cut the Christmas tree and put it up Thanksgiving weekend. This year I had a great idea.

"Who wants to go tree hunting on horseback?" I asked my daughters.

"Really, Mom? I can take Wilson?" Sonja almost squealed.

"And Belle!" Sandy was not to be left out.

We bundled up and saddled the horses. Bill and I walked alongside our girls, who never stopped laughing. *What a wonderful memory they can look back on* I thought as we strolled up and down the rolling hills of our property. We walked among the tree lines looking for just the right one.

"It can't be too tall," I gently reminded everyone. "We have to carry it back home." I heard a snort from Wilson and I assumed he agreed.

A fall day like this was a blessing indeed. The sun was out, even though it was cold. Colorful leaves crunched under our feet, and I enjoyed hearing the thud of the horses' hooves and the laughter. Wearing brightly colored helmets and fleeced gloves, riding on the backs of their horses, my girls looked like a Currier and Ives painting.

At last, after much debate, a tree was chosen. Bill cut it down with his axe, and soon we headed home for tea and homemade cookies.

We left the tree in the garage overnight to thaw out. I remembered a story Gail told me of a friend of hers who tried to decorate a partially frozen tree and the limbs snapped off. To make matters worse, when it thawed, beetles and bugs fell off the tree onto her floor, and not all of them were dead. So I decided to dodge that bullet; the tree would spend a night or two in the garage.

U U U

Within a week the snow came as I knew it would. Like the song, it was beginning to look a lot like Christmas. With a hot, fragrant cup of tea in my hand, I looked out the big pane glass windows of our loft and watched Wilson running at full gallop in the snowy front meadow. I could not believe my eyes. I had never seen him move that fast. His white and silver mane and tail were flowing behind him as his hooves slammed onto the ground, sure and steady. He was having fun, and with each turn, he slid in the snow, showering it into the air. I was elated; his feet were doing much better. If he were in pain, he could not have run about like this. The snow must have felt great.

I called to Sandy and Sonja to come watch with me. As Wilson approached the corral, he did something really funny. He stopped running and started hopping straight up in the air, landing on all four like a giant bunny rabbit. The girls laughed, happy to see him feeling so well. "Merry Christmas, Wilson," I said.

The girls found the fresh snow too good to resist, and asked to go sledding after their school day was over. They bundled up in their hats, scarves, snow pants, gloves, and boots, and then trundled with their sled across the yard to the steepest slope in our front meadow. Depending upon icing conditions, it was possible to build up enough speed and momentum to take them right up the corral gate. As a precaution, we put the horses in their corral before the girls jumped on their sled. Sandy was in the back, anchoring the light weight foam sled, and Sonja knelt in front to steer it. With a push, they started flying down the hill, Kobi running alongside

300

them. Unexpectedly, both dog and sled shifted directions and crashed into one another. There was a flurry of white snow, legs belonging to girls, and legs belonging to the dog, all flailing on top of one another. It really was comical.

Next came the hard part, trudging back up the hill, with sled in tow. It had to be easier than pulling the heavy wood and metal sled that I had as a child. After a few minutes they were ready to try again. Kobi thought of a much more fun way to get down the hill. As the girls pushed off, he made one giant leap and tried to land on the back of the sled. He missed, almost knocking Sandy off the back. He must have been thinking that riding would be much more fun than running alongside. He tried several more times to leap onto the back of the sled, but there simply was no room. On the last run down the hill, the girls put him on the sled and gave him a ride. Almost half way down he jumped off, perhaps deciding it was more fun to jump on the sled than to actually ride on it.

I was not the only one watching the girls play. Belle and Wilson were at the gate looking on with amusement as the girls skidded down towards them, stopping only inches from the gate. Wilson put his nose over the panel to greet them.

It did my heart good to see this, and I mused how different it was from suburban and urban life. Gone were the days of worrying about the air quality index, which sometimes read so poorly that schools back east would cancel outdoor recess. This did not mean the weather here was always ideal. In fact, it could be quite unforgiving, and downright dangerous in the winter. We endured violent, sudden whiteouts, where visibility dropped to zero, and black ice so slick that tires couldn't grip the road. The temperature might drop to thirty degrees below zero, and on some days I would look out the window and feel like I was living inside a snow globe. The wind can be vicious too, especially when combined with the cold temperatures to produce a deadly wind-chill factor, or blanket our road with heavy drifts. We learned these lessons, sometimes the hard way, and now always check the weather, and plan around it. Even with the challenges winters possess, I would not trade this life for another, especially on a magical day such as this one had been.

Go West, Young Woman!

50

How the West Was Fun

L IFE IS FULL OF HUMOR, IF ONE WILL PAUSE LONG enough to notice it. It can take many forms—sublime wit, farcical absurdity, slapstick, etc. One might pontificate for hours on the subject, but what would be the fun in that? In Montana, humor can most easily be found in any situation that does not fit the generally accepted norm, be it the female driver who blithely clips her toenails out her car window while tootling down the highway, or the local town council issuing a *fatwa* against a the nearby casino for daring to erect multicolored plastic palm trees that clashed with the more traditional wigwam and giant Hereford statue that graced the town's entrance.

Our own house is not immune to bizarre antics, that's for sure. Whether its Kobi's tail being the only visible sign of him as he digs his way to China in search of petulant gophers. Or Sandy continuing to run in panicked circles around the house, in blind fear of the "deadly" desiccated grass snake skin that Sonya has long since stopped chasing her with.

Even situations that, from another point of view, might be considered tragic or sympathetic, can carry the simple stamp of incongruity that marks them as candidates for the theater of the absurd. Here's a case in point:

I've mentioned Costco often in this book. It was not my intention to plug any business, as we frequented many big box stores: Wal-Mart, Target, K-

303

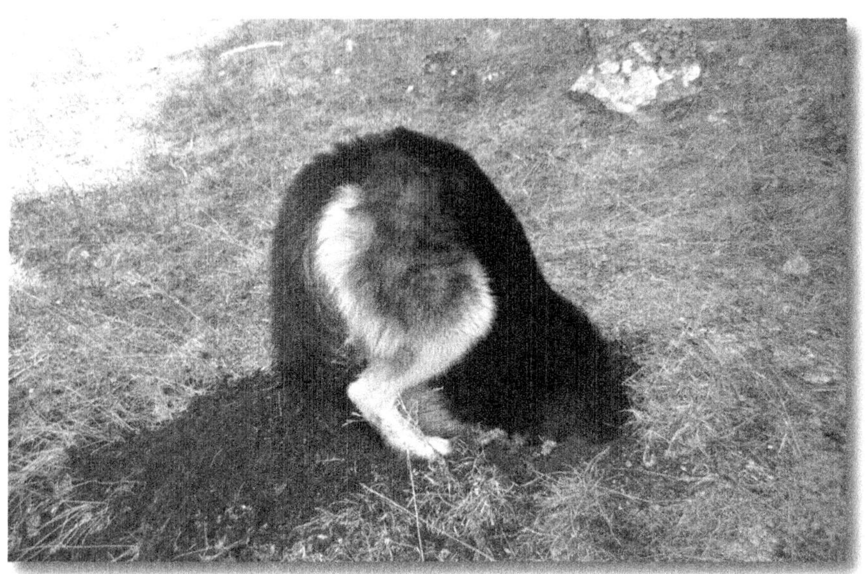

"I know there's a groundhog in here somewhere!"

Mart, Lowes, Home Depot, Shopko, Macy's. We just tended to find ourselves at Costco at least once a week, stocking up on pantry supplies. It really is quite shocking how much food two young girls can eat. And of course, there are the samples. That's how I met my dear friend, Michelle.

After retiring from teaching, she took a part-time job there handing out samples. Each time we dropped by her table, she would inquire about our latest misadventure. I was surprised she was so interested, but it seemed I always had some new story to tell.

Ironically, one of the oddest took place in that very Costco parking lot. We were loading the groceries into the back of our car, when out of the corner of my eye I saw a large pickup truck and flatbed trailer pull up and park nearby. It was not the truck that I found interesting, but the enormous front paw that was hanging off the edge of the flatbed trailer. I walked over and saw the body of a cougar. He was huge, a big male weighing perhaps

180 pounds. He was draped across the flatbed with one leg tied down. He was gorgeous, strong and muscular, with a coat of gold, brown, and gray hair, the epitome of his species. The cat's eyes were open in a lifeless stare, and despite this fact, I felt as though he was looking directly into my own eyes. He obviously was the recent trophy of some local hunter, but the driver had gone inside before I reached the vehicle, so I could not ascertain any details.

"Look at this, girls!" I said, feeling both excitement and regret. "It's a cougar!" My girls had never seen one up close, and they stared with curiosity at the incredible animal.

"I can't believe it!" Sandy squealed. "At Costco! What's it doing here?"

"Someone shot it and probably will have it mounted," I explained. I have personally hunted for food, and I knew I would always choose a human or a pet's life over the life of a wild animal, but sport trophy hunting held no allure for me. Because of my background in conservation law enforcement, I realized the importance of game management, and the need to raise revenue through hunting and fishing fees. But killing something you don't intend to eat never made a great deal of sense to me. But I had to admit, he was a beauty. I suppose when you shop at Costco, you never know what you will find—inside or outside.

ʊ ʊ ʊ

Humor need not always be achieved at the expense of others. Sometimes we just have to laugh at ourselves.

The weeks were slipping by quickly, and I could see the changes in the sky as the days grew a little shorter. With daylight savings time in effect, it would be dark by five o'clock. I didn't like it and found it depressing. I decided to go down to the barn and brush out the horses, taking advantage of the last of the sunny days. As I walked down the hill, I took a few moments to breathe the fresh air and listen to the birds that serenaded me along the way. As I entered the corral, the birds stopped singing, and it became very quiet. The only sounds I heard were my own footsteps crunching dirt as I crossed the dry ground.

I went to the tack room to get a halter, and happened to glance into the open stall to make sure the automatic water station was working. I had to look twice because the water was black. I noticed something in it; it looked like….*Oh no ! I am not seeing this!* A few steps closer confirmed my fears. Sitting in the drinking container was a huge pile of horse manure, stacked up like a pyramid. I closed my eyes and shook my head.

"Who did this?" *That was a stupid question.* I should have asked, "Why do this?" I turned around to see two innocent equine faces that seemed to be saying, "I'm so glad you're finally here. Look what happened to the water." Obviously one of them had backed up to the waterer when the urge struck.

"This is not a commode!" I scolded them to no effect. They could not drink out of this mess, but I couldn't make them clean it up. And since nobody else was around, the only practical solution was for me to try. I put on some rubber gloves, rolled up my sleeves, and went to work. After several gags and grimaces, I succeeded in scooping out the mushy, foul smelling and disgusting gift of nature. Another thirty minutes were spent scrubbing the container and making sure it was fit to drink out of again.

"This was not in the brochure," I announced to the heavens above. Horse ownership was never as glamorous as the movies made out. When I was done, I had to go home and make dinner. It could wait a few minutes; I was not in the mood to eat.

ʊ ʊ ʊ

Humor is not confined to the present. What at the time seems uninteresting, or even stressful, can be presented as something funny in retrospect.

Our last visitor of the year was my old friend, Mark, whom I had known since college. He's the one who had helped us fell that Griswold Christmas tree our second winter here. We have remained friends all these years, through good times and bad, and have stayed in touch, no matter how many times I moved or where I lived. Perhaps it is because we shared some similar hardships in our lives, along with the fact that we are both artists. Whatever the reason, our friendship has endured for over thirty years. Whenever possible, Mark would join us for Thanksgiving or Christmas. This year it would be Christmas.

Bill and the girls were on their way to pick up Mark at the airport. His flight was coming in late at night, but I let the girls stay up to meet him. As they drove through the darkness, the window began to fog. When Bill turned on the heater in my Highlander, it emitted a strange sound and began vibrating. *Wham, wham,* the noise continued in a rhythmic cycle until he turned the heater fan off. They pulled into the saloon in Mullan where there was enough light to inspect under the hood. Several locals that we knew were just leaving the bar, so they offered their advice. A cursory inspection revealed nothing mechanically wrong, so Bill decided to press on to the airport. The noises continued, but only when he turned on the fan, which he had to do periodically to prevent the windows from fogging. The sound proved so intense, that he finally just rolled the widows down, and everyone endured the cold blast there and back. When it got too cold, he'd roll them back up, turn on the heater for a few minutes, and then roll them back down. Mark took it in stride, except that he had not brought a heavy coat from Florida, so for him the ride home proved brutal.

When they got back, Bill told me about it, so we decided to take it into the dealership and have the vehicle inspected the next day. We waited in the lounge until a young mechanic waved at us and approached, wiping the grease from his hands with a blue service towel. He asked us to come out and see what had caused the terrible noise. What he had found was a headless mouse caught in the fan, the rest of its bloody body dangling precariously. Apparently, it had built a nest near the heater fan, and there was evidence it had birthed babies in there.

Gross! I have to have my entire car sanitized. No, I need a new car!

"When you started the heater fan, the mouse stuck its head out and got decapitated. That was what made all the noise. It was her body thumping against the fan. I couldn't find the head, but I did find the nest. It was blocking up the heater. We'll remove the nest and clean up the blood. I can spray some disinfectant in the area so you don't breathe in any airborne diseases. Some of these rodents carry the hantavirus. It's found in mouse feces."

Bill asked, "I wonder how much this repair is going to cost. I suppose it isn't covered by the warranty?"

The mechanic shook his head.

"That's what I thought." He smirked and mumbled something unflattering.

We had always kept my Highlander in the garage to prevent any animal from building a home in it. When we first came to Montana, the garage had not yet been finished, and so we had to leave our new truck outside. A few days later when we went to town, we noticed we did not have any windshield wiper fluid and the wipers were not working. Since we were already in town and the truck was brand new, we took it into the dealership for an inspection.

The repairman opened the hood and showed us the hoses and wiring that were chewed through, and an incredible amount of grass, twigs, leaves, and nesting material all under the hood. This was not just a nest; it was an entire condo unit. It looked like multiple dwellings, all linked together. I had never seen such a mess. "It happens all the time," I was told. "The rodents like the warm engines, so they move in." That first time, the rodent relocation had cost us about $200 in repairs!

"This is worse than the first time with the truck," I remarked to Bill as we looked at the total charges. He nodded slowly. I later told Gail about the headless mouse and she let out her usual snort.

"I don't like mice either, Nancy, but they're a part of life. One time I had to remove an entire muffler on my four-wheeler just to dig out a mouse nest. Most likely, there's more of 'em in your garage, probably hiding in the woodpile. Best get some mouse traps, and maybe a few rat traps as well. And move your woodpile outside next year."

We did, and we did. *Again, this was not in the brochure.*

◡ ◡ ◡

In theory, pain should never be the subject of humor, yet, invariably, we find it so, provided it isn't we who are suffering from it.

Linda had just finished giving the girls their lessons when we noticed Wilson was having trouble urinating. The urine came out in little splashes that hit him in the underside of his belly. It did not look right at all.

"I think Wilson has a bean," Linda remarked, as she crouched under him to inspect closer. "You better call the vet."

"I don't know what that is," I replied, still watching the odd way Wilson's man-part twitched as he tried to continue his business. Linda explained that dirt and body oils can build up and cause a blockage. To prove her point, she reached up and gently removed a black, almost tar-like substance from inside Wilson's sheath.

"I might be able to clean some of this out, but he probably needs a sedative and Hanna needs to come do this."

Originally, I planned to have Linda trailer Wilson to Hanna, our vet, but she was recovering from the flu, and in no condition to help. Since we had no trailer of our own, I made arrangements for a "farm call" by Hanna. Later, when Bill came home for dinner, I told him about Wilson and the plans I had made before we ate our meal.

"Hanna is coming out tomorrow to help Wilson," I said as I continued to stir the vegetables sizzling in the pan.

"What's wrong with Wilson?" He showed equal concern for Wilson and the larger bill that went along with a farm call.

"Well," I paused, trying to think of exactly the right words. "He's having a 'man visit.'"

"A man visit?" he repeated, and looked at me, puzzled.

"His penis is blocked up with some kind of body oil and dirt mixture. It looks like black tarry paste, and it's stuck in his canal and around his sheath. Hanna will have to give Wilson a sedative so she can dig in there and clean...."

"Don't tell me anymore, I get it!" Bill said with a grimace.

I just laughed, "Thank goodness Hanna can come out right away. Can you imagine how painful that is? I feel bad for Wilson."

Bill shook his head, "Enough, already."

Hanna arrived in the afternoon and I explained Wilson's symptoms to her. Standing in our corral, she gave him an examination and decided to clean his sheath. She explained to me some horses need this once in a lifetime, others once a month; there was no way to predict which. She had me hold the lead rope, but warned me he might quickly lie down or he might remain on his feet.

"Just be ready either way," she said as she gave him an injection. Within a few minutes his eyes and bottom lip drooped, and he fell asleep standing up.

Hanna quickly went to work. She reached up and extracted his penis, pulling gobs of black tar off the shaft, and then soaped him with a cleaning solution. Within moments it was over.

"He really needed that," Hanna remarked. "He'll feel better and should urinate normally now. He'll continue to be droopy and sleepy for about a half hour more, so keep an eye on him."

I turned to Kobi, who had been standing by. "Kobi, guard Wilson while he sleeps. He can't protect himself while he is under anesthesia. I have to go write a check for Hanna, and then I will come back."

Kobi obediently settled down next to Wilson's droopy head, which by now almost touched the ground. His glazed over eyes looked straight ahead, but focused on nothing in particular. He was in a stupor.

"Do you really think Kobi will watch over him?" Hanna asked.

"I really do," I said earnestly. "He often watches the girls on their swings when I'm away for a few minutes. I think he senses when someone is helpless."

Back at the house I wrote Hanna a check, while keeping an eye peeled on Kobi through the dining room window. He never left Wilson's side, and sat with him until Hanna and I said our goodbyes and I returned to the barn. Bill stayed away the entire time, locked in his shop. Go figure.

51

Everything's Normal

THE GIRLS LOVED TO RIDE ANY DAY AND ANY PLACE that weather permitted. We had been putting in some extra time riding in our corrals to get ready for the horse show. The horses were on their hitching posts when I heard Sonja's voice loudly call out, "Penis is normal!"

I turned around and looked at her beneath her horse, rather startled by my eight-year-old's remark. She smiled at me and continued her examination. "Wilson is urinating normally. His penis doesn't have any of that icky black stuff on it. I have been paying close attention, Mom. If Wilson gets sick again, I know I have to tell you right away."

"Good work, Sonja. I know you love your Wilson and will take good care of him." It was another reminder that children growing up with livestock learn a lot about anatomy and reproduction at an early age. By observing some of the animal "activities," life lessons come quickly and naturally.

Sonja saddled up and continued to report on the health of her horse during her ride. When Wilson paused for a moment by the big tree in the corral, she turned in her saddle to watch him as he lifted his tail.

When he was done, she called out, "Manure is normal!" She walked him over to me and said, "Wilson is doing much better now, Mom. His manure is round; it's not runny like a cow's anymore." She turned his head back, and with a clucking sound queued Wilson to walk on.

We had been keeping an eye on him because he had been experiencing digestive upset for two days, which was evident when you looked at the black puddles on the ground. I had talked to our vet about it, and she had suggested we wait a couple of days to see if it cleared up on its own. Sometimes just a change of food, or grass with a high water content, can cause such symptoms. Odd as it sounds, I was relieved Wilson had normal manure. I just can't believe I wrote it down.

52

Missing Lynx

CHILDREN, DOGS, AND HORSES—I WAS BEGINNING to think there was not a better combination. I watched a sweet vision of Sonja's little legs carrying her up the hill from the stable. The blue-and-white stocking cap I'd made her last year bounced on her head as she hurried home. Kobi ran alongside, jumping in front of her numerous times, racing back and forth across the path. *What a nut-ball.* Sonja stopped and looked back at her beloved Wilson. He called to her with a loud whinny, asking her to return to the corral. I could almost hear her struggling with her thoughts, as I watched her from the window of the loft. She wanted to answer Wilson's call, but she knew she should continue home. Her heart-shaped face showed her distress, but she had schoolwork to finish. Kobi knew it too, and spun in circles, trying to remind her to follow him and continue home. She turned back toward the house, and began to skip happily home, knowing in an hour or two she would be reunited with Wilson.

She burst into the house with pink cheeks and puffed, "Wilson wanted me to stay, but I knew I had to hurry home. I just told him I would see him soon and he understood."

"I'm sure he does, Love Lamb," I reassured her. I was beginning to wonder if Sonja shared my gift of animal communication.

313

◡ ◡ ◡

Another winter was finally over, and the spring thaw melted the snow, leaving heavy ruts in the road where the water had rushed down the sides to feed the thirsty pastures. The grass once more turned green as it emerged from its winter blanket, the flowers began to bloom, and the quaking aspen trees blossomed. I spent this glorious dawn sitting on the back patio, eating my cereal, and watching the birds flutter around my feeder, singing their morning songs.

But today they were bothered by something. My ears perked up as I listened to several Chickadees sound scolding warning chirps instead of their usual singsong whistle. *I wonder what is bothering them.* Since I was more interested in my cereal, I continued eating. After I finished, I stood up to take my bowl inside to the kitchen, and noticed a small movement in the grass beside my flower garden, along the edge of the patio. I took a closer look and saw a small baby bobcat hiding in the tall grass. *So that's what the birds are alarmed about.*

Male or female, I could not tell, but I called to Bill and the girls to come see him. He was so frightened, I felt sorry for the little tike. He hunkered down in the grass trying to hide, hoping I was not looking at him. As we gathered around him, he remained frozen. I looked for the mother; I knew she would not want us near her kitten, and I had no desire to tangle with an angry mom. She did not appear, though I kept scanning the area for any sign of her. I was glad Kobi was in the house. I had seen the kind of damage an adult bobcat could inflict on the largest of dogs. And besides that, I did not want him to hurt this little guy.

I took a step closer. "Go find your mom!" I told him, waving my hand in his direction. Nothing, he did not move. I dared not come any closer and risk being bitten, but I wanted him to leave for his own safety. Bill picked up a pebble and threw it about a foot from the little kitten, thinking that would spur him on. He refused to budge. He just hunkered down even more. After a few more pebbles, he finally jumped up straight in the air and took off for the clump of Aspen trees just below us. I had to smile; this was just another reason why I loved my rural life. There was always a new experience waiting around the corner, and they just kept coming.

As I turned to go inside, a swift movement caught my eye. A hummingbird was fluttering at the door lock. His wings hummed and blurred with his swift movement. His neck flashed bright ruby red as the sun glinted on his throat. He tried to drink from the keyhole in the door knob, and after a few failed attempts, he flew away. *I think I've found my next greeting card,* I thought to myself. I often painted what I saw in nature; it was a never-ending source of inspiration for me.

Go West, Young Woman!

53

A "Swell" Time

S PRING PROMISED ANOTHER WELCOMED ARRIVAL in the form of "Aunt
Grace" and "Uncle Russell," my old friends from Florida. They
were making their annual sojourn to Alaska in their RV, and this year
had swung by to spend a few days with us. I awoke to the sound and
smell of bacon cooking and coffee percolating downstairs. Bill was
making breakfast for them, and the aromas wafting up the stairs lured me
from my bed. I opened the patio doors on our small balcony, and cool air
flooded the room, settling around my bare legs. It chilled me slightly, but
was so fresh and clean that I stepped out to listen to the songbirds for a
minute. Their music drifted through my ears, and I closed my drowsy
eyes in order to focus clearly on their sounds. The air was sweet with
morning dew, and when I opened my eyes again, I watched the soft,
downy clouds drift through the vast blue sky. *This is the way to start a
morning.* I would have enjoyed it a bit longer, but bacon was calling to
my empty stomach, and I could hear the voices of my friends downstairs.

My girls were already up and in a hurry to get to the barn to show off
their riding skills to Uncle Russell. I had found some horse glitter at a local
ranching supply store, so after breakfast we all made our way to the stable
to begin the grooming. After the brushing, the girls combed pink glitter
into Wilson's mane and tail, and painted designs on his body.

"Uncle Russell!" they called in unison. "Come and see how nice Wilson looks."

Russell rounded the corner, shook his head and mockingly groaned, "Oh no! You can't put pink on a gelding! No pink on the boy horses!"

The girls found his reaction so hysterically funny that they laughed and teased him about it for the rest of their visit. Even three years later, they would call him on the phone and threaten to paint Wilson pink again. Russell always responded with mock indignation, begging them not to do it.

After the girls had their first big laugh on Russell, he came inside the tack room to have a look at my "new" saddle. We were about to discuss it when we heard a loud shout. Sandy stumbled towards us with her hand over her face. "Belle kicked me in the eye!" she cried.

"Let me look at it," I said calmly, not wishing to show my alarm.

"No! I can't!" she sobbed, and she kept her dirt covered hands over most of her face. Russell and I spent some time coaxing her to let us examine her eye. Once we convinced her we wouldn't touch it, she agreed to move her hands. The area around her eye had already begun to swell and turn purple-blue. There was a small scratch across the side of her face near the eye, but it was just a red streak. There was no bleeding, just that red dirty mark. I felt some relief, but my investigation had only just begun. I put my arm around her and reassured her that she would be alright.

"Do you have any blurred vision, or a headache?"

"No," was her tearful reply. "I can see just fine and my head doesn't hurt."

"Good, let's get you back to the house and clean up your eye. You also need some ice on it to help with the swelling. On the way you can tell me what happened."

Russell and I each took an arm and helped Sandy back to the house. After settling her in the blue recliner in our master bedroom, she told us what happened. She had been cleaning Belle's left front foot when Belle tried to pull the foot away. Sandy was determined not to let go, so they struggled. With Sandy's face bent too close, the jerking foot caught her around the eye. While there was definitely some operator error here, I was upset with Belle for being so fussy and unintentionally hurting Sandy. I had cleaned Belle's feet before without a problem. Belle was not being respectful and I was fed up with it. We were lucky this was not serious this time, and I reminded her why wearing a helmet was so important.

Sandy's face was bruised for two weeks, but the injury left no scar. Even though it was approaching summer, Belle was skating on thin ice.

Go West, Young Woman!

54

"Porcupine in Parking Lot"

THAT WAS THE ENTRY FROM AN ACTUAL POLICE BLOTTER, which always appeared as a column in our weekly local newspaper, *The Gold Standard.* It remains one of my favorites, along with "Bear in Dumpster," "Inappropriate snow blowing," "Large hay bails blocking eastbound lane," "Stop sign ran over Maryland & Carter," and the cryptic log entry "Animal call, two dogs walked into a house."

Sometimes even people are the subject of the blotter. One such entry read "Unwanted person at the corner bar," while another stated "Report of a mystery shopper at Wal-Mart" (we don't have a Wal-Mart, hence the mystery). In the summer you see numerous "water violation" reports, but among the most memorable entries were "Request to turn off coffee pot for resident that is out of town," "Tumbleweeds concern local resident," and "Complaint about neighbor's garbage can."

My limited time as a wildlife duty officer in Florida produced more than one memory that would have fit well into the Cheyenne County police blotter. I remember one call I handled from a rather irate woman who insisted we come and remove all the squirrels from her yard because they bothered her so much. After a lengthy discussion, I suggested she simply stop watching them with binoculars from her 14th story condominium.

But my favorite incident was the frightened woman who called saying, "Help! I must save Henry!"

"Who's Henry?" I asked.

"He's my duck! An alligator got in my pond and is trying to eat my ducks. He got hold of Henry and won't let go. I went in the pond and wrestled with it, but I couldn't get Henry out of his mouth. Please send someone to help!"

I explained to her that wrestling with an alligator can be extremely dangerous; she could have been maimed or killed. But she would hear none of it; somebody had to save Henry, so back in the water she went.

Many people asked me if trading alligators and water moccasins for grizzly bears and blizzards was a worthwhile exchange. I take the jokes in stride, knowing it was not the wildlife or the weather, but the urban environment, which drove us here. While I admit there are some things I miss about city life, such as the greater convenience of nearby shopping, good restaurants, museums, concerts, and plays, there are more important aspects I do not miss—the crowds, the traffic, the noise, and the incessant need of indifferent neighbors, and strangers alike, to monitor and control my every action, no matter how seemingly innocuous.

Living in Maryland, just outside of D.C., was a classic case in point. I got a taste of what we were in for the day we moved into our new home. A neighbor came into our backyard where I was standing with Sandy, who had just turned one. "Sunny," my friendly mixed breed Shepherd-Labrador, was sitting next to us. I presumed my neighbor had come to welcome us, but without introduction she announced, "You'd better keep that vicious dog at home."

Sunny just sat there, wagging his tail and smiling. I tried to introduce myself and give her my reassurance that Sunny was gentle as a lamb, but she just turned her back on me and walked away. *Welcome to the neighborhood.*

I also don't miss having property stolen out of my yard, or neighbors pressing their faces to my window to see if I am home. I don't miss being repeatedly harassed when my husband, while mowing our lawn, once accidentally crossed the imaginary boundary separating it from another. I don't miss finding a note in my mailbox from someone who did not like the color of the roses I planted in my own front yard.

But what I don't miss most of all occurred the day after the September 11th Pentagon attack. Bill had only been home a short while and had to go back to the Pentagon early that morning. Of course, everyone was nervous and upset, not really knowing what would happen next. I left the TV tuned to a news channel so I'd be aware of any breaking events. It kept me tense all day. When evening came, I heard the door bell ring, and my heart skipped a beat. My first thought was that something had happened to Bill, and they were sending an officer to notify me in person. When I approached the front door and peeked through the opaque glass inset, I was relieved to see whoever was there was not in uniform. I answered the door and found a neighbor standing there with a look of irritation on his face. "Your grass is too long and your husband should cut it."

I was stunned. I smiled kindly and replied, "He was at the Pentagon when it was attacked by terrorists, and I've hardly seen him since. He's back at work there today, so he doesn't have time to cut the grass. I think he's going to be busy for quite some time."

He said, "That's no excuse, and if the grass gets too long, I'm going to report you to the neighborhood association."

I politely suggested, "If it's really a problem, I'll pay you to cut it for us, or maybe you could recommend a lawn service."

He replied curtly, "It's your responsibility alone to keep up with grass." Then he turned and left.

Yet another neighbor who knew that Bill was assigned to the Pentagon, asked me if he could do something about the helicopters that kept flying over everyday. She said they were disturbing her baby's nap time. Ever diplomatic, I suggested she might want to change her child's nap time because the area was being heavily patrolled to prevent another terrorist attack.

I chalked the former incident up to indifference and the latter one to ignorance. But both shared a common theme of beltway life: *What's in it for me?*

I feel so blessed that we rarely have crime of any note where we now live. It's refreshing to read about these more innocent police calls, instead of the murders and assaults that were so commonplace back east that they only rated back page news. That does not mean we have no serious crime; there is the occasional assault, and the rare murder or prison escape. But taken on a per capita basis, the crime rate here is very low.

Since we've lived in Montana, I've not had to deal with any such concerns. My first year here I planted roses in a variety of different colors in my front yard, and I have yet to hear a single complaint. The wild animals may enjoy them a bit too much, but the feeling has been liberating.

The two most notable frustrations I have experienced were limited to the caribou hide that a salesman promised me would not shed hair (shed, no; cascade, yes), and a civil servant who could not adequately answer my question regarding whether I was supposed to sign or print my name at the bottom of a form. Each time I inquired, he repeated the same mantra, "Put your name on it." Aside from these trivial experiences, and the chronic habit of most locals never identifying themselves when they phone, there simply isn't anything outside of politics worth voicing a comment about.

55

Batman and Robin

Iᴛ ᴡᴀs ʟᴀᴛᴇ ɪɴ ᴛʜᴇ ᴇᴠᴇɴɪɴɢ ᴀɴᴅ ᴡᴇ ᴡᴇʀᴇ ᴀʟʟ ʀᴇᴀᴅʏ for bed. I heard a knock at my bedroom door and a little heart-shaped face peeped in. "Mom, there is a bird in the house. It flew by my head just a minute ago. I really saw it. I think it's a Robin." She was calm but her eyes were big and round against her fair skin.

"I believe you, Sonja; show me where you saw it."

Sonja's little hand waved upward, pointing to the high ceiling above our loft. We were standing near the staircase, which led to the family room below. I looked up and saw it fluttering wildly in circles above us, a dark mass with featherless wings. It couldn't be a bird. I looked at the shape of the wings and its erratic wing beats and I knew…. "I see it, but it's not a Robin. It's a bat."

"A BAT!!!!" Sonja shrieked, as she ran back into her room, slamming her bedroom door behind her. I think I even heard the lock click. Her muffled voice came from behind the door. "Mommy, can it get in here with the door closed?" I told her she was perfectly safe, and quietly thought to myself, *She won't be any help; it's up to Bill and me.* Sandy also was nowhere to be seen.

In the meantime, I heard Bill's voice calling to me, asking me where the net was that we used to clean out the fountains and ponds. He had run

325

downstairs, and the bat had followed him, circling his head. We frantically tried to turn on all the lights so we could see it, and I came down into the hallway, trying to shoo it back into the main room. As it whizzed by my head, my thoughts immediately returned to the memory of one of my high school friends who had a bat get caught in her hair in a Florida orange grove. Thinking of that, I instinctively raised my hands every time it flew by.

I followed the creature back up to the loft, where it fluttered above the railing. Bill found the pool skimmer in the garage, and raced back up the stairs, two steps at a time, with the net in hand. "Where is it? Where is it? Aren't you watching it?"

"Of course I'm watching it!" I replied. "In fact, it's making me feel dizzy. It's over by the piano now."

Bill saw it coming toward us, and he swooped the net on its long pole at the bat, but missed (did I mention Bill was never a very good baseball player?). It buzzed by again, and Bill swung the net, missing it by inches (strike two). As it came towards me I waved my hand frantically, and tried to send him back towards Bill. As long as it remained upstairs, the bat was trapped. The only exit was through our bedroom balcony, and I was not letting it in my bedroom. We'd either have to net it upstairs or shoo it downstairs and out a door.

What a sight we were in our pajamas! "I feel like I'm chasing Grandpa from the 'Munsters' TV show," Bill called to me as he raced up and down the stairs after the little monster.

"Don't lean too far over the rails, you'll lose your balance and fall," I called to him, as he stretched and swung the net wildly. Catching this bat was turning into an Olympic event. I mentally gave Bill an "8" for form and grace, as I watched him dancing with our unexpected guest. The net kept moving through the air, missing the furry fellow by inches. Minutes continued to pass, and I started feeling sorry for the little guy, but he couldn't roost with us. I drew the line at bat guano.

"I missed him again," Bill yelled in frustration. "He's so fast." With one more silent swoosh of the net, Bill called out, "I think I got him!"

In sheer desperation and frustration, Bill had swatted the net at him from partway up the stairs. Amazingly, he connected, stunning the poor bat, and it fell onto the loveseat below—of course, the side where I sit. Bill raced back down the stairs with me at his heels. As he placed the net on top of him, the bat began to squeak and chirp. It moved and flapped, trying to get up. "Don't touch him with your bare hands; they bite," I said emphatically.

"You hold him down with the net and press hard, while I get my gloves," Bill commanded.

With the precision of a special response team, we made the hand-off. I held the net while Bill ran to the garage and got a pair of leather work gloves. I held the net firmly, and the satin edge of my blue nightgown sleeve again reminded me it was late at night. *Why do these things always happen when I am clean and tired? I just hope it doesn't take this moment to turn into a vampire.*

When Bill returned, he took the pole handle from me and gently picked up the net.

"Be careful," I cautioned again. "When my cousin Dave was bitten by a bat while camping, he had to have rabies shots."

With it still squeaking loudly, Bill took the bat outside. He placed it on the driveway and removed the net. The little bat bared its tiny sharp fangs at Bill, and flopped around on the ground.

"I don't know if it's stunned or has a broken wing," he called to me. He moved it into the flower garden and came inside the front door. We stood talking in the hall. "I didn't mean to hurt it," he said flatly.

"I know that was not your intention. Maybe he'll be okay if he rests awhile," I said consolingly.

"I don't know how he got in—do you?" Bill remarked.

"No, we must have had a door open somewhere. Only one of the reasons why I'm so concerned about keeping the doors closed around here. Honestly, if something came in, I thought it would be a mouse. But whatever happens, I know you will save us. After all, you're Batman."

Go West, Young Woman!

56

Home is the Hunter

"Lost" was the operative word of the day. I was cooking spaghetti and mulling over recent events, when I heard the door bell ring. I was sure it was Jack, our UPS delivery man. Between my art business and Bill's work, Jack was a regular visitor at our place. As I approached the door, I did not see his delivery truck or familiar form through the beveled glass. I was puzzled, but opened the door to see a man completely collapsed on our front doorstep. Before I could say a word, he murmured breathlessly, "Sorry ma'am…I'm lost…I was hunting…I've been wandering the mountains for hours…I saw your house…and just kept walking down toward it. I'm so exhausted…I can't take another step."

I looked down at him; he was of medium height, build, and age, with short blond hair peeking out from his camouflaged baseball cap. He was dressed in an orange safety vest and hunting clothes. He looked weak, shaky, dehydrated, and plenty scared. He was also breathing very hard. His rifle was laid against the garage door, likely to show he was no threat. Still, my mind was always on the alert, and I quickly scanned around my house and yard. I assessed him and the general situation. Sometimes this is just how a home invasion starts. While the person is distracted, trying to help someone, the accomplices take control, and it can be life threatening for the homeowner. Of course I would help this man, but there was no sense in letting my guard down. I smiled reassuringly.

"The first thing you need is a big glass of water. Then we can talk about how to help you. Are you having any chest pain?" I wanted to know because he looked a bit pale and clammy. He shook his head no, and only murmured that he was having leg cramps and was tired. *Lactic acid buildup in his legs, no doubt.*

"You're going to be alright and will have any help you need. Just rest here; don't try to get up. I'll be right back with the water."

I went back inside and closed the door, gently turning the lock behind me. While it was doubtful, I still did not want to find this man standing behind me in my own kitchen. Bill was in his shop behind the house, so I called him on the intercom, and told him what I knew so far, asking him to come over to the front porch.

When I returned to the front door, the lost hunter was sitting up. He drank the glass of water down quickly. I cautioned him to go easy so he wouldn't get stomach cramps. Bill showed up, and after the hunter had rested a few moments, we found out his name was Donald, where he lived, and his phone number so I could call his wife.

Still breathless, he said, "I was supposed to go hunting…with my buddies…but they all cancelled…I decided to go alone….I went up to the public lands…on Powder Keg…I found a camp…someone had set up…I parked my truck there…I looked around…spotted some elk…started to trail them…I didn't know…you can't hunt elk by trailing it [that was true enough; they always stay just far enough ahead of hunters because they can smell and hear them]…I had followed them for miles…realized I was lost.

"I spent all afternoon…wandering around the mountain…trying to find my way back…to my truck. I didn't have any food or water…no compass. I was so thirsty…I had started eating snow."

That was a bad idea. Snow only makes you thirstier if you don't melt it first.

Bill said, "You're lucky it was not too cold out or you could've added hypothermia to the list. It's fortunate you spotted our rooftop."

Donald nodded and said, "I spent two hours finding…a way down…to your house."

He was surprised to learn just how far away he was from where he had parked his truck, about eleven miles. He declined any food, and when he was looking and feeling a little better, he asked Bill if he would drive him back up to his truck. He looked tired, and I suggested we take him back to Helena; he could get his truck tomorrow. He did not want to do that, so Bill agreed to drive him back up the mountain where he had his truck parked. It was getting dark, so they needed to get started. Bill told me he would be back in about a half an hour. I kissed his cheek and gently whispered in his ear to take his phone and his gun. He smiled and patted the pocket of his brown coat with his left hand.

Nearly two hours later, I was feeling very uncomfortable and beginning to worry. *What was taking so long? Was Bill alright? Had they had an accident? Was this man not what we thought he was? Was there some violence or trouble at the camp where this truck was parked? Had they broken down? Had they skidded off the ice and tumbled to the bottom of the cliff?* The longer I waited, the more scenarios my mind created. I was ready to call the Sheriff's office in Clark Fork, when the phone rang. I picked it up on the first ring. It was Gail; she heard my anxious voice and asked me what was wrong. I told her what had happened and that Bill had not called or returned. I had tried his phone but it went to voice mail.

"I know where he is," she said, "he's up White Branch road. There's no way he could have returned in a half an hour, and phone service is sketchy there. Have either of you been up there before?"

"No." I was feeling even more apprehensive.

"Nancy, that road is dangerous in the ice we're having right now in the higher elevations. It'll take him a long time to travel it. He'll have to go really slow in the dark, and there's only one trail and hardly any room to pass. It has steep cliff areas; I got stuck up there once looking for my cows."

This news wasn't making me feel any better. Hearing my labored breathing, she quickly added, "I'm going to try to call him myself. If you hear from him, call me." She clicked the phone off before I could manage a goodbye.

What I did not know was that Gail was right. Bill had spent a long time climbing the mountain and going down rabbit trails to where Donald had parked his truck. The return drive home was even worse. My phone rang again, and I heard Gail in an excited voice say, "I heard Bill say, 'hello,' when I called, but the signal dropped out. I think he's okay."

"I feel better, Gail, thanks," I said, relieved. "I just won't feel right until I see him come through the door."

"I know; call me when he gets home."

I agreed and hung up the phone and waited. The waiting was horrible. I am of a personality that would rather be doing than waiting. *He must be fine and will be home any time now.* I looked out into the darkness with my eyes fixed on our road, as if I could somehow will his truck headlights to come around the curve and up the driveway. I turned on all the outside lights, anticipating his arrival.

I jumped when the phone rang, being lost in my own thoughts. Gratefully, it was Bill. He said he was off the mountain and had just left Mullan, only a few miles away. He promised to tell me everything when he got home. I returned to the upstairs window and waited until I saw the headlights round the curve and climb up the driveway, just as I had seen it happen in my mind numerous times that evening.

Bill looked tired; he sat down at the dining room table with a thud, and filled in the details for me.

"If I had known what I was getting into, I would not have attempted to go up that mountain at night." His voice was stressed and his face looked dark and serious. "I would have taken Donald home to Helena, and let his buddies pick up the truck in the daylight."

He went on to explain that everything Gail had told me was right. "It was hard getting up the mountain. At dark several trucks were coming off the mountain. The road was so narrow there was hardly any room to pull over to let someone pass. The logging road was full of ice, and in some spots there was nothing but a sheer drop-off. When we found the turn-off to the side road where Donald had parked, we had to go another few miles to find his truck. It was in a campsite like he said. There was a big wall tent, but no sign of any campers or other vehicles. I could hardly turn around in the narrow space. Donald pulled out ahead of me, but I just spun on the ice. I'd forgotten to bring my tire chains. Thankfully, he had his, so I was able to get enough traction to pull me free. Then we headed back out with him in front.

"We crawled down that mountain in first gear, and more than once the truck slid on the ice. About halfway down, I hit a bad patch of it on a sharp turn, and was turned nearly sideways near the edge of a drop-off. Donald had rounded the corner and didn't see me, so I started blowing my horn, trying to get his attention. Donald had his heater going and his windows closed, so he couldn't hear my horn and continued on. A few minutes later he noticed I was no longer behind him, so he backed up and helped me get it straight. I didn't go over five miles per hour the whole time. I had a deuce of a time controlling my speed on that ice. Even in four-wheel drive, I could feel my tires constantly slipping."

I called our lost hunter's wife and explained he should be arriving home any minute, and to please call me when he did. She thanked us for our help, and, true to her word, called a few minutes later to tell me her own husband was home safe and sound.

That experience had turned into the most agonizing day I'd known since 9/11. It reinforced once more to me that the wilderness of Montana remains largely untouched by humans, and the weather is always a force to be reckoned with. Often, one can scrape by, as Donald and Bill had, but nobody wants to repeat any of it. After that incident, we bought a truck tool box and loaded it down with tire chains, tow cables, and anything else we thought might be handy under similar conditions. Now our winter motto is "Tire chains, don't leave home without them."

Go West, Young Woman!

57

Magnum

ONE AFTERNOON DURING A LESSON AT OUR HOUSE Linda called out to me from the center of the round pen, "Is a seventeen-and-a-half hand horse too big for Sandy?" She was sitting on a stool as Sandy trotted around her on Belle.

I was truly shocked, thinking it must be as big as an elephant. "Yes, it is!" I said, laughing. I thought she might be joking with me.

"Oh, I was thinking about Magnum. He's for sale. My customer has to move out of town and she can't take him."

"Magnum? I didn't know you were talking about Magnum. I actually like that horse," I responded to my own surprise. I had seen Magnum many times at Linda's stable. He was a very big, tall gelding, but I always thought he was equally sweet and obedient. I had watched the trainers work with him and I liked his moves. He was an Appendix, a Thoroughbred-Quarter horse mix, with long legs, a grey body, and black mane and tail. I had spent some time sitting with him when the trainers were busy with other horses.

I stood there thinking about what Linda had said. "Do you really think Sandy can handle him?"

"He's safe enough. Do you want to try him out?"

"I'll ask her tonight."

Sandy continued to trot around the ring, oblivious to our conversation, and I watched my then twelve-year-old move Belle to the center and dismount. She had come a long way with her riding skills, so I decided to let her try Magnum if she wanted to. But what would Bill say? Bill said yes, he was agreeable, and Sandy was excited to ride Magnum.

Within a few days we were back at Linda's barn. When we came through the door we saw Linda on Magnum. She showed us everything he had been trained to do, and she moved him through the walk, trot, canter, side pass, backup, and a small jump.

"Are you ready, Sandy?" I asked her, as she stood at the mounting block.

"Yes, of course, but I am a little nervous."

"It's normal to feel that way," I told her with a reassuring smile.

She looked so grown up in her English riding clothes—avocado green breeches with beige suede knees and tall black boots. They fit her slender frame perfectly. She was no longer a little girl. After several minutes of watching her in the arena, I asked her how she felt up there, and did she like him.

"Mom, Dad, I love him!" she called out.

Bill's eyes were fixed on Sandy and Magnum. "You know, Nancy, she rides him better than any other horse."

"I noticed that too. They seem to fit well. Magnum responds immediately to every queue without fuss. Maybe we should let her spend some more time with him."

Sandy blossomed riding Magnum during that first hour. When she returned to the mounting block, she was all smiles. As she dismounted, she told me how much she wanted him. I told her I wanted her to spend more time with him before we made a decision. While Linda was still holding the reins I announced, "I want to get on him."

"You want to get on Magnum?" Linda's mouth actually fell open; she bent slightly at the waist, and took one step back at the same time. With a chuckle she said, "Are you sure?"

"Yes, I want to see what all this is about. If we're going to consider buying him, then I have to be able to handle him. You can lead me on him this first time. I just want to know how he feels."

As I climbed on Magnum, I realized just how far I was from the ground. I suddenly questioned the wisdom of my decision, but in for a penny, in for a pound. It was like sitting on a skyscraper. As Linda took her first few steps, I let out a breath and enjoyed the ride. He was the smoothest horse I had ever been on. His long graceful legs made it feel more like floating in a boat instead of riding a horse. *I know why Sandy likes him. One needs a step ladder to get on him, but it's worth the climb.*

After my ride I gave Magnum a thank you and a rub on the neck. Sandy talked about Magnum all the way home in the car, at dinner that evening, and for weeks afterward. We were all watching an episode of her favorite show, "The Wild, Wild West," when she announced she would love to ride Magnum alongside the heroes, James West and Artemus Gordon. Both girls adored the characters of Jim and Artie played by Robert Conrad and Ross Martin so many years ago. I even placed their pictures in a little locket for Sandy to wear. I hoped it might satisfy her never ending obsession and major crush on them.

The following week, her emotional high came crashing down after we discussed Magnum with our vet, and learned he had a heart murmur. Hanna thought it was stable, and most likely would not cause a problem, but we were still worried. The owner also would not negotiate on his price of $3,000. Sandy took the news hard, but I promised her we would find her a competition horse, so we decided to keep looking.

58

Whiskey for My Sandy

I T HAD BOTHERED ME FOR QUITE A WHILE THAT Belle and Sandy were not getting along well. I feared that Belle now had Sandy's "number." Sandy could be timid, and with each succeeding year, Belle was becoming more surly, definitely ignoring Sandy and being plain disrespectful. I did not want that to continue. Sandy was not enjoying her riding as much as she used to, and riding should not be a constant struggle of wills. She was also doing well in her English and Western riding competitions, and Belle could not compete, being a gated horse. I painfully made the decision to sell her. Her primary rider needed to be a little more confident. My feelings were confirmed when one afternoon Sandy was thrown from Belle and landed squarely on her face.

I once saw a tee shirt that said, "The hardest thing about riding is the ground." I knew this to be true from my own experience, and finally, so did Sandy.

Sandy had some scrapes, but was otherwise unharmed. She felt bad that her perfect record of staying in the saddle was broken, but I told her most people see the ground long before she did. Gail told her she had been thrown some twenty times in the years she has been riding. I just told Sandy not to break Miss Gail's record!

"Oh, Linda told me it would happen *someday*, but I wanted to hold onto that record as long as I could."

That incident only confirmed my thoughts that Sandy needed a different mount. After this, she would not enjoy Belle the way she used too. I also knew this from my own experience. When it came to horse riding and ownership, it was one of those many things "not in the brochure."

Belle was a good horse and most anyone could ride her, but I decided to advertise her as an intermediate horse. Our vet, Hanna, gave Belle a checkup before she went to the catalog sale. She confirmed that Belle was in excellent health and had great feet. I explained to Hanna that Sandy needed a horse she could take to shows and would better fit her riding needs. Hanna offered to keep her eyes open for any horses that might be good for Sandy.

We had a difficult search and had only found one possible candidate. His name was Weston, a little strawberry roan quarter horse. She loved him, but he had an eye condition, and eventually lost sight in it. We couldn't have a half-blind horse; Sandy was not yet that skilled of a handler, but I still felt bad.

It was several months later when Hanna told us about Whiskey, a Morgan gelding she owned. He had been used in a therapeutic riding program in which Hanna and Linda were on the board of directors. The program was disbanded due to financial concerns, and they were now placing all the horses in new homes. Whiskey sounded like he was worth seeing, and I trusted Hanna's judgment when she recommended a horse in good health and with a temperament suited for Sandy. There was one concern; Whiskey was twenty-five years old.

"Twenty-five! He's twenty-five?" Bill exclaimed, his voice rising in pitch.

"I want to go look at him," I replied firmly. "Hanna says he is in excellent health, and Morgans live longer and have a longer saddle life than most horses. Will it hurt to look?"

I assumed his grunt and mumbling qualified as a yes. Within a couple of days we were standing outside a large pasture. I could see Whiskey at the far end standing with the cutest little Appaloosa pony that was about two years old. Linda went out and approached him. He jumped and turned away the first time, but then stood still and let her put the halter on him. Linda walked him over to us. I was already making my assessment. He was slightly smaller than Belle, but with a solid copper colored body and a wavy red-caramel mane and tail. I thought he looked handsome. Best of all, he was well trained and had a gentle disposition. *He does not look his age at all. He is a stocky fellow, but his feet look good. What a beautiful color—and that wavy mane! He has big expressive eyes.*

Linda threw the saddle on his back while he remained still and patient.

"Well, let's see what he's all about," Linda said, as she put her foot in the stirrup and mounted with ease. With a small cluck, Whiskey moved off and Linda rode him around the field, turning, trotting, galloping, and walking again. He moved quickly and silently.

"He's so responsive," Bill remarked. "He does everything you ask him. I must admit I wouldn't think he was twenty-five."

Bazinga! One point for me. I did not know how this would turn out but I knew Bill's mind was made up before we got here. At least he was rethinking his previous opinion; I had to give him credit for that.Whiskey might just make a nice gift for Sandy's thirteenth birthday.

Linda finished her trial ride and stopped him in front of us. Her face was cloudy, and she shook her head. I felt instant dismay. "What's wrong Linda? Is there something you don't like about him?"

"No, I like the horse; he's just fine. I think he may be too fast for Sandy. He really moves. She may not like him."

We all sat for a moment and digested the fact that a twenty-five-year-old horse might be too much to handle. I looked at Whiskey and noticed that, despite the workout, he was not even breathing hard.

"Do you want to try him?" Bill asked Sandy. "It's up to you."

I offered a suggestion. "Why don't you just sit on him and let Linda walk you around first, just to see how he feels."

Sandy smiled and said she wanted to try him out. After mounting him, Linda led him by the reins. Sandy looked relaxed in the saddle, so Linda gave her the reins.

"She looks like she's enjoying herself, and she's riding him well. I don't see any head tossing or attitude from this horse."

Bill agreed and we quietly talked about it. Sandy trotted over and stopped

Whiskey, leaning back and saying "Whoa" in a quiet voice. "I love him!" she said without hesitation. "I feel safe on him." The smile on her face was the same one she had when riding Magnum.

"You really like him," I repeated with a short sigh. "I'm glad you told me."

"I like him, too," Linda piped in. "I think he's just what Sandy needs right now, a good confidence builder. Older horses are great for that. He shows his age in his teeth and his back, but he's in excellent shape."

I agreed. Again, I noticed Whiskey was breathing normally. All that trotting had not affected him.

"Take him around the field once more and then we should go." I turned to Bill and said, "Honestly, this migraine is getting worse." It was true that throughout all this I had been dealing with a nasty migraine that was beginning to affect my stomach. It was something I dealt with regularly for over twenty-five years. As she moved away, I told Bill that I thought even if she rode Whiskey for five more years, she would be eighteen and ready for another horse anyway. I wanted him to at least consider it. He agreed that Sandy had not looked that happy on a horse since Magnum, and therefore did not reject the idea out of hand.

When Sandy returned and unsaddled Whiskey, he stood at the fence with us. I had wanted to see if he would walk away as soon he was released, but I was quite pleased to see he remained and sniffed us curiously. We stood there for some time, getting to know him, and he did not leave us to be with his little Appaloosa friend.

"I forgot to ask you if you can pick up his feet," I said to Linda's young assistant, Eva, who had hopped on Whiskey's back.

"Let's see," Linda replied, and to my surprise, and without asking Eva to dismount, she picked up his back leg. Whiskey appeared not to have noticed and seemed fine with the whole idea. She then went around and lifted every foot. "If I can lift his feet with someone on his back, I don't think Sandy will have any trouble with him."

I agreed, "Neither do I."

"That is the beauty of old horses like this one," said Eva, "they've seen and done it all."

We told Linda to inform Hanna we were very interested in Whiskey, but wanted to talk it over tonight. We would call Hanna in the morning and let her know, one way or another. Linda again reminded us that she thought Whiskey was a good choice for Sandy, and Eva echoed her sentiments.

When we finally said goodbye, Whiskey stood at the fence and watched us leave. It was not until we were down the road that I saw him in the rear view mirror turn and walk away.

Whiskey was the subject of our conversation at dinner, and later that evening I had a private talk with Sandy. I asked her how she really felt about the horse, and if she wanted him for her own. She promised she did, and I explained the potential problems with having an older horse. They needed extra care, and because he was older, she would not have him as long as Sonja would have Wilson. She still wanted him, so I decided to have the "epic talk" with Bill.

I was sticking my neck out again. I truly had the same concerns he did, but I believed Whiskey was a good choice and I thought we should try to come to an agreement with Hanna. Bill gave in, with reservations, only because he trusted my judgment. Normally that would have made me feel better, but I thought about Belle. I did not think I would ever sell her; and it was nagging at me. Everyone had said she was really my horse. It was true she was attached to me more than anyone; but I also knew she was not being ridden enough to reach her true potential, and she was bored. I asked myself if I was making the right decision. I felt as though I had made a big mistake thinking Belle was mine.

We came to an agreement with Hanna that Whiskey would come home for a two week trial, so everyone would be sure they would be right for each other. Because I found out that same day I had to have a rather difficult breast surgery, Whiskey's homecoming was postponed. We decided to have him come home the day Linda was to pick up Belle, to take her to the catalog sale in Billings. That way I would have time to recover and help Sandy with Whiskey, and Wilson would not have to be alone, left without a friend. I also thought having a smooth transition would help Sandy, and make it easier for her to say goodbye to Belle if Whiskey was already here.

I was recovering nicely when the big day came. I had said my goodbye to Belle in private, so when she was loaded on the trailer, I gave her a gentle

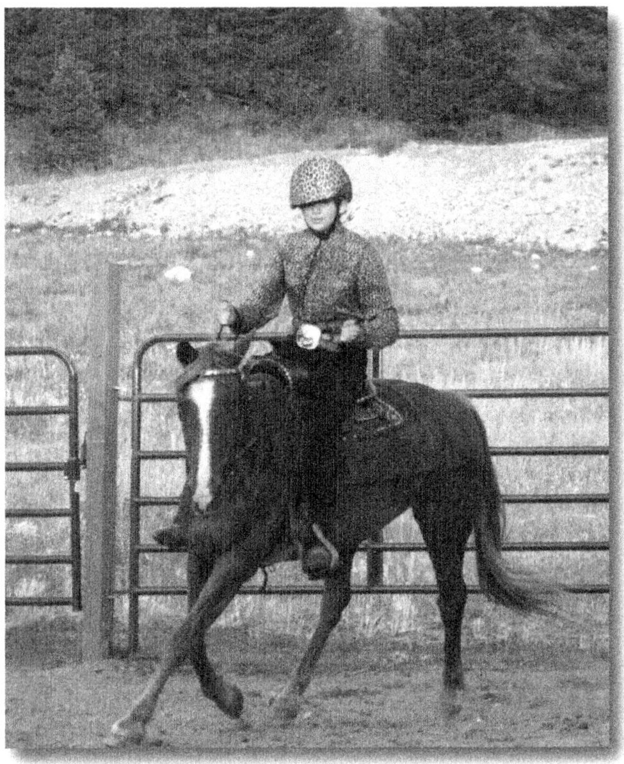

Whiskey practicing for a blue ribbon

pat and wished her well. She would not look at me. I think she knew she was leaving for good. My stomach churned all the next day as I wondered when Belle would go up for sale. I had not heard from Linda, so I supposed the sale had run late. When I called the next morning, I found out Belle had been sold to a woman in Mullan! She would be living only a few miles from us.

Linda also told me that the woman who bought her really wanted her; she stood by her pen all day and late into the evening. Nearly all the buyers had gone home, so Belle sold practically for pennies. Of course, her sale was never about the money. The fact that she was bought by someone who clearly would love her softened the blow, and I decided everyone ended up where they needed to be.

59

School Daze

I T TOOK NEARLY TWO YEARS IN MONTANA for our life to develop into a fairly predictable routine. The trips to town became less frequent, but more hectic, as we tried to jam all our shopping into one day a week. Each morning would begin with the usual chores—let the dog out, start preparing breakfast, and get ready for school.

In our case school meant home study. I had been teaching both children since they were four and neither expressed any desire to attend public school. Given that winter weather often left our road snow- or ice-bound, the safer and more practical arrangement seemed to be home schooling.

As Sandy's studies became more advanced, I had to enlist my husband's aid. Originally we divvied up courses between us, but we soon found this arrangement impractical. In the end I taught Sonja, and Bill instructed Sandy. Initially, Bill thought it best to conduct courses for Sandy at his shop, while I used the craft room in our house for Sonja. But the girls had other ideas, and both of them would migrate daily to the dining room table where the warmth of the fire provided them a more comfortable atmosphere in which to study.

Sandy, in particular, preferred to spread all her books on the dinner table, where they often remained through lunch. I was not pleased, but no matter where I sent her, eventually she returned to that cozy setting. Bill wasn't happy about it either, as it required frequent trips from the shop to instruct her or check her work. I finally convinced the girls to share the craft room, which we had set up as a school room, and I was adamant that all other chores be placed on hold until after school was finished in the afternoon. Bill grumbled that this arrangement interfered with his work, which often required him to engage his suppliers in the east while they were still open. Since they were two hours ahead of us, he fretted whenever the large clock in the hall neared 2:00 p.m., the witching hour for him, lest the companies close before he could place any orders.

For a while this was a chronic problem, but in time we all became more efficient at schooling, and the girls started getting up earlier, realizing the sooner they began, the sooner they could finish. Eventually a new routine set in, but it took several more years of adjustment and experimentation.

By now, the girls had somehow migrated again, this time to the loft—my loft—where I ran my own art business. This proved to be too much for me and my professional work. By the time they finished school each day, two rooms has been turned into disaster areas, the craft school room and my loft. I must have complained more often than I realized because Bill came to me one day with a suggestion.

"I have a cunning plan," he announced slyly, "that will solve all your problems."

"What, we're sending the girls to boarding school?" I said sarcastically.

"Okay, that was my backup plan. No, actually, we've been thinking of building another garage. Maybe I can design part of it as an art studio. That way everybody has a place to get their work done. I'll have my shop, you'll have your studio, and the girls can have the run of the house."

I had to admit the idea had merit, but another building? First the shop, then the house, followed by the stable. We were creating a compound, piece by piece. *When would it end?*

While we worked on yet another plan, the girls continued to refine their routines. No longer wishing to share a table with Sandy, Sonja had discovered another location from which to study. I didn't give it any thought, but Bill was slow to notice the change until one day when he heard a loud commotion emanating from the loft.

"You stepped on me!"

"Sorry, it was an accident."

"No, you did it on purpose!"

"I did not, Sonja."

"Yes, you did! Get out!"

"Hey, you hit me!"

"Well you deserved it for stepping on me!"

"What's all the racket about, you two?" Bill bellowed.

Sonja was sitting, wrapped in her favorite pony blanket, inside the double-door closet that formerly served as my art storage. Indignantly, she looked up at her father, "Sandy stepped on me."

"It was an accident…" Sandy began, before her father cut both of them off.

"What the devil are you doing in this closet in the first place?" he fumed.

"It's where I do my school work," she sobbed, noting the irritation in his voice.

"I was trying to get a book," Sandy began explaining. "I didn't see her."

"Liar! You know I'm always in here. You stepped on me on purpose!"

"Well you hit me on purpose!"

"Knock it off, both of you…NANCY!"

"I'm right here, Bill," I spoke softly as he abruptly turned.

"Did you know about this?"

"Yes, Bill. Sonja has been using the closet as her classroom for the past month. I thought you would have noticed before now."

"Why the blazes is she studying on the floor of a closet? She has a perfectly good table and chair right here."

"Because she wants her own private space. The two don't share any class work, so it's easier to let them work apart, and now that my closet is used for school books, they both need access to it."

Bill sighed and relented, "I guess it's about time to start planning that studio garage."

Go West, Young Woman!

60

Spring Has Sprung

"COW PEAS," SAID GAIL, SMILING. I SHOOK my head and laughed.

"Give it up, Gail," I replied. We were sitting at my dining room table with my daughters, enjoying the afternoon sun shining through the windows.

"I'm telling you," she said to Sandy and Sonja, "plant them this spring and you'll grow cows all over your yard." She swept her arms around in a wide arc to emphasize her point.

"No way, not really," the girls said shaking their heads.

Gail put the packet of seeds in Sonja's hand and said, "Plant them, sprinkle them in the yard, and you'll see."

As the girls scampered out of the room, I began to tell Gail my latest news.

"I was in the second-hand building supply store. You know, the one by the railroad tracks?" Gail nodded in agreement, taking a sip out of her tea cup, holding it with recently manicured nails.

"I was looking at the fixtures, when I saw the most interesting bathroom sink. It was solid cast iron, with a porcelain enamel glaze." I saw Gail's eyebrows go up in a curious fashion, as her blue eyes stared into my hazel green ones.

"It was filthy, and you could not see the color very well because of the scale. It was blue under there, I was sure. So I scraped off a little corner and I saw a beautiful deep marine blue color. It also had the most gorgeous brass Victorian fixtures. The handles were all carved with ornate leaves and scroll designs."

I was watching the bewilderment on Gail's face. I knew she was wondering why I was telling her about a sink, even if it was in one of my favorite colors. She knew I was interested in restoring furniture and other items, but what would I do with an old sink? I had nowhere to put it in my house.

"I showed it to Bill," I continued. "We stood around, talking about it, and he offered to somehow fit it into the loft where I currently work, so I could use it to wash my paints. I thanked him, but I really did not see how we could retrofit it into the room. Then he told me we still needed to build the garage for the new tractor. We could make it our summer project, so why not build a room on top of it to use as a work area for me?

"He said he had always wanted to build a place for me because he knew the girls had taken over the loft where I work, and it was hard to get anything done there. After talking about it for a while, we decided then and there, in the store, to build the garage for the tractor and the extra room for me! So I went and asked how much the blue sink cost. I was given a price of $35.00 and told it was mostly for the brass fixture attached to it. We put it in the car and took it home."

Gail grinned, "A blue sink made you decide to build a garage and an art studio?"

"Yes, isn't it amazing?"

"Duh."

61

The Good Earth

I WATCHED AS TWO GOLDEN EAGLES FLEW over the front meadow, circled, and returned to their nest in a tall Ponderosa pine on the hill above my backyard. They were a majestic pair, with rust colored feathers and a wing span of almost seven feet. I could see the juveniles that were almost ready to fledge, and wished I could be there when the time came for them to take their first flight. I was worried all the noise and activity from the recent garage/studio construction would upset them, but it appeared to have no effect, and they went about their business as usual.

We had settled on a final design and a contractor after several months of research. The structure consisted of two large single-car garage bays, one on each side of the building. In the center was my art studio, a big airy room with a small loft on top. In the corner was a bathroom where my pretty blue sink sat. Regrettably, we were not able to salvage the brass fittings—they were too old, and no replacement parts could be found.

The front face of the studio angled outward like the prow of a ship, and was made up of a double stack of large windows for natural light. It also served as a deterrent to my claustrophobia because the rest of the building was built into the hillside next to the house.

The soil from the excavation was used to widen the turnaround area in the driveway. Looking at all the dirt reminded me of the time Bill left

Washington, D.C., to come to Montana to check on the progress of the shop our contractor was building for us.

"What do you want me to bring you from Montana?" Bill asked me as he was packing his suitcase. I thought about that for a moment. Bill usually brought gifts for me and the girls when he traveled.

"I want a dirt bag," I grinned. Usually, Bill was used to my sense of humor, but this time he just looked at me with a blank face. I did not prolong his puzzlement. "I want you to bring back a handful of soil from Cimarron, just a small zip lock bag full. That way when I feel like we are never going to get there, I can hold it in my hand, and remind myself it really belongs to us, and all I have to do is just hang on a little longer. But more important than that, I want you home safe with us, wherever we are."

That memory made me smile because Bill did bring me that bag of dirt from our property, and I brought that little dirt bag all the way from the east coast and dumped it back in our front yard, where it and we belonged.

After we finished the inside of my art studio, I was at last able to work with minimal interruption, and focus on new projects. I could not begin to describe how much I enjoyed my privacy and freedom. Everything was organized just the way I liked it, and, for once, things always remained right where I left them. I especially enjoyed washing my hands in the blue sink that had inspired the whole project.

I was able to complete the Golden Eagle painting that I had spent years thinking about. I started a new line of sterling silver jewelry, and I managed to design and print three new greeting cards in a matter of a few weeks. It amazed me how productive I could be if left alone for only a couple of hours a day. But I was not completely alone. While working at my drafting table, the very one my dad sat at when he was alive and working as an artist, I would look up to find Wilson staring at me. We did not have our pastures subdivided with permanent fencing yet, so he was free to roam. When he realized I was in the studio, he would stand outside and look in at me for hours, just watching me work. I think he liked the company. It became an almost daily occurrence. Whiskey would accompany him on these sojourns. They often dropped by and looked in the windows, hoping I was there. If I was not sitting at the window or by the fireplace, they'd walk away. I remember thinking when late summer came and we fenced, I was really going to miss them keeping me company during the afternoons.

Go West, Young Woman!

62

I Am No Lineman for the County

W HEN I TALKED ABOUT US BECOMING MORE INDEPENDENT, it wasn't just about doing our own maintenance. It also involved making our own repairs. One would think a new house would not need much repair work, but we found we were having problems with nature. Twice, Bill's shop had flooded. He also suffered through a period when the plumbing pipes in the shop wall would freeze, though this problem would self-correct itself the next winter.

But the other problems did not fix themselves. Our second phone line in the house that connected to Bill's shop went dead. We tried everything we could, replacing parts and splicing new wires. The phone company was no help and wanted a great deal of money just to inspect the wiring. So like the little red hen, we had to do it ourselves. We researched the problem and ordered new cable over the Internet. Finally, we dug up the yard with our trusty backhoe, and found the cables had not been secured in any pipe or conduit, and needed replacement. Chase helped us, often working in the pouring rain, which made a muddy mess of everything. At one point we were having a "Green Acres" moment because the only functioning phone box was on the back of the shop where Bill had installed a temporary phone. When the weather would not permit him to use it, he ran a phone cable through a window and stood inside to talk. At least we did not have to climb up the telephone pole to talk, like Oliver and Lisa did.

One afternoon we were discussing our ongoing telecommunication woes with the computer rep at Costco, and munching on food samples, when I heard a voice behind me say, "Remember me?"

I turned to see a middle-aged man with blond hair and a familiar face, smiling at me. "I'm your lost hunter. You probably don't recognize me when I'm not dressed in camouflage."

"Well, hello, Donald," I said with surprise. "How are you doing?"

"You know it took me three days to feel better. I was so worn out I could barely move. Thanks again for helping me."

"I'm just glad you're alright."

He walked away with a wave of his hand, heading towards frozen foods. It reminded me again that, despite its size, Montana was a small community.

63

All Not Quiet on the Western Front

I WAS STILL AWAKE. I TOSSED AND TURNED, listening to the symphony that was my husband. Even after his surgery for his sleep apnea, he had slowly worsened to the point of making so many odd sounds, that eventually I gave each of them distinct names. There was, of course, the generic snoring, but some of the sounds stood out and deserved special recognition.

Bill always fell asleep first. If you counted to five after he laid his head on the pillow, he would be comatose. I never understood how he did it, but I wished I could. Within another moment or two, the "music" began. Usually it started with the helicopter assault. This consisted of a *puh, puh, puh* sound made by blowing out air between his lips in short swift bursts. He usually had his arm over his face, and I guess he was trying to blow it off so he could breathe better. I would gently lift it and rest it by his side, but then the helicopter would turn into a whale.

The whale noise was quite irritating because it was composed of both sound and motion. One long burst after another would exhale from his blowhole and usually hit me square in the face, normally right after I'd just managed to fall asleep. The whale blow also offended my sensitive nose. It looked like exhausting work, and was hardly restful for either of us. His chest would heave up and down, and I would watch with amazement, wondering how much we could benefit mankind if we could only harness that power.

Next on the list was the turkey gobbler. It was a high pitched garbled gobbling sound that nearly made me burst out laughing every time I heard it. I don't know how he slept through it. I am surprised that in the middle of the night we were not surrounded by hens. The female turkeys would like it. I'm sure they could hear it throughout the county.

There were numerous choking sounds that I found frightening, and I always woke him up immediately, much to his annoyance. Then there were apnea episodes, when he would just stop breathing for a moment or two. That was not funny.

I must mention the smoke alarm noise. It is a high-pitched screeching chirp or whistle, like a smoke alarm makes when the battery is low. Eventually I would turn over and fall asleep from sheer exhaustion, but the first time I awoke to the chirp, I honestly thought the smoke alarm was malfunctioning. I lay there nervously for several minutes before realizing the sound corresponded to his breathing. So I calmed down and just added it to the play list.

I had hoped the fresh country air would help us all sleep better. Surprisingly, Bill sleeps better than I do, even while playing his symphony. Occasionally, he wakes himself up with one of his sounds and asks me about it. I give him the name of it and he goes back to sleep. I think his favorite is the helicopter because of his previous military life, but that is only my opinion.

In the morning he always makes fun of his sound effects in an effort to coax me out of my fatigue. He enjoys my descriptions of them and remains unaffected by his own concerts. I only know that every evening I can expect a new symphony arrangement, and especially after a hard day of physical labor, the volume of his woodwinds will match anything Beethoven ever composed.

64

Night of the Predator

As usual for the springtime, I opened my eyes to the sun and listened to the singing and chirping birds. Our bed is next to the French doors that open to our private deck, with a view of all the mountains that roll further in the distance. I always open the doors and begin my morning by getting dressed with the fresh air and the free, more pleasant concert of birds. But this morning, before I was out of bed, I heard the chirping voice of Sonja. She and Bill had already gotten dressed and gone down to the barn. They had just returned, and she came running into the bedroom very concerned.

"Mom, Wilson was out of the corral this morning. He jumped out and crushed one of the panels down. He was just standing there wanting to get back in with Whiskey when we went down to see him. Whiskey stood beside him, just inside the corral. Why would Wilson jump out?"

"Is he hurt?" I asked, and I went to the window and looked out. Bill had tied a rope with ribbon across the missing panel area and I saw the panel on the ground. It was completely caved in, crushed in the center. It lay mangled and twisted in the grass.

"No, Mom, he's not hurt, just a small scrape on his left leg," Sonja replied, still looking very worried. "Do you think he wanted to get out and eat the grass?"

"I don't know what to think until I get a look around. Let me get dressed, Honey Girl, and we will go down there and see if we can figure out what happened."

I dressed quickly, skipping my breakfast, and Bill told me the same story that Sonja had relayed. We walked to the barn together with Kobi. I examined Wilson, and other than the scrape, he was unhurt. I also took a look at Whiskey and he was fine. I could hardly believe Wilson could get over that panel; it was almost as high as his head. *How did he not break his leg or sustain a major injury? There was only one thing that would make him jump over it and it was not food; it was fear.*

The damaged panel had been near a corner section formed by the joining of the corral with the round pen. Something had trapped Wilson there, and the only way out was over the top of the corral. My first thought was the grizzly bear, but I figured it would have done more damage, and truthfully, we would have been looking at remains, not two healthy horses.

I had studied forensic evidence of animal kills in my game commission years. Bears will eat the internal organs and often the udders of female animals, while Cougars will not. Generally they want the neck area and the limbs, often leaving the belly and organs untouched. The corral was dry, so there were no signs of tracks or a scuffle. When Bill and I went into the pasture to look around, I saw ripped up areas of grass, and scrape marks where Wilson had dug in his feet, spun, and turned. Something had pursued him. The grass was still moist and a hoof was clearly outlined where Wilson had been. It was then I placed my money on a mountain lion.

"Bill, something chased Wilson. See these marks in the ground—the pattern and how the grass is dug up." I looked down in dismay. *Wilson, why didn't you call for us? We would have helped you. Were you too scared to scream?*

Bill walked over to where I was standing. He looked around and agreed. "You're right; I see them."

"I'm going to expand my search and see if I can find anything else."

It took awhile and I was glad that my hat shadowed my face. I felt very worried about this incident. I thought about the big cougar we'd seen by Bill's shop door that afternoon when Belle was on the picket line. If he was our predator, we were in for trouble. I started a short way down the road that passes the corrals. I took Kobi with me; I was not in a big hurry to turn the corner into the area thickly wooded with trees. A large shade tree offered respite from the sun, and it was there that the dirt road was still slightly damp. I knew the cougar had walked this way before. This was the area I had made a cast of the cougar track some time ago for the girls' science project.

Kobi and I followed the road, and about fifteen feet from the corral I saw it. "Stop Kobi, sit," I told him. I did not want him to step where I was looking. I bent down for a closer look; the Aspen trees rustled as if they were telling me their secret. There was a track, and it was cat.

It was not as large as the one the big cougar had made. So that only told me it was a different one. It was not a great track, not good enough to cast, but enough for identification. It was then I started putting together my theory. I believed a young puma got into the corral and frightened Wilson over the top of the panel, and it crushed under his weight. Then I surmised it chased him into the pasture, and then gave up, deciding it was too much work, or maybe it was scared away by something else. Wilson stayed by Whiskey and wanted back inside where he felt safe, but in reality he was at risk in an enclosed area. *Good for you, Wilson. You got away.* I was puzzled by why it didn't attack Whiskey, he being an older horse. But maybe it had seen Wilson first, or it tried and Whiskey proved too fast.

Bill and I discussed the theory and began a plan of action. We agreed we would never know for sure, but all the evidence pointed to a cougar. I called Gail and told her everything, and she also agreed with me. She gave me a few tips to discourage the cougar, but gently reminded me that this was the West, and the predators here were a way of life. She had lost many animals to them, and although she hoped it would never happen to us, we had to face that possibility.

I knew she was right on one level, reality. But I could not let this happen. The idea of a senseless loss sickened me. What a violent horrible death to happen to either of our sweet boys. I could not even think of the complete and total devastation it would cause for Sonja, being so attached to her Wilson, not to mention the fact she was his bodyguard. She wore his picture in a little heart locket I had given her for her birthday. No, we were an

American military family, and a cougar can't take us on and win. We would not helplessly stand by; but we needed a plan.

I hung up the phone and went straight to Bill. "We need a plan."

"I'm already on it," he said. Bill had started sighting in several rifles, and had secured them at different vantage points in the house. He also fitted them with flashlights, in case the cat came in the dark. He cleared "fields of fire," as the military called them, between the house and stable.

We went to town and purchased two new panels from Lowe's. All our friends in the store were very concerned for Wilson and Whiskey. We decided the extra panel would widen the area more and eliminate the narrow corner of the corral where Wilson had been trapped. It would give the horses more room to maneuver. We also purchased eight more solar lights that changed colors, and two motion-activated solar spot lights and poles on which to mount them. With Chase's help, we put them next to the round pen to give us extra light if needed. I placed all the colored lights around the perimeter. We got a radio and turned it on in the tack room. We left the window open so the sound would carry. We turned on all the flood lights surrounding the corral. We tried to think of everything we could do to deter any predators, using noise and lights, and if in the end all else failed, there was always the rifle.

The beautiful sun started to sink under the weight of the night sky. After dark there were more stars than I could count, but I had no eye for it that night. Like any other defensive military plan of action, it was not all action. So much of it was waiting to see what the enemy would do. All evening I thought of why a cougar would bother a horse. They normally do not attack something so large because the cats themselves do not want to get hurt. They are better off catching prey that is smaller and weaker. They usually eat an average of one deer a week, or smaller prey like rabbits. Sometimes desperate cats that are starving or crazed with pain will try something like this. I knew the elk were late having their calves, and I wondered if that fact had something to do with it. My best hope was that this cat had seen an opportunity and given it a try, then seeing it was too hard, gave up. I still worried he would be back.

We tried to watch some TV, but neither of us could concentrate. I started researching the idea on the Internet of getting a llama or a breed of dog that protected livestock. I heard that llamas can kick, bite predators, and make loud screeching noises that scare them off. Sonja asked if she could sleep in the upstairs loft area by the window. It had a great view of the yard and barn area. She wanted to wake up periodically and check on Wilson and Whiskey. Understanding her fear, I told her to get her sleeping bag.

Before bed, Bill and I stood on the deck and looked out. "It all looks so peaceful," I said wistfully. "How did all that commotion go on last night and we did not hear it?"

"We'll hear it if it happens again. We're sleeping with the window open and the blinds up."

"If we sleep," I responded.

It was a long night. Neither of us slept well, and we were up and down all night looking out the window, searching the shadows for the figures of our two horses, and listening for any sounds that did not belong among the rushing creek and the rustling leaves. The peace and quiet I loved so much only felt ominous that first night. Sonja had a fitful night too, and when she heard me stirring, came in to offer her report. When morning dawned, we were all bleary-eyed and tired. This was only the first night of a continued vigil.

Chase came by to begin fencing the interior of our property. We hired him because Bill and I knew nothing about fencing, and it was one of Chase's primary jobs at his family's ranch. Who better to learn from than a professional? We used our backhoe to dig the holes for the large corner braces. I had a real appreciation for this kind of work as Chase explained how the wire is wrapped around the braces to push and pull at the same time. I learned about stays, long twisted pieces of wire that are turned and twisted and pushed down across all the wires to hold them in place, and T-posts that offer the support for the structure. We used smooth wire without barbs to fence three separate sections of our land. It was miles of work, with gates added for easy access. It was such a relief when it was over. I found out something else about ranchers—they work in the rain. Many an evening everyone came in wet, cold, and soggy.

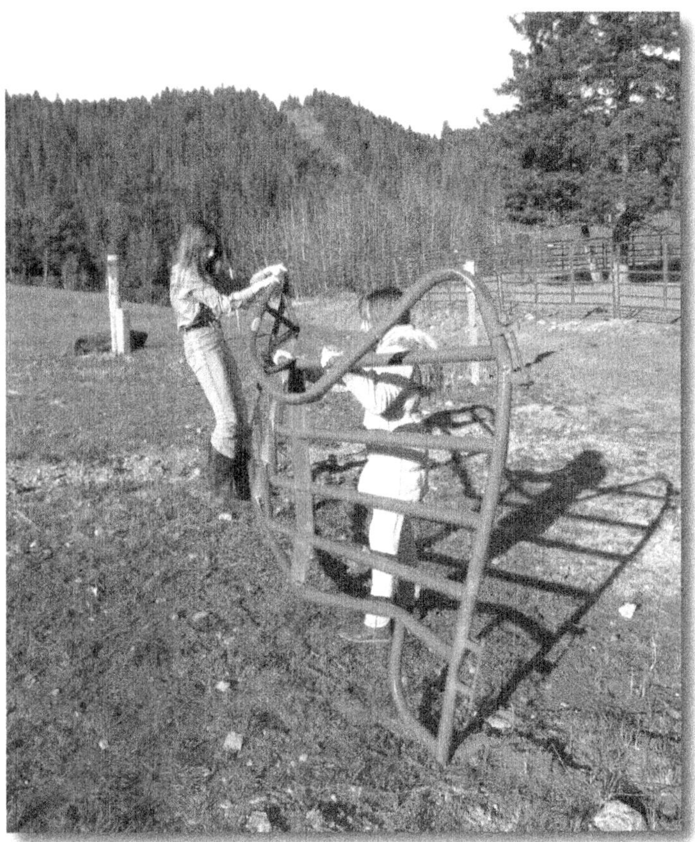

Assessing the damage after Wilson's "great escape"

ʊ ʊ ʊ

The cat never returned; so now that we had an evening off to relax, the first thing the girls wanted to do was ride. I walked to the barn with them, with Kobi racing alongside, jumping back and forth as always. You'd think he was excited about riding. The girls were trying to learn, but I still put the snaffle bit in for both horses; the girls did the rest of the saddling.

When Wilson was ready, I went over to him and started to put it in place. I was surprised when he started to back away. "Now Wilson," I chided, "it's time to ride; you've had a few nights off." I tried again, and while he stood still, he would not open his mouth and clamped it down. I tickled his mouth and moved my thumb up and down in the back where he does not have teeth. When he started to open, I gently placed the bit in his mouth, but he quickly shut it firmly and bit the side of my finger!

The pain shot through my hand like a bullet. He did open his mouth and I pulled it away with a squeal. Before I could react and correct him, Sonja swatted Wilson hard on the nose telling him, "NO, you can't bite Mommy!" She backed him up, and ran to me, horrified. By now my finger was quickly swelling and turning purple, but the skin was not broken.

"I'm okay," I said. I saw the look on her face and she was almost in tears.

"Are you going to sell Wilson?" she asked with her blue eyes wide and fearful.

"No, I'm going to bridle him," I replied curtly, because my hand really, really hurt. I rubbed my hand a few times while walking over to him, and tried again. This time Wilson took the bit just fine, like he had a hundred times before. It only proves the point that even the best and most docile horses can still hurt you. My guess was he was still traumatized by having the cougar in front of him. These sorts of things do happen.

Go West, Young Woman!

65

Let Them Eat Cake

WHEN I SAW CHASE COMING UP THE DRIVE to see Bill, I knew they would be busy for awhile, since they were going to work on Chase's shotgun. I decided to try a recipe I had wanted to make for some time. This cake went together quickly, and I had it baked and ready to eat in less than an hour. It was a recipe I modified. I don't follow cake recipes to the letter. I like to add a little more vanilla and sugar and anything else I deem necessary. This was an Irish Cream cake. We had purchased some Irish cream for company, and I wanted to bake with it and use my doughnut glaze as a frosting.

Soon, the cake was ready, and it was lucky for Chase's brothers that they showed up just in time to have some. So I had three of Gail's sons at my table: Greg, the oldest; Chase; and Allen, the youngest. The boys really liked the cake, so I wrapped up some for them to take home so Gail and Herman could have some. I cautioned the boys again that I was going to check with Gail to make sure she got it. Without naming names, I knew I had sent home treats that never made it to Gail. The four miles home was too tempting and the treats didn't always survive the journey.

Chase laughed out loud, "Allen, go ahead and eat it, it's so good, and having the extra piece of cake is worth getting yelled at."

367

"Chase, are you contributing to the delinquency of your brother?" I turned to Allen. "I'm following up on this," I said, looking him straight in the eye.

The next day I did call Gail, who had not seen or heard anything about the Irish Cream cake. She did get it about two days later, after it had been sitting in her son's truck the whole time.

"I'm so sorry, Gail. Next time I'll give it to your husband."

"My husband!?"

"Won't it arrive safely with him?"

"Yeah, in his stomach."

66

The Price of Freedom

I ASKED GAIL WHAT HER PLANS WERE FOR MOTHER'S DAY. Since we are both moms, I'd sometimes surprise her with a gift, like a plant or some baked goods. She told me this year they planned to go out in the truck to shoot the gophers that were tearing up her meadows, and then have a picnic lunch.

"It sounds like a real Montana Mother's Day," I said laughing. "I understand about the gophers. They're causing problems on my land too. I'm afraid the horses will fall and break their leg in a hole."

"It happens, Nancy; one of my neighbors lost his colt that way. It was running in his field and fell and broke its leg so badly, it had to be put down."

In fact, gophers were such a problem, that a long article appeared in *The Gold Standard* newspaper, dedicated to the issue. It was written by our county agent, who wrote a regular column devoted mainly to farm and ranch issues. As much as everyone enjoyed the deer and the elk, they too caused a lot of problems, and could be quite destructive. They tear down or damage fences, and since we always have large herds passing through, fence walking had become an annual repair event.

The presence of deer is so common, that my daughters once found a newborn deer in the Aspen trees near our stable area, and we watched it grow up. Our other experience with a fawn was quite different. I was looking out the patio doors, when I saw something lying on the ground near the girls swing set. *It looks like Kobi killed another animal and possibly skinned it.* I called Bill on the intercom and asked him to pick it up. He brought it to the door and asked me to come out and see what he was holding.

"What do you make of this?" he said, his tone quizzical and somber at the same time.

I studied the shiny, smooth, pink mass in his hands, noting the nearly formed eye socket and delicate limbs.

"It's an unborn deer," I replied sadly. "It looks like it may have needed another six weeks or so to come to term. There's not a mark on it anywhere. The mother must have aborted."

We were both still, and the silence hung in the air.

"At first I thought Kobi had skinned it out," I said reflectively. "Now I can see how careful he was with this fawn. He often rips up his prize and plays with it, or brings it directly to me. Perhaps he wanted to help this poor creature; maybe that's why he brought it home."

I looked into Bill's face. "We have to bury it in the garden. I can't just throw it away or let other animals get hold of it. Whether the mother's alive or dead, it's our responsibility to bury it."

"I'll get the shovel," Bill responded.

I rounded up the girls while Bill dug a hole near our house. He carefully placed the remains in the grave and shoveled dirt over it. Each girl said a few kind words, and Kobi sat nearby, respectfully observing the ceremony. All in all, it was a proper Christian burial.

ʊ ʊ ʊ

The animals in Montana are as wild as the skies they live under, and just about as dangerous. We were all still worried about the cougars returning, or finding bear droppings nearby. And there are the pesky coyotes and occasional wolf to consider.

After our last cougar incident, Gail had asked me, "Have you had anymore problems with cats?"

"No, and I'm glad, but we're still watching. I guess it will be this way from now on."

"There's plenty to eat now, so I'm hoping this is over for awhile, but keep up your plan. Just keep changing between the lights and the radio at the barn. If you leave them on all the time, they get used to it. It would also help if you left a jacket or something out there hanging on the fence once and awhile. It'll have your scent, and that may discourage predators. You may also want to switch the lights in different color patterns and spots."

"I also hung out some wind chimes. Maybe that'll help."

"So, is there anything else going on?" Gail inquired.

"Yes, there's one thing I wanted to ask you about, but if you tell anyone I'll deny it."

"Oh?" I heard a mixture of puzzlement and concern in Gail's voice.

"Who does that cute little black-and-white baby cow belong to at the bottom entrance? It's so darling. It was in the road and we had to stop. It's a friendly little thing, and he came by my car window. I liked him."

"I should have thought of that! You like the Guernsey cows! They're cute and friendly. You want one? You should get one!"

"No, no, I don't want one. I only said it was cute. I knew you'd get too excited."

"Cute is the first step. I should have known you would like the pretty ones; I'm talking you into a cow." She was positively gleeful.

"No cows, Gail," I said firmly, and I meant it.

"Remember, I talked you into horses. Well, I gotta bolt…." The receiver went dead. Some things just need to be in the brochure.

Go West, Young Woman!

Epilogue

T HERE IS SOMETHING SPECIAL ABOUT STEWARDSHIP of your own land and learning how to share it with wildlife. I find the mountain peaks heal my spirit, and the wild unpredictable skies connect me to nature, making me feel alive and filled with hope. We have carved out a great life here on the mountain. It is not a perfect one, but a happy one, filled with laughter, times of peace, beauty, hard physical work, and an extreme sense of accomplishment. During our first few years here we built a home, a stable, an art studio, two garages, a work shop, a playhouse and swing set, two stone patios, a waterfall, a greenhouse, several retaining walls, and miles of fences.

Most importantly, we hope to build lasting friendships and adapt to a new lifestyle and different way of living. As Gail would say, "It's better than a coyote in the washing machine."

Go West, Young Woman!

Recipes

I HAVE A RECIPE FOR HOMEMADE HOT CHOCOLATE I think anyone would enjoy. I make it every year and give it as Christmas gifts. It is a healthier alternative to store bought cocoa and we think it tastes better too. It is rich, but delicious. I spent an entire afternoon in the kitchen trying to perfect it. I had my family tasting it so many times that day, that by dinnertime, they were not hungry and tired of chocolate! I hope you enjoy it too.

Nancy's Hot Chocolate

3 cups of dry milk
2 cups of powdered sugar
1 and ½ cups of granulated sugar
1 and ½ cups of unsweetened Dutch cocoa
1 cup of mini chocolate chips

To make this even more decadent, I include a spoon that has been dipped in milk chocolate and wrapped in cellophane.

This makes about 5 quarts. I put it in jars with the directions printed and attached. Combine 1/3 cup of mix with one cup of hot water. Stir in chocolate spoon.

I find the spoons in the thrift stores and look for the prettiest designs on the handles.

I serve this with my banana or corn bread. Since this is not a cookbook, I did not want to put in too many recipes, but try one of my breads with the hot chocolate and you won't be disappointed.

Banana Bread

½ cup butter
1 cup sugar
2 eggs
1 ½-2 cup mashed ripe banana (very ripe is best)
¼ cup sour cream
3 teaspoons vanilla extract
2 cups of flour
1 teaspoon baking powder
½ teaspoon baking soda
¼ teaspoon salt
1 or 2 Tablespoons of milk

Preheat oven to 350 degrees and line a 5"x9" loaf pan with parchment paper in the bottom. Spray the sides with nonstick cooking spray.

In a mixer, cream the butter and sugar. Add the eggs, banana, sour cream, and vanilla to the mixture and mix on low. Add the flour, baking powder, baking soda, and salt. Mix on low. If the batter looks too thick, you can add a tablespoon or two of milk. I often do.

Spoon the batter into the pan and bake for 50-55 minutes. I like to put my cake pans on cookie sheets and bake them in the oven. I think it prevents burning the bottoms of the cakes.

Corn Bread

1 ¼ cups of flour
¾ cup of corn meal
½ cup sugar
2 teaspoons baking powder
½ teaspoon salt
1 cup of milk
1 cup of vegetable oil
1 egg
¼ cup maple syrup

Preheat oven to 400 degrees and spray an 8" or 9" pan with nonstick spray. Mix together flour, corn meal, sugar, baking powder and salt. Then stir in the milk, vegetable oil, egg, and maple syrup. Stir well until combined. Pour in pan and bake 25 minutes or until golden brown on top.

CPSIA information can be obtained
at www.ICGtesting.com
Printed in the USA
BVOW06s2011080617

486424BV00008B/337/P